The Lord Shepherding His Sheep

Psalm 23

Joel Beeke

EP BOOKS

1st Floor Venture House, 6 Silver Court, Watchmead, Welwyn Garden City, UK, AL7 1TS

web: www.epbooks.org

e-mail: sales@epbooks.org

EP books are distributed in the USA by:

JPL Fulfillment

3741 Linden Avenue Southeast,

Grand Rapids, MI 49548

orders@jplfulfillment.com

Tel: 877.683.6935

First published 2015

Revised and expanded from an earlier book *Jehovah Shepherding His Sheep*

British Library Cataloguing in Publication Data available

ISBN: 978-1-78397-144-2

Scripture references are from the King James Version

With heartfelt appreciation for
Larry and Linda VanBeek
faithful friends, always kind and self-denying,
lovers of Christ-centered preaching;
many thanks for all the truck loads of books
and trips you made to numerous conferences
all over America to sell Reformed literature with me.

Contents

Preface   7
Psalm 23   9
Introduction   11

Part 1
Psalm 23:1 "The LORD is my shepherd; I shall not want."

1 The Shepherd-Lord   17
2 Who Lacks Nothing?   33
3 How the Lord's Sheep Shall Lack Nothing   45
4 Why and When the Lord's Sheep Shall Lack Nothing   59

Part 2
Psalm 23:2 "He maketh me to lie down in green pastures:
he leadeth me beside the still waters."

5 The Shepherd's Gift of Divine Rest   75
6 The Shepherd's Refreshment   93

Part 3
Psalm 23:3 "He restoreth my soul: he leadeth me in the paths of
righteousness for his name's sake."

7 The Shepherd's Restoration for the Diseased and Downcast   107
8 The Shepherd's Restoration for the Wandering Sheep   121
9 Unrighteousness Uncovered and Righteousness Imputed   135
10 The Shepherd's Righteousness to Sanctify and Preserve   149

Part 4

Psalm 23:4 "Yea, though I walk through the valley of the shadow of death, I will fear no evil: for thou art with me; thy rod and thy staff they comfort me."

11 The Shepherd's Protection and Spiritual Growth   165
12 The Shepherd's Protection and Spiritual Courage   179
13 The Shepherd's Companionship   193
14 The Shepherd's Comfort   205

Part 5

Psalm 23:5 "Thou preparest a table before me in the presence of mine enemies: thou anointest my head with oil; my cup runneth over."

15 Divine Provision   219
16 Divine Anointing   233
17 Divine Joy And Liberty   245

Part 6

Psalm 23:6 "Surely goodness and mercy shall follow me all the days of my life: and I will dwell in the house of the LORD *for ever."*

18 God's Gracious Pursuit   261
19 At Home with the Shepherd   275

Notes   289

Preface

Scripture abounds with illustrations of shepherds and sheep, which are metaphors for the loving care of Christ for His people. The Bible speaks of sheep 176 times, lambs 164 times, and shepherds 80 times. No shepherd-sheep image, however, is as well-known as that of Psalm 23. Though three millennia have passed since the sweet singer of Israel first sang about the shepherding care of God, this psalm still proclaims profound truths and invaluable lessons. The psalmist uses the shepherding practices of biblical times to illustrate the spiritual communion between the Chief Shepherd, Jesus Christ, and His flock, the living church of God.

This book is based on a series of sermons preached thirty-five years ago and was subsequently published as my first book, titled *Jehovah Shepherding His Sheep*. That book has been reprinted several times over the years, but I have long desired to shorten, edit, and in certain parts, rewrite those sermons. *The Lord Shepherding His Sheep* is the result of that desire. My original desire for the book, however, has not changed: I offer this book with the conviction that reading Christ-centered, Reformed, experiential sermons frequently serves as a means of blessing for God's sheep. My aim is to bring glory to God, to edify believers, and to help lost lambs find the Good Shepherd.

I would like to thank Pamela Hartung, Ray Lanning, Paul Smalley, and Phyllis TenElshof for their editorial assistance. You have made this a better book than it would have been without your able work. And without my dear wife Mary generously allowing me (without complaint!) to work long hours on writing projects for the sake of Christ's kingdom, this book would never have been published in its present form. I pray that these chapters bear eternal fruit for the glory of the Lord Jesus Christ, "that great shepherd of the Sheep" (Hebrews 13:20).

Joel R. Beeke

Psalm 23

1. *The* L*ord* *is my shepherd; I shall not want.*

2. *He maketh me to lie down in green pastures: he leadeth me beside the still waters.*

3. *He restoreth my soul: he leadeth me in the paths of righteousness for his name's sake.*

4. *Yea, though I walk through the valley of the shadow of death, I will fear no evil: for thou art with me; thy rod and thy staff they comfort me.*

5. *Thou preparest a table before me in the presence of mine enemies: thou anointest my head with oil; my cup runneth over.*

6. *Surely goodness and mercy shall follow me all the days of my life: and I will dwell in the house of the* L*ord* *for ever.*

Introduction

Psalm 23 is a deeply spiritual meditation. It is a jewel unsurpassed in richness and beauty. It is no wonder that there is no more familiar passage in all of Scripture than this psalm. For countless people it is one of the first portions of Scripture committed to memory in childhood.

The widespread familiarity of Psalm 23, however, can also be dangerous. Millions of ungodly people take its words lightly upon their lips while knowing nothing of the Great Shepherd described in this psalm. They are ignorant of Christ's work as Savior and Shepherd that is woven throughout its verses. And in their lack of knowledge, they have claimed a jewel that does not belong to them. By often repeating this psalm, many self-proclaimed Christians have also abused its words to such an extent that no separation is made between the natural and the spiritual, between common and saving grace, or between sheep and goats.

Even God's flock can take Psalm 23 for granted. Lacking the application of the Holy Spirit, the psalm's sublime truths and experiential depths remain hidden. However, when properly applied, Psalm 23 reveals the highest, deepest, widest, and most glorious experiences into which God leads His people this side of heaven.

For them, Psalm 23 serves as a *pilgrim song.* As God's pilgrims journey through the Vanity Fair of this world, oppressed by internal and external enemies, they look to Psalm 23 for courage. In the hands of the Holy Spirit, the psalm is a balm to soldiers wounded on the battlefield of free grace, a key to unlock the chains of spiritual prisoners, and honey to brighten the eyes of weary saints.

The melodious harp strings of Psalm 23 will never fall silent. Charles Spurgeon aptly said, "I will venture to compare it also to the lark, which sings as it mounts, and mounts as it sings, until it is out of sight, and even then is not out of hearing .... These are celestial notes, more fitted for the eternal mansions than for those dwelling below the clouds."[1]

Psalm 23 also serves believers as a *personal creed.* F. B. Meyer says a thinker who was challenged to declare his creed replied by quoting Psalm 23, then added,

> That is my creed. I need, I desire no other. I learned it from my mother's lips. I have repeated it every morning when I awoke for the last twenty years. Yet I do not half understand it; I am only beginning to spell out its infinite meaning, and death will come on me with the task unfinished. But, by the grace of Jesus, I will hold on to this psalm as my creed, and will strive to believe and live it; for I know that it will lead me to the cross, and guide me to glory.[2]

For believers Psalm 23 is a creed of victory. Every word asserts that God is and provides all that His people need. Sovereign grace rings through every syllable.

Finally, Psalm 23 helps believers experience *profound communion* with God. It becomes at times a spiritual Holy of Holies. Through this psalm, believers commune with God the Father, find reconciliation through the blood of the redeeming Shepherd, and receive the Spirit's grace to rest in the triune God. For them, Psalm 23 is more than a spiritual oasis in the desert, more than a refuge on which all the storms of life break, and more than a rock of safety and blessedness. It is holy ground.

Child of God, when you begin to understand this psalm in the light of the work of the Great Shepherd, Jesus Christ, may the God of all grace become for you a pilgrim song, a personal creed, and a Holy of Holies! May it become not only a soul-captivating psalm, but also a soul-conquering one, so that unbelief no longer intrudes between your soul and Christ. Instead, by God's grace, may faith triumphantly set Christ between your soul and all else. May you fall before God in humility, be grounded in Christ as the only firm foundation, grow in the grace and knowledge of the Great Shepherd of your soul, and experience a foretaste of heaven on earth. In turn, your heart will well up with joy and exclaim, "The LORD is my shepherd; I shall not want."

I also pray that the unsaved who attempt to shepherd themselves as they journey to eternity be given a deep impression of what they are missing. May an unquenchable flame of yearning rouse their souls to need, find, and follow the Good Shepherd of Psalm 23.

Part 1

Psalm 23:1
"The LORD is my shepherd; I shall not want."

1

The Shepherd-Lord

The LORD is my shepherd.
—Psalm 23:1a

Centuries ago, a Persian ruler dedicated one room of his palace to the memory of his early days as a shepherd boy. Its bare floors housed nothing but the simple equipment of shepherding: a staff, a rod, a knapsack, and a water jug. A few minutes each day, he would sit in this room to remind himself of what he had been. It served as a warning against the temptations to which he was exposed through royal power and popular favor.

Similarly, David the king—surrounded with power, riches, and honor—did not forget his days as a shepherd boy. Enlightened by the Holy Spirit, David wrote Psalm 23. In it he blended his mature experience as a believer with memories of his humble beginnings as a shepherd boy receiving his first spiritual lessons.

David's autograph is written across every verse of this psalm. Each verse reveals that the one who wrote it had suffered deeply. He had tasted the cup of bitterness and had continually disappointed himself. However, it also cries out of his experiences of spiritual rest and revival. David's faith is alive, his love fiery, and his hope firm. He looks back at the stormy times of warfare and rebellion, of sin and sorrow. But he also sees the green valleys and gentle streams into which God led him. John Calvin said that by "calling to remembrance the benefits which God had conferred upon him, [David] makes them ladders by which he may ascend nearer to Him."[1] The Lord was faithful to David from the time he was a boy to the very end of his days on earth.

"The LORD is my shepherd," say God's children as they begin, continue, and end with the Lord alone. Self falls away. "The LORD" becomes the motto of their lives. He is their all-in-all, their heaven on earth. They receive grace to learn with David that the defining moments in life are when self is pushed to the background and the Lord comes to the foreground. The words "the LORD" are the foundation of Psalm 23 as well as of the entire Word of God.

Do you know what it means to have all the foundations of your life stripped away except "the LORD"? Many people have memorized the entire twenty-third psalm; but friends, do you really believe the first words of it? Do you know "the LORD?" To know Him is eternal life (John 17:3)! Have you met Him in His glorious attributes? Have you been brought face to face with His majesty, His holiness, His justice, His power, His wisdom, His grace, His mercy, and His love? Do you realize that all foundations for eternity—yes, that the very trial and triumph of true saving faith—are contained in the first words of this psalm: "the LORD"?

Without the saving knowledge of the Lord, we cannot walk the journey of Psalm 23; rather, we are on the road to eternal destruction regardless of any wisdom, power, or riches we may have attained. "Thus saith the LORD, Let not the wise man glory in his wisdom, neither let the mighty man glory in his might, let not the rich man glory in his riches: but let him that glorieth glory in this, that he understandeth and knoweth me, that I am the Lord" (Jeremiah 9:23–24).

By nature, we are without God in the world (Ephesians 2:12). Because of our deep fall in Adam, we are no longer the sheep of our Creator. He calls us wolves, lions, adders, and wild beasts. We are the property of the devil. By nature, we follow Satan (Ephesians 2:2), who is a miserable shepherd who looks out only for himself. He deceives and tricks his sheep for his own greedy satisfaction. His goals are contrary to those of God. Satan's flock is thin, weak, and riddled with diseases and parasites. His pasture is dry and barren. His fold is broken down. He does not care for his flock but rather hates his sheep. If he were a shepherd among earthly shepherds, he would be despised.

However, his sheep know no better than to follow him. They are blind to their own misery. They have never known a better life. They have never tasted the green pastures of God's Word. The dry, empty grass of the world is their constant diet. Abraham Hellenbroek wrote, "With the exception of Satan, there is not a more miserable creature than natural man."[2] As sheep blindly follow one another into places that eventually destroy them, so we blindly follow Satan, allowing him to guide us into hell.

Nevertheless, by grace David could say, "The Lord is my shepherd." The word he uses for "Lord," printed in capital letters, is the highest and most personal name of God: YHWH or Jehovah. Nearly 7,000 times in Scripture, the Lord calls Himself by this name. The Lord means the Living One, the Self-existent One, the unchangeable God who establishes and keeps His covenant from eternity to eternity, and the powerful and sovereign God who works the salvation of His creatures (Exodus 3). David is saying, "The Lord, who is the great I AM THAT I AM—He who dwelt in the burning but never consumed bush, who inhabits eternity and yet dwells between the cherubim—He, the triune God, is my Shepherd."

David's Shepherd is *God the Father* who sovereignly chooses His flock from eternity. He is *God the Holy Spirit* who brings all the elect into the flock in the time and hour of His sovereign good pleasure. Yet especially in Psalm 23 He is *God the Son*, the Messiah, the Lord Jesus, David's personal Shepherd. The Word of God, particularly in Psalm 23, reveals that shepherding is the special task of the Lamb of God, the Lord Jesus. Scripture describes the Lord Jesus Christ as exercising a threefold shepherd ministry. In John 10:11 Christ calls Himself the "good Shepherd" who gives His life for His sheep. Thus we see Him forsaken and crucified in Psalm 22. In Hebrews 13:20–21 Christ is called the "great Shepherd of the sheep" who was "brought again from the dead" and through whom God works His holy, sanctifying will in His people. Thus we see Him in Psalm 23. In 1 Peter 5:4 the Lord is designated "chief Shepherd" with reference to His Second Advent when He will give to His sheep "a crown of glory that fadeth not away." We see Him as the King of glory in Psalm 24.

Christ, therefore, is the good Shepherd, the great Shepherd, and the chief Shepherd. As the good Shepherd, He is the Shepherd-Redeemer who on Calvary's cross laid down His life for His sheep, rightfully purchasing them back from the fold of Satan with the full approval of God. As the great Shepherd, He is the Shepherd-Owner who lives to find His lost sheep, irresistibly bringing them back to His fold to care for them for all eternity. As the chief Shepherd, He is the Shepherd-Keeper who gathers, defends, and preserves His flock as He sits at the right hand of His Father, waiting for the divinely appointed day to return to earth and bring them to dwell with Him forever in the Father's house.

Is Christ your Shepherd? Do you belong to Him? Can you say wholeheartedly and experientially with David, "The LORD is my shepherd?" Do you need Him as Shepherd? Can you live without Him as Savior? If you dare not claim Him by possession, can you claim

Him by desire? Can you say He has drawn you to the point where you cannot live without Him?

The Shepherd Purchasing His Flock

Before we can become acquainted with Christ as our Sheep-Owner and Sheep-Keeper, we must need Him as our Sheep-Redeemer. We must recognize our need for the blood of the Good Shepherd to be applied to our souls. How does the Lord show His people this need? How does He convince them of the need for the Lord Jesus as their personal Shepherd? The Lord teaches the elect their need by showing them that they are nothing more than sheep.

Sheep are unique creatures. They have special natures, qualities, and characteristics. Allow me to give you four characteristics of sheep. These characteristics correspond plainly with the nature of God's people and, therefore, reveal man's urgent need for the good, the great, the chief Shepherd.

(1) A sheep is *dependent*. Left alone, a sheep would soon perish, for it needs assistance in every aspect of its life. A sheep cannot provide its own food. It has no means to defend itself from enemies or injuries. It cannot take care of itself when it is injured. It needs care, guidance, and protection day and night. Without its shepherd, it must surely perish.

Do you recognize your own dependence? Has the Lord taught you that *independence* is the word mankind chose to place as a banner above the gate leading out of the Garden of Eden? Has the Lord shown you that by nature you pursue independence to your own ruin? Has He revealed to you that all your ways end in death, thereby making you dependent upon Him for life? Can you agree with William Huntington who said that it is good for God to give us our portion one little hand-basket at a time, for "the hand-basket portion is the best, both for soul and body, because it keeps us to prayer, exercises our faith, engages our watchfulness, and excites to gratitude"?[3] Do you acknowledge your utter dependence in physical and spiritual things? God's child is totally dependent on the Shepherd Jesus who says, "Without me ye can do nothing" (John 15:5).

2) A sheep is *foolish*. It will leave a rich pasture to go to a barren one. It knows how to get lost but not how to find its way home again. Left to itself, it would not know what pasture should be fed upon during the summer, nor where to retire in winter. Such is God's child. "So foolish was I, and ignorant," says Asaph; "I was as a beast before Thee" (Psalm 73:22). Do you recognize that you are a foolish sheep in the sight of an all-knowing, holy God?

(3) A sheep is *prone to wander*. It will go anywhere except in the direction it should be heading. A wandering flock is a picture of God's erring people, of whom the Lord complained in Hosea 11:7, "My people are bent to backsliding from me." Believers learn that Isaiah was right: "All we like sheep have gone astray" (Isaiah 53:6). They confess, "Lord, from my side I can do nothing but wander away as a backsliding sheep. I cannot walk in the narrow pathway of salvation one step without the Great Shepherd."

(4) Finally, sheep are *stubborn*. When a loving shepherd attempts to wash his sheep, the animal will fight it. It will struggle to be freed as long as there is ground beneath its feet. Only when its feet are knocked away from beneath, causing a sheep to lose its foothold and float in the bath water, will the stubborn animal finally give up the battle and submit to the washing.

As long as you can stand on your own feet, do you strive against being washed with the Savior's blood of justification as well as the Shepherd's water of sanctification? Only when the Lord causes you to lose your foothold and you expect to drown will you find yourself floating in true submission, experiencing that "underneath are the everlasting arms" of the Great Shepherd. Oh how sweet it is to bow before the Lord by acknowledging Him, confessing Him, approving Him, and cleaving to Him in love!

The Lord teaches believers such lessons to bring them to confess, "Lord, I am as dependent, foolish, wandering, and stubborn as a sheep. Sweep me off my own legs; destroy my own strength and righteousness. Lord, I need the Redeemer-Shepherd if it is to be well with me for time and eternity."

Have you become as a sheep before the Shepherd-Lord? Or do you wander over the earth with an empty heart, a guilty soul, and a condemning conscience, looking and crying for the divine Shepherd but finding that you are your own greatest enemy? Without Him there is no possibility to be saved. We all are foolish sheep that have gone astray. However, with God, and in God, there is both possibility and opportunity. What we have made impossible, Christ has made possible.

Even if all the sins of the entire human race were laid to your account, there would remain an abundance of pardon available for you in the blood of Christ. There is hope for those who have no hope.

For the needy but chosen sinner, Christ offered from eternity to lay down His life as Sheep-Purchaser and Sheep-Redeemer. He paid a higher price to obtain his flock than any earthly shepherd has ever given. He laid down His life for His sheep (John 10:15).

In the Ancient Near East, shepherds purchased sheep with money earned by long hours of sweat and labor. Their flocks were their livelihood (Proverbs 27:23-27). Even a lamb was exceedingly precious to a shepherd (Matthew 18:12). From the moment of purchase, a true shepherd's heart was bound to his sheep.

How much more is Christ's flock bound to His soul in intimacy, for it was bought not only with sweat and labor but also with His precious blood. In Gethsemane, He labored and agonized in prayer, sweating great drops of blood. At Gabbatha He took the place of His sheep, accepting the condemnation pronounced by the Roman governor. He willingly submitted to the decree of His own Father as Judge: "Awake, O sword, against my shepherd, and against the man that is my fellow, saith the LORD of hosts: smite the shepherd" (Zechariah 13:7). At Golgotha He was forsaken by His Father and led as a lamb to the slaughter (Psalm 22:1; Isaiah 53:7). In His sacrifice, He purchased His sheep and redeemed them. He bore the penalty of God's law and satisfied God's justice (Galatians 3:10, 13). He redeemed His flock with the blood of the everlasting covenant. He submitted Himself to the wrath of the Father. The death of the Shepherd is the life of His sheep (John 10:10-11). He was bound that they might be freed, suffered innumerable reproaches that they might never be confounded, was condemned that they might be acquitted, was cursed that they might be blessed, and was rejected that they might be accepted.[4]

May the Shepherd lead you to confess with faith and amazement that the Great Shepherd-Redeemer gave His all on Calvary to pay the full price for the redemption of His foolish and wandering sheep. Stand still with sacred astonishment, cover your mouth in holy silence, and bow your heart in reverent adoration. "Behold the Lamb of God which taketh away the sin of the world!" (John 1:29).

Truly, Christ gave His all. He gave Himself (Ephesians 5:25). Therefore, He cannot be separated from His sheep. His sheep are bound up in His very identity. He is the Head and they are the body. When one member suffers, the whole body suffers. He is touched by the infirmities of His flock (Hebrews 4:15). Therefore, "fear not, little flock" (Luke 12:32), but exhort one another, saying,

Now with joyful exultation let us sing Jehovah's praise,
To the Rock of our salvation loud hosannas let us raise;
Thankful tribute gladly bringing, let us come before Him now,
And, with psalms His praises singing, joyful in His presence bow.
To the Lord, such might revealing, let us come with reverence meet,
And, before our Maker kneeling, let us worship at His feet.
He is our own God and leads us, we the people of His care;
With a shepherd's hand He feeds us as His flock in pastures fair.[5]

The Shepherd Owning His Flock

The purchase of sheep is only the beginning of the shepherd's work. Immediately following the payment of the purchase price, a shepherd is obliged to confirm his ownership of the new sheep by marking and naming them.

Sheep marking was a painful process. Catching each young animal in turn, the shepherd had to lay its ear on a wooden block and notch it deeply (according to the unique shape of his earmark), using the razor-sharp edge of his knife. This procedure was painful for both shepherd and sheep, yet through this an indelible mark of ownership and relationship was established. Indeed, each shepherd's earmark was sufficiently distinct to enable a neighboring farmer to detect even from some distance to whom a sheep belonged.

A parallel to sheep marking is how a slave in the Old Testament who desired to remain a lifetime member of his master's home was marked. His master took the slave to his door, put his ear lobe against the doorpost, and with an awl bored a hole through his ear (Exodus 21:5–6). This mark publicly declared, "I love my master, my master's family, and my master's service, and I desire to remain his willing slave forever."

Jesus Christ, the Great Shepherd, was marked by His Father to be the suffering Lamb and willing Servant from eternity. He gave Himself to His Father saying, "Lo, I come, I delight to do thy will, O my God" (Psalm 40:6–8). He bore the bloody marks of Calvary's cross (John 21:25).

Christ also marks His people when He draws them into His flock. The old writers refer to it as "the blood-mark of the covenant."[6] This covenant mark is not painless jewelry worn about the neck but a painful mark on a believer's heart. It is described in Matthew 16:24, "If any man will come after me, let him deny himself, and take up his cross, and follow me."

This mark acknowledges the failure of God's people to shepherd themselves and a willingness (Psalm 110:3) to follow the Great Shepherd. This mark is painful to the flesh, but through the mutual suffering of Shepherd and sheep, it is increasingly precious, necessary, and profitable to the sheep. It binds them closer to their once bloody, but now ever-living and faithful Shepherd.

Some people think it is possible to possess both the mark of Christ and the mark of the world. They think they can enjoy the benefits of Christ's shepherding care without having to renounce self and Satan. But as Matthew 6:24 says, "No man can serve two masters: for either he will hate the one, and love the other; or else he will hold to the one, and despise the other. Ye cannot serve God and mammon."

As an earthly shepherd's earmark provided both proof of ownership and protection, so Christ earmarked His flock for distinction and security. Sheep of God, there is no greater security than seeing and knowing that "the LORD is *my* shepherd." It is the Lord Jesus who marks *me* with God's mark of free, sovereign grace!

Unhappily, just as sheep can see earmarks on every sheep in a flock but their own, some of God's sheep do not see the mark of Christ on themselves. They exclaim, "Is it possible for all to belong to Christ, except me?" Truly, it is a great blessing to be able to embrace Christ as a personal Savior and Shepherd, leader and guide.

Blessed are they who can say with the Heidelberg Catechism, "I with body and soul, both in life and death, am not my own, but belong unto my faithful Savior Jesus Christ."[7] Blessed are those who have experienced that the Shepherd owns them, and they own the Shepherd. They know Him as their personal Shepherd. They confess with deep joy, "The Lord Jesus is *my* Shepherd."

The shepherd's ownership of sheep also involves naming them. While sheep-marking symbolized public distinction and security, sheep-naming was an act of intimacy. Each shepherd gave to each animal a name that it would respond to when called. The relationship between shepherd and sheep was so intimate that he could identify each animal in the darkness. If a strange shepherd called the name of a certain sheep, the sheep would not respond for it did not recognize a stranger's voice. A well-trained flock would flee in panic upon hearing the voice of a stranger (John 10:5).

The sheep-naming of Christ's flock remains an eternal secret between the Chief Shepherd and His sheep, for each sheep will one day receive from its Shepherd "a white stone, and in the stone a new name written, which no man knoweth saving he that receiveth it" (Revelation 2:17).

Such is the relationship between Christ and His flock. He knows all His sheep by name. They are names He received from His Father in eternity: "Thine they were and thou gavest them me" (John 17:6). So intimate is the communion between the great Shepherd and His sheep that even on Calvary, Christ still knew and remembered His sheep: "To day thou shalt be with me in paradise" (Luke 23:43).

In the hour of God's good pleasure (Galatians 1:15), He calls His sheep to become His property, bringing them under the banner of the Shepherd-King and causing them to obey His word. Christ says, "My sheep hear my voice, and I know them, and they follow me. I give unto them eternal life; and they shall never perish, neither shall any man pluck them out of my hand" (John 10:27-28). Christ not only purchases and owns His flock, but as Shepherd-Keeper, He also preserves His sheep forever.

The Shepherd Preserving His Flock

A good shepherd also obligates himself to keep and care for his sheep so they might flourish. He spends his life pursuing his sheep in all their wanderings and curbing their obstinate misbehavior.

A good shepherd neglects nothing that concerns his charge. He is with his sheep in all seasons. With sound judgment and discretion, he exercises his authority over them. Just as every sheep committed to his care is personally known to him, so the shepherd takes responsibility for their safety. He leads them to the most abundant pastures and protects them against every danger. He searches after wanderers from the fold, cleanses those that are defiled, and administers medicine to the diseased. He will not leave any sheep entangled in a thicket, or allow another to be swept away by overflowing waters. He tenderly leads the lame and the blind, and patiently bears with the weak and the wayward. He watches over the young and old, the weak and strong. Day and night, he provides food for his flock and a fold for their safety.

In like manner, Christ, the Great Shepherd not only purchases and owns His sheep but also preserves them. Sitting at the right hand of His Father, He pursues them moment by moment with divine watchfulness and tender loving kindness. In heaven's courts, He continually lays down His life on their behalf, interceding for them in the presence of His Father, and guiding them with His Word and Spirit. He spares no pains for the welfare of His sheep. His preservation involves all of His shepherding gifts and operations:

(1) He has a *shepherd's heart*, which beats with pure, overflowing, and unconditional love towards His chosen flock.

(2) He has a *shepherd's hand*, which rules, guides, leads, and directs His sheep, steering them away from sin, Satan, the world, selfishness, and false doctrine.

(3) He has a *shepherd's eye*, which takes within its scope His entire flock—even those wandering far from the path.

(4) He has a *shepherd's ear*, which responds to the bleating cry of one sheep as if there were no other sheep in the flock.

(5) He has a *shepherd's nearness*, remaining beside His flock with majesty and grace. He never sleeps nor slumbers.

(6) He has a *shepherd's knowledge*. He knows His flock within and

without. He knows them better than they know themselves. He is minutely acquainted with all their weaknesses, infirmities, diseases, sorrows, and joys; and He meets their needs with His shepherding wisdom.

(7) He has a *shepherd's skill.* He leads His sheep to pasture suitable to their individual circumstances, characters, and needs. He knows how to give the right medicine and dosage to the sick, to furnish the mourning with comfort, and to bolster the weak with strength.

(8) He has a *shepherd's experience.* When a Welsh shepherd was asked how long it took a shepherd to become competent, he replied, "About four generations." Jesus Christ is not a novice shepherd; from eternity past, through all of time, He has shown divine wisdom, power, and ability in sheep-management.

(9) He exercises a *shepherd's faithfulness.* He does not leave nor forsake His flock. He will not flee when enemies attack His sheep by day or by night. During the day, He stands beside them, fighting off the adversary; at night He is the door of the fold, behind which they find protection. His faithfulness will not allow one sheep to be lost. He loses none of the sheep entrusted to Him (John 6:39; 17:12).

(10) Finally, He has both a *shepherd's strength* and a *shepherd's tenderness.* With His shepherd's rod, He disciplines His beloved sheep and guides them into the right path. He delivers them from the jaw of the lion, the paw of the bear, and the teeth of the wolf. However, He is also tender. He will not overdrive His flock (Genesis 33:13). No lamb is too small for Him to carry in His bosom (Isaiah 40:11). No sheep is too weak for Him to feed with gentle strength. None is so faint that He cannot give it rest. This Great Shepherd pities His sheep as a father and comforts them as a mother.

The Great Shepherd will gather, defend, and preserve His chosen flock until the end of the world. He will gather His sheep from the east and from the west, from the north and from the south, until the last day. He will bring them under the banner of His covenant and confirm His own promise: "I shall be with thee always, even unto the end of the world" (Matthew 28:20).

He is the Lord, the God over all, and blessed forever (Romans 9:5). He is the self-existing, uncreated, and eternal Lord, whose love and care, whose providence and power are unlimited and inexhaustible. Who, then, can deny that He is an all-sufficient Shepherd? In strength, He is almighty; in wisdom, He is omniscient; in love, He is unequalled; and in resources, He is unbounded! What evils can He not foresee? What danger can He not avert? What enemy can He not subdue? What need can He not meet?

The members of His flock are as different in their age, dispositions, and temptations as they are in their language, country, and ethnicity. Yet the eye of the Shepherd-Lord observes each of His dispersed sheep as if they were all gathered before Him in one place. He hears their requests individually. Indeed, His hand can administer blessings that will prove most suitable to each sheep. To the troubled heart, He can impart peace; to the weary, rest; to the penitent, pardon; to the hungry, food; to the blind, sight. To the sick, He gives health; to the weak, strength; to the tempted, deliverance; to the foolish, wisdom; to the guilty, pardon; to the proud, humility; to the censorious, charity; and to the bereaved, submission. To the living, He administers undying hope; and to the dying, He promises endless life.

So is Christ your Shepherd and are you His sheep? Has He purchased you? Is He your Keeper? Does He have the keys to your heart? Are you acquainted with the marks of sheep plainly laid out in John 10: knowing the Great Shepherd, listening to His voice, loving Him, trusting in Him, and following after Him? Do you know the inward joy of bowing under His loving authority, acknowledging His wise ownership, finding freedom and contentment in willing slavery to Him alone, and experiencing a confidence that "all things shall work together for good to them that love God" (Romans 8:28)?

Examine yourself closely, for goats are often found amid the sheep. Be honest with yourself. Is the Shepherd-Lord everything to you? Is He the foundation of your hope, the object of your faith, the center of your love, the guarantee of your safety, and the pledge of your prosperity? Can you say that you belong to the covenant of grace, which is "the way by which God through Christ becomes the property of the sinner and the sinner becomes the property of God"?[8]

If you are strangers to God's grace, are you determined to shepherd yourselves into death, hell, and damnation? Can you not see that Satan's shepherding seems sweet in the beginning, but soon becomes bitter and leads to a tragic end? Do you not see the frown behind the accuser's outward smile and the hatred beneath his silver tongue? That false shepherd is a roaring, devouring lion!

The way of Christ may seem bitter in the beginning as it hedges you in with thorns to keep you from sin, but in the end, it leads to sweetness. These two shepherds differ from each other as much as burning hatred differs from burning love. Oh, that the Lord may yet win over your soul, and bring you to confess with Joshua, "As for me and my house, we will serve the Lord" (Joshua 24:15)!

Praise to our eternal and Almighty God, the Shepherd of sheep. He is the exalted Creator, the Shepherd of the weak and helpless. He is Wisdom, the Shepherd of the foolish and ignorant. He is the Lord our Righteousness, and Shepherd for unrighteous sheep. He is the perfect, holy, undefiled Lamb of God, the Shepherd of polluted, guilty, death-bound, and hell-worthy sinners. He is the purchasing, owning, and keeping Lord Jesus, the Shepherd of sheep who were bound for death and condemnation.

Will I not then love my Shepherd with all my heart, soul, mind, and strength? He gave His life to rescue mine, He is alive again and my Shepherd still! He regards me as His ransomed sheep. He lives to claim His blood-bought property, to rescue, rule, and defend it. Unworthy and unstable as I am, my Shepherd is the gracious and unchanging Lord! Feeble and defenseless as I am, my Shepherd is Almighty God! His fullness supplies me and His wisdom directs me. His power protects me, and His right hand upholds me. And He receives me into His everlasting fold! Help me understand Thy marvelous love, O Lord. Cause me to cry out in adoration, "The LORD is my shepherd."

2

Who Lacks Nothing?

I shall not want.

—Psalm 23:1b

The Lord never promises His people an easy life. Holy warfare against sin and their mortal enemies, the devil, the world, and their own flesh,[1] is inevitable. The Master warns His sheep, "In the world ye shall have tribulation" (John 16:33), yes, even "much tribulation" (Acts 14:22).

Of all the enemies believers encounter while engaged in spiritual warfare, their own heart is the greatest culprit. The old nature within them stands on the front line of opposition to the seed of regeneration, never ceasing to fire at every fruit of the new birth. Self becomes their greatest enemy, obstacle, and disappointment.

Self creeps into everything, frustrating the child of God's desire to live to the honor and glory of God. Self cleaves to all the Lord gives. Self always gets in the way. The Holy Spirit uses self to help God's children see the depths of their misery. They learn to confess with Job, "I abhor myself and repent in dust and ashes" (Job 42:6). They look at themselves and cry out, "I am lacking in everything."

You might say, "That sounds like a tragic and hard life." Yes, it is a hard life, but not a tragic one. There is a joy in the emptiness of God's children that they would not trade for all the shallow joys of the world. Furthermore, their emptiness is not an end in itself but serves to make room in their soul for Jesus Christ. The Holy Spirit drives them to God's throne with this sense of emptiness and the desire to be filled with His grace. When they learn to find nothing in self, they also learn to possess everything in God.

God's people live in the paradoxes of 2 Corinthians 6:9-10, "As unknown, and yet well known; as dying, and, behold, we live; as chastened, and not killed; as sorrowful, yet always rejoicing; as poor, yet making many rich; as having nothing, and yet possessing all things." They are a unique people with a unique life.

Jehovah's sheep have nothing yet they possess everything. In the words of Psalm 23:1b, "I shall not want." To understand the unique life of believers, we must examine who they are and why they shall not want. This chapter will focus on the question: *Who shall not want?*

Our text is bold, wonderful, profound, and sweeping in asserting: "I shall not want." Based on, "The Lord is my shepherd," this statement is the confession of sheep that are utterly satisfied with their purchaser and owner—the Jehovah-Shepherd. David is saying, "as a poor, foolish, dependent, and wandering sheep, I shall not want. I shall not lack. I rest in the Great Shepherd's all-sufficient care." The words "not want" literally mean, "not lacking" that is, not deficient in proper care and management. It also suggests utter satisfaction and submission to the Lord's shepherding. "I shall not want," is the exclamation of a sheep that puts wholehearted trust in its Shepherd and is content with its portion in life.

No one likes to experience want or discontentment. By nature, we want to be satisfied and happy. We want to say with David, "I shall not want." We are prone to include ourselves too quickly in our text's words. Therefore, it is crucial that we maintain from the very beginning that only God's people, as living members of His flock, can be included in the confession "I shall not want."

Who really are God's true sheep? What marks of grace confirm that I am a member of the Shepherd's flock? Of the numerous signs that a sheep belongs to a certain shepherd, one sign is foundational to all others. This mark quickly reveals the rightful shepherd of a flock as well as the ultimate sign of the sheep that belong to him. The love of sheep for their shepherd is the mark of a good shepherd. If this distinguishing feature is missing, all is missing.

Even to a stranger, it is obvious that faithful sheep are so fond of their shepherd that they are aware of his every movement. When he stops, they stop; when he moves, they move. They want to keep close to him at all costs, even if he should lead them to poor pasture. They love good pasture, but they love their good shepherd more.

This love is the mark that cannot be missing. "And now abideth faith, hope, charity, these three; but the greatest of these is charity," says 1 Corinthians 13:13. Love is essential if we claim we have spiritual life. As 1 Corinthians 13:2 says, "Though I have the gift of prophecy, and understand all mysteries, and all knowledge; and though I have all faith, so that I could remove mountains, and have not charity, I am nothing." Love was the great test Jesus imposed on Peter (John 21:15). Love is the test by which we must examine ourselves. Do you love God?

Many people say too easily, "I love the Lord." If we say love is the mark, there is a danger that we include many in Christ's flock who are not His real sheep at all. This danger, however, does not call us to change the mark of love, but to explain it. Many people who say they are Christians love an imaginary god, not the God of the Bible. God's sheep have a true love for the living God. They are drawn to love their Shepherd because He first loved them (1 John 4:19). Examine yourself to determine if you really love God in light of the following ten marks of love in the true sheep of God:

(1) The first mark of love toward the shepherd is a *desire* for his presence and fellowship. A faithful sheep is restless and discontent apart from its shepherd. No fellow sheep, pasture, work, or play can be a substitute for his shepherd.

So it is with God's spiritual sheep. When the Lord takes believers into His flock in the moment of regeneration, they soon discover what it means to have every desire of their renewed soul long after God. They say with Isaiah, "With my soul have I desired thee in the night; yea, with my spirit within me will I seek thee early" (Isaiah 26:9), and with David, "My heart and flesh crieth out for the living God" (Psalm 84:2).

As a couple in love fervently desire to converse with each other, so the goal of God's child is communion with the Lord. God's children can never love the Lord as He deserves, yet they know something of an intense love that flames forth with burning desire towards the Lord, causing them to say at times with the psalmist, "My soul followeth hard after thee" (Psalm 63:8). Love desires union, and joy flows out of that union. He who loves God loves His appearing and His abiding. Ralph Erskine said, "It is their purpose to live and die with him; and to live upon him, for wisdom, righteousness, sanctification, and redemption."[2]

Panting after God goes far deeper than merely wanting God to fulfill our selfish desires or to quiet our consciences. Believers desire communion with God for God's honor and glory. Their desire perseveres, for it is not the fleeting desire of temporary faith. It is an earnest desire that arises from a sense of having lost God in Adam's fall. Samuel Rutherford said he would rather be in hell with Christ (if it were possible), than live without Him in heaven.[3]

Is communion with God the desire of your soul?

(2) Love for the Shepherd evidences itself in *delight* in Him. God's true sheep rejoice in the Lord Jesus as a hidden treasure (Matthew 13:44), experiencing greater joy and power in one day of communion with Him than in a lifetime of worldly pleasures (Psalms 4:6–7; 63:3; 84:10). When faith is exercised, and love is fiery, believers are so set on the Lord that they desire nothing more. "Show us the Father," Philip said, "and it sufficeth us" (John 14:8). They agree wholeheartedly with the first question of the Westminster Shorter Catechism: "What is the chief end of man? Man's chief end is to enjoy God, and glorify Him forever."[4] If God is our treasure, there our heart will be also.

What is your delight and joy? Do you know something of the hatred of sin described by the Heidelberg Catechism as "sincere sorrow of heart that we have provoked God by our sins, and more and more to hate them and to flee from them"? Do you have a "sincere joy of heart in God, through Christ, and with love and delight to live according to the will of God in all good works"?[5] Believers can relate to Rutherford's wonderful experience: "Since He looked upon me, my heart is not my own; He hath run away to heaven with it."[6] God's people delight in Him (Psalm 37:4), while for the wicked, "God is not in all his thoughts" (Psalm 10:4). Which description suits you?

(3) Sheep also have a deep *admiration* for their shepherd. By their actions, they reveal that no shepherd can match their own. If it were possible to gather all the shepherds in the entire world, and a sheep could pick out the best, strongest, and most courageous shepherd, a faithful sheep would choose its own shepherd.

Think back to when you were a child. If you had brought together all the fathers of the children in your class in order to pick the best, strongest, and most courageous father, I imagine you would have picked your own father. Such is the love of a child for his father. My wife and I were once in the home of a man of small stature. While we were visiting, a very tall man stopped in. One son said to him, "You are very tall—almost as tall as my father." Admiration for his own father was so strong that his short father stood tall in his imagination.

Even more are believers led to admire their shepherding God. They have the greatest Shepherd of the universe as their Leader. His greatness is not a product of their imagination. He is the wisest, strongest, most courageous, and most faithful Shepherd. There is no god like Jehovah. "To whom then will ye liken me, or shall I be equal, saith the Holy One" (Isaiah 40:25). Jehovah's sheep choose their Shepherd above all others. Their love for Him causes them to tell of Jehovah's excellencies so that others also may fall in love with Him. With heart, voice, and life, true believers yearn to honor their Master above all others, in all circumstances and through all the days of their lives.

They desire to proclaim His greatness and glory throughout the length and breadth of the world (Psalm 96). They sing for joy when their Shepherd is exalted. Their prayer is that the preaching of His gospel may bring forth much fruit to the glory of His worthy name.

Thou art, O God, our boast, the glory of our power;
Thy sovereign grace is e'er our fortress and our tower.[7]

Is the glory of God the supreme purpose of your soul? Even though you often fall into temptation and sin, can you appeal to heaven's courts that all the prevailing evil in your life is against your soul's committed purpose and your deepest desires? Can you say, "I can have no rest until I am brought to that place where God is exalted to the highest and man abased to the lowest"?

(4) A sheep loves its shepherd so much that *the shepherd can do nothing wrong.* A sheep thoroughly loves its shepherd, and therefore thoroughly loves what its shepherd does. Such love moved Moses to sing, "He is the Rock, his work is perfect: for all his ways are judgment: a God of truth and without iniquity, just and right is he" (Deuteronomy 32:4).

Jehovah's spiritual sheep love their Shepherd so much that they do not want to change Him at all. They come to love their Great Shepherd for His perfections: His spotless holiness, His unfathomable wisdom, His unconditional faithfulness, His abounding grace, His sovereign goodness, and His unflinching justice. They come to love Him for His conduct, for what He withholds and for what He grants. They love Him for His rebukes and for His approval. They love Him even for His disciplining rod, knowing that He makes and keeps all things well. Grace sees beauty in all that the Lord does. Such love declares with Job in his sorrows, "the LORD gave, and the LORD hath taken away; blessed be the name of the LORD" (Job 1:21).

Such love causes believers to confess with David, "One thing have I desired of the LORD, that will I seek after; that I may dwell in the house of the LORD all the days of my life, to behold the beauty of the LORD, and to enquire in his temple" (Psalm 27:4). Petty criticisms fall away as a complaining spirit gives way to a growing inclination to praise.

(5) The fifth mark of love for the shepherd is *trust*. A sheep does not worry where it will pasture tomorrow or where it will find shelter as winter comes on. Sheep rest in the confidence that their master knows how to meet their needs.

The true sheep of the Lord are defined by their faith in Christ. To outsiders, the Shepherd says, "Ye believe not, because ye are not of my sheep" (John 10:26). Sheep have experienced the struggle and joy of expressing all the needs of their bodies and souls to the Lord in prayer. They know there is nothing so difficult for flesh and blood as to hand itself over to another. Yet blessing results, for it is their "only comfort in life and death" to be "not my own," but to "belong unto my faithful Savior Jesus Christ."[8] Their prayer is, "Lord, grant me to know Paul's assurance that, 'Whether we live therefore, or die, we are the Lord's'" (Romans 14:8).

While trust is the mark of every true sheep, it is also a pathway of growth. Believers learn to give everything over to the Lord in trust through a fourfold lesson in the school of free grace. First, they learn that they cannot manage the least matter by themselves, for they will spoil everything. Second, they learn that the Lord is worthy to receive everything. Third, they learn that the Lord alone can make and keep all things well. Finally, they learn that the Lord has full right to possess them entirely, for they belong to Him.

Seek grace to give your unanswerable riddles, your impossible responsibilities, and your unbearable burdens to the Lord. His shepherd heart cannot bear to hear one sheep bleating in distress. He will not tarry; He will come. When He comes, He brings everything that is needed along with Him. He knows our frame; He remembers we are but dust. Let your prayer be: "O God, grant us trusting grace, for if our hand is in Thy hand, like a little child whose hand is held by his father, we shall 'not be afraid for the terror by night; nor for the arrow that flieth by day'" (Psalm 91:5).

The seal of the American Baptist Foreign Mission Society in 1814 shows an ox standing between an altar and a plow, with the motto, "Ready for either," written below. It warns us to be ready to work in God's field yoked to the plow, or ready to fall beneath God's sacrificial sword upon the altar. Love for Christ leads us to say, "Lord, I am Thy willing sheep. Thy will be done."

(6) Another mark of sheep love is *humility*. Love is humble. The love of God revealed in the cross of Christ strikes a decisive blow against believers' worldly pride (Galatians 6:14). They become as children as they trod the kingdom road to increasing humility (Matthew 18:3–4). The more fruit a tree contains, the lower it hangs to the ground.

Publicly, a hypocrite may appear humble, but he is presumptuous in assuming that he is with the Lord (Luke 18:11). True humility is publicly as bold as a lion when God's truth is called into question, but it cannot come low enough when alone with the Lord. Witness

Elijah. On Mount Carmel, in the presence of all Israel, this prophet stood tall in courage. However, when he prayed, he "cast himself down upon the earth, and put his face between his knees" (1 Kings 18:42). God's ambassador, clothed with boldness, was clothed with humility before Jehovah.

Why was there such a drastic change in Elijah? Because true humility recognizes that man is nothing before God. True humility strips us of vanity and makes us less than "the small dust of the balance," or a mere drop of water in a bucket (Isaiah 40:15). Thus Elijah was filled with holy amazement that the smoking fire of God's holiness had left not one of his hairs singed.

(7) Sheep are *sensitive* to things that displease their shepherd. Spiritual sensitivity causes grief over and hatred of sin as well as a childlike fear of the Lord's name. We must hate sin with a holy hatred because it stands in the way of the two greatest goals in our life, namely, to honor and glorify God above all, and to enjoy communion with the God whom we worship and adore. Is that your life's purpose, too?

Sorrow over and hatred of sin is inseparably bound up with a tender fear of Jehovah. This causes the people of God to be swayed more by the smiles and frowns of God than by the smiles and frowns of man. With Joseph we say, "How then can I do this great wickedness, and sin against God?" (Genesis 39:9). It is also fear mixed with holy jealousy for the Lord's name and His church.

(8) Love for the shepherd displays itself by following the shepherd with *childlike obedience*. When the shepherd-sheep relationship is strong, a shepherd can lead his flock through dangerous territory and even to death without the slightest bleat of protest from his sheep. They follow as if they see nothing but him.

Likewise, Jehovah's sheep unashamedly follow Christ with a faith blind to all but Him. Hebrews 11:8 tells us, "By faith Abraham, when he was called to go out into a place which he should after receive for an inheritance, obeyed; and he went out, not knowing whither he went." Beyond all reason, God's children receive grace to obey the Word and do the will of the Lord. Think also of what Peter said to Jesus: "Master, we have toiled all the night, and have taken nothing: nevertheless at thy word I will let down the net" (Luke 5:5).

Sheep do not obey their shepherd perfectly, but they do so with sincerity. The Heidelberg Catechism says, "Even the holiest men, while in this life, have only a small beginning of this obedience; yet so, that with a sincere resolution they begin to live, not only according to some, but all the commandments of God."[9] Do you exercise this obedience, even if it is only a small beginning?

(9) Love for the shepherd progressively produces sheep who are *like-minded*. The Lord teaches His flock to think biblically rather than as the world thinks. He trains them to love what He loves: His glory, His truth, His grace, His kingdom, His people, and His Son. He teaches them to hate what He hates: "a proud look, a lying tongue, and hands that shed innocent blood, a heart that deviseth wicked imaginations, feet that be swift in running to mischief, a false witness that speaketh lies, and he that soweth discord among brethren" (Proverbs 6:16–19).

The Shepherd trains His sheep to be discerning in all that they see, hear, and do. He carefully instructs them how to detect false shepherds, heretical gospels, and unfit pastures. He causes them to want only the nutritious feed of the doctrines of grace. He directs them to walk before Him in the land of the living and to do nothing that He cannot bless.

(10) Finally, Jehovah's flock experiences that all marks of grace are *rooted in the everlasting love of their Shepherd*. Sheep who love the Shepherd will eternally endure because the Shepherd loves His flock according to the triune God's unalterable, eternal decree. "We love him because he first loved us" (1 John 4:19). Our Shepherd's love is eternal, sovereign, unchangeable, sacrificial, condescending, patient, and infinite. He is worthy of all our love in return. Just as children

will never be able to repay their parents for all they have done out of love for them, so God's children will spend eternity unable to repay what the Lord has done on their behalf.

Are you experientially acquainted with these ten marks of love for the Jehovah-Shepherd?

- desire for Him
- delight in Him
- admiration for Him
- confidence that He does no wrong
- trust in Him
- humility before Him
- sensitive reverence in His presence
- following Him in childlike obedience
- biblical like-mindedness with Him
- knowing everlasting love from Him

Be honest with yourself. Apply the touchstone of these biblical marks of grace to your heart. Though you may be the weakest, smallest, and most helpless sheep, if you belong to the Great Shepherd, you shall not want. Never forget that the smallest lambs in the flock have the choicest portion of all true sheep, for He carries them in His arms where they can hear the beating heart of their Shepherd (Isaiah 40:11).

Are these ten marks increasing in your life? If you have left your first love you are in serious trouble. Remember from where you have fallen, repent, and do the first works (Revelation 2:4-5). Stephen Charnock wrote, "We must not only examine whether we have a wedding garment, but also whether it be well kept and brushed; whether no moths be got into it, no new spots dashed upon it …. Graces are to be purified, as well as sins purged out; grace, as well as metal, for want of rubbing and exercise, will gather rust."[10]

Whether you are young or old, prepare to meet your God. If the weight of eternity registers with you as it should, every day should be a day of self-examination. Allow yourself no rest until you can say with the psalmist, "The LORD is my shepherd, I shall not want."

3

How the Lord's Sheep
Shall Lack Nothing

I shall not want.
—Psalm 23:1b

We have seen that the Shepherd's sheep have experienced something of ten marks of grace flowing from a Spirit-wrought love towards their Shepherd: desire for Him, delight in Him, admiration for Him, confidence that He does no wrong, trust in Him, humility before Him, reverence in His presence, childlike obedience in following Him, biblical like-mindedness with Him, and the knowledge of everlasting love from Him.

Now we will consider *how* the Shepherd will provide so that they lack nothing.

His Sheep Can Lack Temporal and Spiritual Goods

The first principle of lacking nothing is that the Lord's sheep *can suffer want temporally and spiritually.* By confessing, "I shall not want," David was not saying that believers will never be placed in the crucible of material lack or the furnace of spiritual want.

Psalm 23 does not advocate the heretical viewpoint that has become common among preachers who teach that if a person is prospering temporally, it means that God's blessing rests upon his life. Conversely, if a person is not prospering materially, his faith has been too small. We shudder when God is presented as an imaginary Santa Claus whose purpose is to make us rich. Rather, Revelation 3:17 says, "I will spue thee out of my mouth because thou sayest, I am rich, and increased with goods, and have need of nothing; and knowest not that thou art wretched, and miserable, and poor, and blind, and naked."

Job, Elijah, John the Baptist, and even Christ Himself experienced great hardship. From experience, David knew better than to say that sheep in the Shepherd's care will never experience a lack of physical prosperity. Had he not been hounded for years by the forces of Saul as well as those of his estranged son Absalom? Obviously, David was a sheep who had known intense hardship and anguish of spirit. David's psalms testify that God's comfort and help often seemed to be far from him, while sin, doubt, terror, enemies, and God's judgments seemed near. To say it bluntly: *sometimes God's sheep feel their lives are only a bundle of wants.*

To truly say, "I shall not want," we must see with our faith and not with our eyes. Martin Luther said that if we follow our feelings instead of God's Word, we may find ourselves thinking, "If the Lord is my Shepherd, why does He impose this burden on me, that the world torments and persecutes me so cruelly through no fault of mine? I am sitting in the midst of wolves, I am not sure of my life for a moment; but I do not see any shepherd who would protect me." Luther says we may then ask, "Why does He permit the devil to harm me so greatly with terror and doubts? Besides, I find myself totally unfit, weak, impatient, still laden with many sins. I feel no security but only doubt, no comfort but only fear and trembling because of God's wrath. When will He ever begin to manifest in me that He is my Shepherd?"[1]

So what did David mean when he wrote, "I shall not want"? Philippians 4:19 says, "But my God shall supply all your need according to his riches in glory by Christ Jesus." Psalm 34:10 tells us, "They that seek the LORD shall not want any good thing." In the simple words of Psalm 23, David proclaims that Jehovah will meet all the needs of His sheep and work all things, both temporal and spiritual, for their good. How will He do this?

The Shepherd's Provision for This Temporal Life

In the first place, David is confessing that the Lord's sheep will not lack what they need for this temporal life. God has everything to give, for all gold and silver is His (Haggai 2:8). The earth is the Lord's, and all that fills it (Psalm 24:1). God says, "Every beast of the forest is mine, and the cattle upon a thousand hills" (Psalm 50:10). However, that does not imply that God promises His flock earthly abundance. Psalm 75:6–7 says, "For promotion cometh neither from the east, nor from the west, nor from the south. But God is the judge: he putteth down one, and setteth up another." He is able to give His sheep earthly wealth, but His promise only extends to earthly necessities. In famine, in calamity, and in old age He shall fulfill His own word: "I have been young and now am old; yet have I not seen the righteous forsaken, nor his seed begging bread" (Psalm 37:25). He who feeds the ravens and makes the lilies bloom will not starve His children.

"I shall not want" is a great comfort to the poor, tested family of God. It assures them: "Do not be afraid. Lift up your head. Whatever is truly needed shall be given by the lavish hand of a faithful Shepherd." True believers possess more riches than all the banks in the world. Even if nearly bankrupt outwardly, they still possess the rich bank of faith.

Like Abraham, even on the way to the mount of sacrifice, they learn
to say, "God will provide" (Genesis 22:8).

The Heidelberg Catechism summarizes God's temporal provisions
for believers in expounding the fourth petition of the Lord's Prayer:
"Give us this day our daily bread." It says, "Be pleased to provide us with
all things necessary for the body, that we may thereby acknowledge
Thee to be the only fountain of all good, and that neither our care
nor industry, nor even Thy gifts, can profit us without Thy blessing;
and therefore that we may withdraw our trust from all creatures and
place it alone in Thee."[2]

The catechism is saying that living in the providential care of the
Shepherd enriches believers more than all the diamonds in the world.
It implies that the Lord teaches us profitable lessons and produces
precious fruit in our lives through His dealings with us, confirming
Romans 8:28: "We know that all things work together for good to them
that love God, to them who are the called according to his purpose."

The Lord brings us distress to teach us important lessons. First, He
teaches us to look to His hand in *total dependence*. Trials often come to
us to teach us that our supplies come from the Great Shepherd, who
is the Heir of all things. The Lord is indeed our "only fountain of all
good"; He teaches us total dependence upon Him for the least blessing.
In this way the Holy Spirit teaches us to "withdraw our trust from all
creatures" and place our trust alone in the Lord.

Second, the Great Shepherd instructs His flock through afflictions
that He is rich to *show His mercy and compassion* to those who fear Him.
Matthew Henry wrote, "Man's extremity is God's opportunity," that
is, God's opportunity for "magnifying his own power."[3] People of God,
look back on the path of your pilgrimage. Can't you see times when
God has met you and helped you? Haven't you received deliverance
in a remarkable way? By His providences, the Lord teaches His sheep

to call Him by the same name that Hagar gave Him, "Thou God seest me" (Genesis 16:13).

Third, the Shepherd gives His sheep trials to help them *treasure His grace* more than His gifts. The favor of God becomes more precious to them than riches. Moses' prayer becomes theirs: "If thy presence go not with me, carry us not up hence" (Exodus 33:15). Can you say, "I would be happier with God's favor in a lowly cottage than to dwell with the wicked in a luxurious palace? 'Better is little with the fear of the Lord than great treasure and trouble therewith'" (Proverbs 15:16). Truly, "a little that a righteous man hath is better than the riches of many wicked" (Psalm 37:16).

Fourth, God leads His sheep down paths of difficulty to teach them *submission*. They learn to look beyond man, the devil, or accidents to acknowledge that everything comes from the Lord's hand. Submissive believers pray, "I opened not my mouth, because thou didst it" (Psalm 39:9). They bow before the sovereignty of God and justify Him in all His doings. The Lord's sheep learn that hell and condemnation are what they deserve. When suffering affliction, instead of saying, "Why me?" they come to say, "Why not me?" In the furnace of affliction they sing Psalm 46:10, "Be still, and know that I am God." Like Job, they not only acknowledge God—"The Lord gave and the Lord hath taken away"—but praise Him: "Blessed be the name of the Lord" (Job 1:21). They learn to cling to God as their dearest Friend even when He appears to act as their greatest enemy. Do you know the fruit of true submission as a result of the Lord's providential dealings? Can you confess with David, "It is good for me that I have been afflicted; that I might learn thy statutes" (Psalm 119:71)?

Finally, the Lord bestows upon His sheep the grace of *godly contentment*. True contentment does not depend upon what we *have* but upon what we *desire* to have. Food and clothing were enough for Paul, but "they that will be rich fall into temptation and a snare, and into many foolish and hurtful lusts" (1 Timothy 6:8, 9). Because of our fallen nature, the more a man has, the more he wants. Instead of filling the vacuum, possessions only multiply it. Blessed are those who have learned to pray like Agur, "Give me neither poverty nor riches; feed me with food convenient for me: lest I be full, and deny thee, and say, Who is the LORD? Or lest I be poor, and steal, and take the name of my God in vain" (Proverbs 30:8-9). As Charles Colton quipped, "Our incomes should be like our shoes, if too small, they will gall and pinch us, but if too large, they will cause us to stumble, and to trip."[4] Paul said, "Godliness with contentment is great gain" (1 Timothy 6:6). With the apostle, let us learn to be content in every situation, knowing that "I can do all things through Christ which strengtheneth me" (Philippians 4:11-13).

The Shepherd's Provision for Their Spiritual Life

David also teaches that the Lord's sheep will not lack anything necessary for their spiritual life. He who provides for the body will also provide for the soul. The proof of this can be found in Psalm 23 itself. Listen to David's bold proclamations:

- I shall not lack spiritual *rest*, for, "he maketh me to lie down in green pastures."

- I shall not lack spiritual *refreshment*, for, "he leadeth me beside the still waters."

- I shall not lack spiritual *restoration*, for, "he restoreth my soul."

- I shall not lack spiritual *righteousness*, for, "he leadeth me in the paths of righteousness for his name's sake."

- I shall not lack spiritual *protection*, for, "though I walk through the valley of the shadow of death, I will fear no evil."

- I shall not lack spiritual *comfort*, for, "thou art with me; thy rod and thy staff, they comfort me."

- I shall not lack spiritual *provision*, for "thou preparest a table before me in the presence of mine enemies."

- I shall not lack spiritual *anointing*, for "thou anointest my head with oil."

- I shall not lack spiritual *liberty*, for "my cup runneth over."

- I shall not lack spiritual *blessings for eternity*, for, "surely goodness and mercy shall follow me all the days of my life: and I will dwell in the house of the LORD forever."

God's grace abounds for the Shepherd's sheep. It internally and effectually calls them to repentance (Galatians 1:15), regenerates them (Titus 3:5), justifies them (Romans 3:24), sanctifies, and preserves them (Romans 8:29, 39). Grace offers everything to Jehovah's sheep: pardoning grace to forgive them; restoring grace to return them; consoling grace to heal their broken hearts; upholding grace to strengthen them in time of trouble and warfare; preventing grace to keep them from sin; accompanying grace to go with them moment by moment; and following grace to pursue them to the grave. Truly we may give our "Amen" to God's promise, "My grace is sufficient for thee" (2 Corinthians 12:9). We can sing,

> Now to God, our Strength and Saviour
> Render praise and loudly sing;
> In our father's God rejoicing,
> All your noblest music bring.

> I am God the Lord who saved thee,
> And from cruel bondage freed;
> Open wide thy mouth of longing;
> I will satisfy thy need.

> Yea, with wheat the very finest
> I their hunger will supply

Bid the very rocks yield honey
That shall fully satisfy.[5]

The Shepherd's Surprising Dealings for Their Good

When Paul wrote in Romans 8:28, "all things work together for good
to them that love God," he did not say each thing in itself was good,
but that all things, good and evil, work together in God's providence
for the good of the flock of the Lord. The best things, including the
promises of the Father, the work of the Son, and the graces of the
Spirit, work together for the spiritual good of God's children. Even
the worst things are so planned and controlled by God that they too
work together for their good.

No doubt someone will say, "It is easy to understand how good things
work together for good, but how the worst things can work for their
good I cannot comprehend."

Allow me to show you some ways how even divine desertion and
various afflictions work together for the spiritual well-being of believers,
so that we may enter more fully into David's claim, "I shall not want."

Spiritual Desertion for Their Good

One of the most difficult experiences for a believer is feeling the
desolation of divine desertion when all seems dead and barren. David
wrote of this dark winter of the soul, "How long wilt thou forget me,
O Lord? For ever? How long wilt thou hide thy face from me?" (Psalm
13:1). In this sad condition, the Christian asks, "Lord, why castest thou
off my soul? Why hidest thou thy face from me?" (Psalm 88:14). "I
am weary with my groaning; all the night make I my bed to swim; I
water my couch with my tears" (Psalm 6:6). Thomas Watson called
this kind of spiritual desertion "a short hell."[6]

Wilhelmus à Brakel wrote, "Spiritual desertion is a lengthy
withholding and withdrawal of those normal operations and influences
of the Holy Spirit in the regenerate." However, the Holy Spirit does not

cease to indwell believers and continues to support them. They remain justified and adopted children of God. However, their experience of His presence and grace dims. Brakel said, "This causes them to be in darkness, weak in faith, disconsolate, to fall into sin, succumb to temptations, and to remain grieved and fretful in the bearing of a temporal cross."[7] How can this bitter experience work for the good of God's children? Remarkably, in God's wisdom and kindness even spiritual desertion produces good fruit, such as increased humility, a sense of dependency, spiritual hunger, and treasuring God. Just as a tree's roots go deeper in dry times, so the soul becomes more deeply rooted in Christ when the Lord withholds His rain for a season.

Divine desertion drives you to the throne of grace to seek after God's presence more than ever. It causes you to knock at heaven's gates with unceasing petitions: "O LORD God of my salvation, I have cried day and night before thee" (Psalm 88:1). The Lord can use your sense of divine desertion to help you examine your soul and to put to death the accursed thing within that has caused you to desert God and Him to desert you. The freezing winter of divine desertion can kill the deep roots of the weeds of sin. Knowing that the common cause of desertion is sin, such withdrawals should make you hate sin all the more.

When the comforting sense of God's presence is missing, the bereft believer calls forth a more diligent exercise of the spiritual graces, especially faith, hope, and love. We preach to ourselves, saying, "Why art thou cast down, O my soul? And why art thou disquieted in me? Hope thou in God: for I shall yet praise him for the help of his countenance" (Psalm 42:5). Watson wrote, "Faith as a star sometimes shines brightest in the dark night of desertion."[8] Thus the rough file of God's seeming desertion is used to scrape off much spiritual rust. This awakens the soul to treasure heaven's gifts instead of taking them for granted. Missing God purges a Christian of weakness, laziness, and worldliness.

The Holy Spirit uses this sense of divine desertion to cut off our confidence in everything within ourselves—our experiences, humility, prayers, faith, and joy—to make room for the Lord Jesus Christ. Then, too, the Lord may delay manifesting Himself in our conscious, spiritual experience to teach us that His delays are not denials, but rather that His comings are always at His time and in His way. He may hold Himself back to teach you that His presence is not your right but a gift of grace to a sinner (Romans 9:15). He shows us that He remains worthy of all honor even when He seems to desert us, though He is never absent from us.[9]

Like the bride in the Song of Solomon, believers experience divine desertion to rouse them out of spiritual lethargy and to seek Him, crying: "Saw ye him whom my soul loveth?" (Song of Solomon 3:3). He rebukes our careless complacency and reminds us that we are not yet in heaven. We turn from envying the wicked in their earthly prosperity and long to see God's eternal glory (Psalm 73:24–26).

Feeling deserted by God can also increase our reliance upon Christ, for He was forsaken by God for our sins. He cried out on the cross, "My God, my God, why hast thou forsaken me?" (Matthew 27:46). Yet He persevered through the darkness, bearing the guilt of our sins to save us from being truly forsaken by God. He bore the substance of God-forsakenness, while we endure only a shadow of it. Our sense of feeling forsaken is not real forsakenness, for His promise remains true in Christ, "I am with you alway, even unto the end of the world" (Matthew 28:20). That is a great comfort for believers. John Flavel wrote, "Because he was forsaken for a time, you shall not be forsaken forever, for he was forsaken for you."[10]

Even when the Lord feels absent from us, He is still present as our covenant God in all His majesty and grace (Psalm 73:23). Watson said, "When God hides his face from his child, he is still a Father, and his heart is towards his child."[11] Christ is always the Shepherd of His people, so each one may say, "I shall not want."

Afflictions for Their Good

Afflictions can be heavy for a believer. Ralph Erskine said, "There are two things especially that hinder the comfort and consolation of a Christian. The one is sin, the head of the serpent, and the other is affliction, the tail of the serpent."[12] Yet afflictions also serve as medicine in the hands of the Great Shepherd to promote spiritual health in the following ways:

First, through afflictions the Lord *humbles His people*, showing them who and what they are in themselves. He teaches them the same lesson taught to Israel as the Lord led His people "through that great and terrible wilderness, wherein were fiery serpents, and scorpions, and drought, where there was no water; who brought thee forth water out of the rock of flint; who fed thee in the wilderness with manna, which thy fathers knew not, that he might humble thee, and that he might prove thee, to do thee good at thy latter end" (Deuteronomy 8:15-16).

Second, through affliction God's flock *learns what sin is*. By nature sin is God-dishonoring, defiling, and damning. Through affliction, believers learn that sin has the devil for its father, shame for its companion, and death for its wages. William Bridge wrote, "You see how it is in winter, when the leaves are off the hedges, you can see where the birds' nests were; when the leaves were on in the summer time, you could not see those nests: and so in prosperous times men do not see the nests of their hearts and lives; but when their leaves are off, then their nests are seen. Suffering times are sin-discovering times."[13]

Third, the Great Shepherd uses affliction to *destroy the deadly disease of sin* in His flock, so they may bring forth healthy and godly fruit. Affliction is the Shepherd's dog, sent out not to devour the sheep, but to bring them back into the fold. Sanctified affliction cures sin by grace. "Before I was afflicted I went astray," David says, "but now have I kept thy word" (Ps. 119:67). It is as good for a child of God to be chastised with affliction as it is for a young branch on a vine to be pruned (John 15:2).

Fourth, the Lord uses affliction *to cause His people to seek Him*, to bring them back into communion with Himself, and to keep them close by His side. As sheep stay close to their shepherd in storms, so the Lord said of Israel, "In their affliction they will seek me early" (Hosea 5:15).

Fifth, the Lord uses afflictions *to conform His flock to Christ*, making them partakers of His sufferings and His image. God had only one Son without sin, but none without affliction (Hebrews 12:7). Paul aspired "that I may know him, and the power of his resurrection, and the fellowship of his sufferings, being made conformable unto his death" (Philippians 3:10). He understood that God's afflicting rod is a chisel to carve Christ's image more fully upon His people. Through the way of suffering believers follow the Lamb. Every path of affliction they encounter has already been traveled, endured, and sanctified by their Shepherd. Can you complain about the light crosses you have to bear as guilty sinners when you behold the heavy cross Christ had to bear for your sake?

Sixth, afflictions work for good because *the Lord balances them with spiritual comfort and joy.* "Your sorrow," Christ tells His disciples, "shall be turned into joy" (John 16:20). He brings His people into the wilderness to speak comfort to them (Hosea 2:14). Where godly suffering abounds, godly consolation also abounds (2 Corinthians 1:4–5). As Psalm 30:5 says, "Weeping may endure for a night, but joy cometh in the morning."

Seventh, affliction *keeps God's children walking by faith and not by sight* (2 Corinthians 5:7). If enjoying God and His benefits were always what believers experienced in this world, they could begin to live off of their provisions instead of their Provider. Therefore, with their sweet meals, the Lord orders some sour sauce so His children may live not by sense, but by faith. In prosperity God's people talk of living by faith, but in adversity they come to the experiential knowledge of what it means to live by faith.

Eighth, affliction works for good in *weaning Jehovah's flock away from the world and preparing them for heaven.* Paul wrote in 2 Corinthians 4:17–18, "For our light affliction, which is but for a moment, worketh for us a far more exceeding and eternal weight of glory; while we look not at the things which are seen, but at the things which are not seen: for the things which are seen are temporal; but the things which are not seen are eternal." Affliction lifts the soul heavenwards to look for "a city which hath foundations, whose builder and maker is God" (Hebrews 11:10). Affliction paves their way to glory. "He that rides to be crowned," John Trapp wrote, "will not think much of a rainy day."[14]

Children of God, is not this enough to convince you that affliction is for your spiritual good? You "shall not want" anything necessary or good for you, both temporally and spiritually. The Lord is your Shepherd.

Some years ago a teacher asked her students if anyone could recite the twenty-third Psalm. A little girl came to the front, faced her class, and simply said, "The Lord's my shepherd, *that's all I want.*" Little did she realize the depth of what she was saying, for "If God be for us, who can be against us?" (Romans 8:31). May God give us faith to believe this comforting truth and embrace it.

4

Why and When the Lord's Sheep Shall Lack Nothing

I shall not want.
—Psalm 23:1b

We have considered the marks of grace found in Jehovah's flock. We have also seen that this flock will not lack anything necessary for body or soul. In His providence, the Shepherd makes all things, good and bad, work together for the flock's welfare—even such things as divine desertion and providential affliction. The sheep who love God stand firm upon the promise of Romans 8:28, "And we know that all things work together for good to them that love God, to them who are the called according to his purpose."

The questions that now confront us are: What is the basis for this promise that they shall not want? When can God's children expect the promise to be fulfilled?

59

Why the Lord's Sheep Shall Lack Nothing

In distinction from every other flock in the world, why will the Lord's flock not lack any necessary thing? Is the cause found in believers themselves or in their divine Shepherd? Or is it found in a cooperative effort of Shepherd and sheep? What is the foundation of David's daring confession "I shall not want"?

Many people believe the foundation of this confession, at least partially, is in the flock itself. They attribute the spiritual well-being of God's flock to a decision for Christ made by their own free will, the exercise of prayer, reforming their behavior, doing good works, experiencing convictions of conscience, and/or spiritual exercises and experiences. They attempt, in whole or in part, to attribute the blessing of salvation to the work of man.

Today basically three views of Christian salvation exist. The first view teaches that the gate to salvation is broad and the road is easy to travel. Scripture, however, states, "Strait is the gate, and narrow is the way, which leadeth unto life, and few there be that find it" (Matthew 7:14). This false form of Christianity maintains that man, by his own free will, is able to walk through the gate of regeneration by merely admitting he has sinned and by easily accepting Christ as Savior. The result is a life in which Christianity and the world need not be divorced from one another. This shallow form of Christianity says, "Salvation depends on your decision whether or not you want to be a sheep of the Lord's flock. By accepting Christ you have nothing to lose and everything to gain. Conversion is simple; anyone can be converted anytime he wants to." This view promises forgiveness without repentance, and justification without sanctification.

The second view of salvation is more subtle. It says that the gate to salvation is narrow and the path is challenging, but you can travel it in a progressively easy manner if you want to with some help from God. God has done His part, so now you must do yours. Those teaching this view speak much of God's grace, but they still give the decisive role to man's will and works. They deny the witness of God's infallible Word: "It is not of him that willeth, nor of him that runneth, but of God that showeth mercy" (Romans 9:16).

The third view is the biblical way of salvation. It places salvation fully in the hands of the Shepherd, teaching that the gate to salvation is impossibly narrow for flesh and blood to enter. It presents salvation as nothing less than the divine miracle that Scripture proclaims it to be—impossible for man but possible with God (Matthew 19:25–26). Its watchword is, "Except a man be born again, he cannot see the kingdom of God" (John 3:3). Otherwise all men are blind (2 Corinthians 4:4), and dead in trespasses and sins (Ephesians 2:1).

The biblical view not only teaches that grace is necessary to enter the narrow gate of salvation but continues to be needed to travel the narrow way of salvation and not be sidetracked. In John Bunyan's *Pilgrim's Progress*, Goodwill (i.e., Christ) *pulls* Christian inside the narrow gate and answers one of Pilgrim's questions about the ongoing way of salvation by saying, "Yes, there are many ways butt down upon this, and they are crooked and wide. But thus thou mayest distinguish the right from the wrong, the right only being straight and narrow."[1]

God's sheep do not enter into spiritual life on their own, nor do they then travel onward in a progressively easy way. Obedience to the Shepherd characterizes their life, and His grace provides them with the strength and will to journey along the narrow, difficult path of salvation. Thomas Shepard warned the church of all generations when he said, "Every easy way to heaven is a false way, though ministers declare it from the pulpit and angels publish it from heaven."[2] An easy way to heaven leads to hell. Shepard also warned that trusting in a faith of our own forging instead of one created by God's power is the "most dangerous rock that these times are split upon."[3]

William Gurnall compared the narrow way of salvation to a path between two hedges, behind which archers shoot arrows at God's pilgrims every step of the way. No ground can be gained without a holy war. Believers can even become their own greatest enemy by shooting themselves, for they often find opposition in their hearts and wills. Salvation becomes increasingly challenging, except by God's grace.

Have you experienced the painful way of salvation? Have you cried out for divine grace, knowing that you have no strength to overcome your enemies within and without? Have you found the way of salvation too narrow for self-righteousness and self-reliance? Have you had to lose yourself and fall fully on God's sovereign grace as your only hope for time and eternity?

The greatest reason why the Lord's sheep shall not want is that God has decreed to meet all the needs of His people in Christ Jesus. The Lord was eternally happy within Himself and was not obligated to take one step for His sheep. But it pleased Him to give fallen man full salvation and everlasting life in His Son. Without God's gift, man would be spiritually lacking for all eternity.

Some years ago, a minister visited a school for deaf children. Standing by a small girl at a blackboard, he asked her who created the world. She wrote, "In the beginning God created the heaven and the earth." He then asked how God's people were made a new creation. She wrote, "This is a faithful saying, and worthy of all acceptation, that Christ Jesus came into the world to save sinners; of whom I am chief." Unable to restrain himself, he finally asked her the question that had bothered him since he met these children, "Why has God made you deaf and mute when so many others can speak and hear?" With tears in her eyes she wrote, "Even so, Father: for so it seemed good in thy sight."[4]

God's election of His people is sovereign, eternal, unchangeable, and unfathomable. We can only exclaim with the apostle Paul, "O the depth of the riches both of the wisdom and knowledge of God! How unsearchable are his judgments, and his ways past finding out! For who hath known the mind of the Lord, or who hath been his counsellor?

Or who hath first given to him, and it shall be recompensed unto him again? For of him, and through him, and to him, are all things: to whom be glory for ever" (Romans 11:33–36). God's sheep receive His sovereign good pleasure through the mediation of the Great Shepherd and thus may affirm by faith, "I shall not want."

When the Lord's Sheep Shall Not Want

Who shall not want? The Lord's sheep that have experienced the marks of grace have no want. *How* shall they not want? Out of free grace they shall not want any good or necessary thing, temporal or spiritual. *Why* shall they not want? Out of free grace, Jehovah has elected them to everlasting life. And *when* shall they not want? By the same free grace, they will not want from eternity past, in time, and in eternity to come.

Not Wanting From Eternity Past

God's sheep will not want from eternity past because of the eternal, unquenchable love of the triune God. The eternal fountainhead of love is in the heart of *God the Father* (1 John 4:10). He held His beloved ones in the palms of His hands with His unchangeable and unconditional love. In His justice and love He promised to provide a way of salvation for them, even though they were His enemies. They shall not want because the righteous love of the Father ordained Jesus Christ from eternity to be their Savior, Substitute, and Shepherd (1 Peter 1:19–20). From before the foundation of the world (Ephesians 1:4), the Father gave His only-begotten Son, purposing to deliver Him to death (Acts 2:23). Out of love, the Father promised to turn a deaf ear to the suffering cries of His Beloved One (Psalm 22:1) so that, on the basis of substitutionary justice, God Almighty could listen to His people!

The Lord's sheep will not want because from eternity *Jesus Christ* took upon Himself their cause with unconditional, eternal love (Galatians 2:20). He willingly accepted the elect in the eternal counsel of peace (John 6:38–39). He voluntarily substituted Himself for them to satisfy

God's just demands (Galatians 3:13). Hiding His divinity behind the veil of flesh and blood, He bore their infirmities, endured their sufferings, and was confronted with their temptations (Isaiah 53:4–6; Hebrews 2:14–18). The spotless Lamb of God became sin so that sinners might be free from guilt and condemnation (2 Corinthians 5:21). From eternity He chose to be in want, even to the point of death, so that His flock should never want eternal life.

The sheep of God will not be in want from eternity because *the Holy Spirit*, the third person of the Godhead in the covenant of redemption, was as Thomas Goodwin put it, "the secretary of heaven" who served as "both witness and recorder" of the transactions that took place in the eternal counsel between the Father and the Son (John 16:13).[5] That covenant could not be made without the consent of the Holy Spirit, for both the Father and the Spirit needed to consent to designating Christ as the Mediator of sinners, as Samuel Rutherford clearly shows.[6] But the Spirit's main work in this covenant is His agreement to apply to the elect the saving graces purchased by Christ for them. Thus the Spirit unconditionally gave Himself, out of love with the Father and the Son, to work out the covenant through Christ in time for the elect.[7] He willingly gave Himself from eternity to minister to Christ in His human nature in various ways, from Christ's conception in the womb of Mary until His dying cry, and to dwell in the souls of the elect as their Comforter from the moment of regeneration until their glorification (John 15:26). Though at first their hearts were stone and they hated God, the Spirit would work salvation in them through Christ Jesus and lead them to glory. Christ predicted this, saying, "He shall glorify me: for he shall receive of mine, and shall shew it unto you" (John 16:14).

God's sheep will not want from eternity because their Shepherd is unconditionally bound to love His people. "I will love them freely," He promised (Hosea 14:4). So the three Persons of the Trinity mutually pledged faithfulness to the eternal charter of the covenant of grace.

The Father pledged to the Son, "I shall receive all for whom Thou hast given Thy life as a ransom price." The Son pledged to the Father, "I shall redeem all that Thou hast committed to my charge. Of all that Thou hast given Me, I shall not lose one." The Spirit pledged to both the Father and the Son, "I shall gather them. I shall bring them with weeping and supplication to the throne of grace, and give them faith to believe in the Son of God alone for salvation." Thus before all ages, God bound Himself to Himself in promising eternal life for the elect (Titus 1:1–2).

Sheep of God, the Lord is too jealous of His name and reputation as Chief Shepherd to leave you to yourself. He will not fail; He cannot. God, united within the Godhead, cannot be separated by one divine person failing to take up His portion of the eternal charter. If one hoof of the Lord's flock is left behind or one elect sheep suffers eternal want, God must cease to be God. But that is impossible. Jehovah's sheep have not lacked and cannot lack from eternity because gracious love was established in the triune God's eternal counsel of peace. The entire flock was secured, pledged, and guaranteed from eternity. God's sheep rest on that eternal, unbreakable foundation.

Not Wanting in Time

God's sheep are not only safe from eternity past but are safe in time. In Bible times, a faithful shepherd cared for his flock from morning to evening. In the early morning he would lead his flock from their fold to pasture lands. Armed with rod and staff, the shepherd kept alert for beasts of prey, sickness in his sheep, and the foolish wandering of some. A good shepherd knew that no animal was more foolish than a sheep. They were prone to stumble over steps, hedges, ditches, and poor pastures. The good shepherd gently led them along proper paths.

A conscientious shepherd lived with his sheep day and night. In the evening he brought them into the fold he had constructed. This fold was a large, walled enclosure, open to the sky. A narrow opening in the stone wall served as a door for the sheep to enter and exit. When all his sheep were inside, the shepherd would stand watch in the narrow entrance, filling it with his physical body. Any wild animal or thief that wanted to attack the sheep would first have to kill the shepherd. Thus, with soul and body, the shepherd was bound intimately with his flock.

Christ, the Great Shepherd, is also intimately bound with love for His flock (Hebrews 4:15). Armed with rod and staff, He guards His sheep night and day (Psalm 17:8). He protects them from fatal wounds and enemies. He prevents them from falling into presumption or unbelief. He saves them from harming themselves. He brings them out of the pits into which they fall by their own foolishness (Psalm 40:2). He is the heavenly Physician who applies the balm of Gilead to the diseases of their souls (Jeremiah 8:21-22). He never misdiagnoses His flock's diseases or charges for His services. He built the sheepfold with love in His state of humiliation, and He now stands in the doorway as the sheep's Protector in His state of exaltation. He does not leave His flock alone for one moment. This Shepherd who never sleeps can truly say, "I am the door: by me if any man enter in, he shall be saved, and shall go in and out, and find pasture" (John 10:9).

The Great Shepherd sends the Holy Spirit to make room for Himself in His sheep, glorifies Christ in their souls, and applies Christ to their hearts (John 16:7-14). He does this through the preaching and reading of His Holy Word. He forms in them righteousness, peace, and joy (Romans 14:17). He does His works in time when and as He pleases (Galatians 1:15). For Jacob, twenty years lay between Bethel and Peniel and often he feared, "All these things are against me." Yet he was not forsaken. The Shepherd deals with each person differently. Yet all can say, "Happy is he that hath the God of Jacob for his help" (Psalm 146:5). They are happy because God never ceases to love His flock. The sheep are safe forever for Christ is ever with His flock.

The Shepherd lovingly keeps His sheep till their last breath. Jesus, "having loved his own which were in the world, he loved them unto the end" (John 13:1). The love of the Shepherd includes:

- *sacrificial* love, by which He gave Himself
- *condescending* love, lowering Himself to lift us up
- *unconditional* love for sinners who have forfeited it many times
- *never-fluctuating* love even when we deny Him
- *unquenchable* love that pursues those who wander
- *desiring* love, in which He longs for communion with us
- *unmatchable* love, beyond the love of any mere creature
- *infinite* love, deeper than our misery, higher than our sin
- *patient* love, even when poorly returned
- *unbreakable and unchangeable* love, springing from the heart of God
- *irresistible* love, wooing and conquering and keeping to the end.

As beneficiaries of this love we may exult with Paul, "He that spared not his own Son, but delivered him up for us all, how shall he not with him also freely give us all things? ... Nor height, nor depth, nor any other creature, shall be able to separate us from the love of God, which is in Christ Jesus our Lord" (Romans 8:32, 39). Blessed are the sheep that are hemmed in on all sides by sovereign love from the moment of regeneration to the end of their lives. They shall not want!

Not Wanting for Eternity to Come

As the King's bride from eternity past (Ephesians 1:4; 5:25) and espoused in time (2 Corinthians 11:2), the marriage of the Lamb with the church will be perfected in eternal bliss (Revelation 19:7-9). What begins in eternity goes on for eternity. God's children thus may confess, "The

Shepherd who was faithful from eternity and watchful to shepherd me through all my pilgrimage, will not desert me in the Judgment Day. I shall not want."

What a blessed day it will be for true believers when the Shepherd gathers them at the throne of grace in the courts of heaven! Their day of public acquittal, acknowledgment, and victory over the world will finally arrive. The Great Shepherd will turn His flock over to the Father, saying: "Father, the hour is come. Here am I with those Thou hast given Me. Thine they were and Thou gavest them Me, and I now return them unto Thee. Of all that Thou hast given Me, I have lost none."[8] If heaven resounds with joy over one sinner brought to repentance (Luke 15:7), what shouts of praise will fill its courts when Christ comes for His bride? He who "loved the church, and gave himself for it," will "present it to himself a glorious church, not having spot, or wrinkle, or any such thing," but "holy and without blemish" (Ephesians 5:25, 27).

The Lord's sheep, at long last perfected in holiness, will take the crowns off their heads, cast them at the feet of the King of kings, and confess, "Chief Shepherd, it is all of Thee, through Thee, and unto Thee. Thou hast purchased us with the price of Thy blood freely shed for us. Thou art worthy, O Lord, to receive glory and honor and power: for Thou hast created all things, and for Thy pleasure they are and were created."[9]

The sheep of God's flock will no longer be torn by warfare. No longer will Satan tempt them, no longer will the world oppose them, no longer will sin entice them, no more will unbelief plague them, and no longer will their fleshly, old nature rule over them. No longer will these sheep try to claim Christ's eternally-given robe of righteousness by their own merit. All evil will be walled out and all good walled in. The church triumphant will confess with unspeakable rapture, "The Lord is my shepherd. I shall not want."

Children of God fear not, for your future is secure. As a shepherd goes before his flock, serving as the eyes, ears, heart, and brain for his flock, so God goes before His people and preserves them for tomorrow. He gives enough grace for each day, and His strength is made perfect through our weakness. All our tomorrows have to pass through Him before they get to us. Every tomorrow of His flock will be filled with His presence. Those who possess God will not want.

Often the Lord allows darkness in your life to prepare you for eternal light. Augustine wrote that God pursued him with trouble to prove that he could not find true joy and peace "except in Thee, who teachest us by sorrow, and woundest us to heal us, and killest us that we may not die from Thee."[10] Even though your life may be spiritually battered and broken, God promises to bring you into His heavenly presence. Self must be broken this side of the grave so that we need not be broken on the other side. "A broken and a contrite heart, O God, thou wilt not despise" (Psalm 51:17).

The gates of hell shall not prevail against the church of God for the foundation of the Lord is sure, and the Lord knows those that are His (Matthew 16:18; 2 Timothy 2:19). For all eternity, the flock of God shall not want but proclaim:

> When I in righteousness at last
> Thy glorious face shall see
> When all the weary night is past,
> And I awake with Thee
> To view the glories that abide,
> Then, then I shall be satisfied.[11]

A Warning to Goats

The wicked must be warned of what will also take place on that Day of Days. The goats will be separated from the sheep, gathered together, and sent to eternal destruction. There are no words to express the horror that will overwhelm Satan's goats in that day. Eternal wretchedness, misery, blindness, nakedness, and poverty will be their portion (Isaiah 65:13–14; Revelation 3:17). It will be too late for them to obtain cleansing blood, secure true peace, and seek a place to go with all their needs. The door of grace will be forever shut (Matthew 25:10–12). Oh, how dreadful it will be to stand before the judgment seat of the Almighty without Christ as our righteousness! What misery to be exposed to the wrath of God and the Lamb forever!

If you are perishing, it is still possible for a goat to become a sheep, transformed by grace in true conversion. First Timothy 1:15 promises, "This is a faithful saying and worthy of all acceptation, that Christ Jesus came into the world to seek and to save sinners; of whom I am chief." Christ still offers His grace, saying, "Foolish sinner, receive Me as your wisdom. Diseased sinner, trust Me as your heavenly Physician. Guilty sinner, I am the Priest who can cleanse all sin by My blood. Enslaved sinner, turn to Me as your liberating King."

God comes to you in Christ, proclaiming, "I have no pleasure in the death of a sinner, but rather, that he should repent and live" (Ezekiel 33:11). Sinner, will you hate the Shepherd who can supply all your wants and heal all your wounds? Why will you renounce the only One who can truly make you happy in this life, in death, in judgment, and in eternity?

For your own good, consider what it must be like to be cast into hell after having heard of the Great Shepherd and the way of salvation. Your refusal of His services will earn you eternal torment. The nations who never received an opportunity to hear the gospel will be set, as it were, on the surface of hell, but you will be thrust down to the very center of damnation, in torments even worse than Sodom (Matthew 11:21–23).

Christ says, "Ye must be born again" (John 3:7). We can attend church our entire lives, lead outwardly moral lives, believe the truth with our minds, be convicted of sin, fear hell and damnation, and still be lost. Of such persons, we can say, "And so I saw the wicked buried, who had come and gone from the place of the holy, and they were forgotten in the city where they had so done: this is also vanity" (Ecclesiastes 8:10).

Christ longs to gather you to Himself as a hen gathers her chicks (Matthew 23:37). Do not be unwilling but come to Him. If you do not, it would be better for you if you had never been born. Call upon Him while He is yet near, "for whosoever shall call upon the name of the Lord shall be saved" (Romans 10:13).

Part 2

Psalm 23:2
"He maketh me to lie down in green pastures: he leadeth me beside the still waters."

5

The Shepherd's Gift of Divine Rest

He maketh me to lie down in green pastures
—Psalm 23:2a

A flock of sheep feeding and resting in rich, green pastures by a cooling stream is a pleasing sight in any country. But green pastures are a rare feast for sheep in Israel. Not only are the sheep grazed in the wilderness instead of cultivated fields, but lack of rain allows for verdant grass only two or three months a year.[1] Such a pastoral scene understandably becomes a vivid symbol of spiritual rest and contentment, and David used this symbol in saying: the Lord "maketh me to lie down in green pastures."

Some people are quick to interpret the blessings of Psalm 23 as natural benefits. We will not deny, of course, that everyone needs physical rest. There must be pauses and parentheses in every life, for our hand cannot always be laboring, nor our brain always given to intense thought. Pleasure and relaxation are a part of enjoying God's good gifts. But if we apply the Shepherd's benefits of Psalm 23 only in a natural way, we soon forget the spiritual benefits enjoyed by God's people in addressing their deepest spiritual needs.

Due to our fall in Adam, we lost God and His image as well as true, spiritual rest. Augustine rightly said, "Thou hast formed us for Thyself, and our hearts are restless until they find rest in Thee."[2] To fill the void within, we grasp for the world's promises of satisfaction. Even though the world around us and within us is but a land of deserts, we still pursue its elusive promise of rest. We live as if we could be the first persons in the history of mankind to find true contentment apart from our Creator. "The wicked are like the troubled sea, when it cannot rest, whose waters cast up mire and dirt" (Isaiah 57:20).

Today's generation is living proof of this truth in its restlessness, dissatisfaction, and unhappiness. Millions immerse themselves in senseless forms of entertainment. Millions more grasp illegal drugs, alcohol, and prescription medications to try to lift their moods. Flashing advertisements constantly promise peace, popularity, and happiness for a price. Our society is one mass of restless people, continually returning empty-handed from selfish pursuits.

True rest is to be found by grace in God alone. There is true rest only in the Jehovah-Shepherd. This rest is reserved only for His people and is granted only by sovereign grace. This rest makes a lost sheep willing to follow the Shepherd in the day of divine power, for He alone can lead to rest. The Lord "maketh me to lie down in green pastures."

The Shepherd Provides the Conditions for Rest

It would seem easy to get a sheep to lie down and rest. A shepherd, however, knows better. Kenneth Bailey writes, "A dog can be trained to sit and lie down. Not so a sheep."[3] Sheep will only rest when certain conditions have been met. Just as an earthly shepherd will labor diligently to provide the necessary conditions to grant his sheep natural rest, so the heavenly Shepherd will labor to provide the necessary conditions for His flock's spiritual rest.

The Rest of Safety

Freedom from fear and a sense of safety is something a shepherd must provide his flock for them to feel free to lie down and rest. Phillip Keller writes, "Sheep are so timid and easily panicked that even a stray jackrabbit suddenly bounding from behind a bush can stampede a whole flock. When one startled sheep runs in flight a dozen others will bolt with it in blind fear, not waiting to see what frightened them."[4]

Sheep need a sense of security in order to rest. Keller explains, "As long as there is even the slightest suspicion of danger from dogs, coyotes, cougars, bears or other enemies the sheep stand up ready to flee for their lives. They have little or no means of self-defense. They are helpless, timid, feeble creatures whose only recourse is to run."[5] Indeed, a single predator can kill several, even dozens, of sheep in one night.

How does a shepherd quiet his flock's fears so that they may lie down and rest? Certainly, he seeks to remove as many causes of their fear as he possibly can. Yet nothing brings more of a sense of safety to the flock than the presence of the shepherd himself. Simply seeing him in their midst puts their fears to rest.

Such is also the condition of Jesus Christ's spiritual flock. Due to their helplessness and vulnerability, they are a timid flock with many things to fear. When the Lord begins His saving work in their souls, they learn that they have no strength in themselves to fight against spiritual predators.

First, they come to fear *sin*. Its guilt, penalty, power, pollution, and results presses upon their consciences. They also fear the *law*. Its demand for perfection allows them no rest, but drives them like an Egyptian slave-master to make bricks without straw. They also fear *Satan*. Where can they find rest when they are continually confronted with this roaring lion's fearful attacks of temptation and accusation?

And, they fear *death and judgment.* How can they rest if their everlasting destiny lies in the balance and is found wanting?

Only the presence of their Shepherd can dispel these fears. His blood has brought reconciliation and peace in the midst of all that threatens them (Colossians 1:20). His presence makes them calm as the Shepherd stands with them and leads them in the strength of the Lord. He is their peace (Micah 5:4–5). The Lord Jesus said, "I will not leave you comfortless: I will come to you" (John 14:18). Literally, His promise is, "I will not leave you *orphans.*" By the indwelling Spirit (v. 16), Christ and the Father dwell in the believer, are always present (v. 20), and are "a very present help in trouble" (Psalm 46:1).

The Shepherd stands by His flock and grants them the faith to behold Him and to believe that He is looking on them in His favor. They are thus free to lay all their fears at His feet and to place all their trust and confidence in Him as the Great Shepherd. By protecting the sheep from the things they fear, but especially by staying close to them and enabling them to behold His presence, the Jehovah-Shepherd provides His flock with the first condition necessary to make room for spiritual rest.

The Rest of Harmony

Sheep must also be at peace with one another to rest. Keller writes, "The second source of fear from which the sheepman delivers his sheep is that of tension, rivalry, and cruel competition within the flock itself."[6] Like other animals, sheep fight among themselves, creating strife and tension within the flock. The stronger attack the weaker and claim the best pasture for themselves. As a result, the flock cannot lie down and rest.

Is it any different with Christ's flock spiritually? Did you ever find one of God's children at rest spiritually while striving to be "top sheep"? Do not the head butting and shoving among God's children sometimes cause so much disorder that the entire congregation becomes edgy and tense? Paul's advice in Philippians 2:3 is needed among believers today: "In lowliness of mind let each esteem [the] other better than themselves."

The Good Shepherd responds to fighting in the flock in justice, wisdom, and love. He disciplines the strong for pushing around the weaker sheep. In Ezekiel 34:21-22, He says, "Because ye have thrust with side and with shoulder, and pushed all the diseased with your horns, till ye have scattered them abroad; therefore will I save my flock, and they shall no more be a prey."

The Shepherd also makes known His presence in the flock as Lord and Son of David. Ezekiel 34:23-24 says, "And I will set up one shepherd over them, and he shall feed them, even my servant David; he shall feed them, and he shall be their shepherd. And I the LORD will be their God, and my servant David a prince among them; I the LORD have spoken it." Just as the presence of the shepherd often causes sheep to stop fighting, so the presence of the Lord silences bickering and promotes humility and peace among all who are truly His.[7]

Furthermore, the Good Shepherd shows special compassion for the weaker sheep. Isaiah 40:11 says, "He shall feed his flock like a shepherd: he shall gather the lambs with his arm, and carry them in his bosom, and shall gently lead those that are with young." The Shepherd shows His sheep that the greatest advantages come not from striving to dominate others but from being the servant of all. "God resisteth the proud, but giveth grace unto the humble" (James 4:6).

Then, instead of a *butting order* the sheep respond with a *bowing order*. The Lord's sheep cannot come low enough. Are you seeking grace to become one of the lowliest sheep of God? Have you learned that the closer you are to the bottom the closer you are to the Shepherd? Let this be your prayer: "Lord, give me grace to come down, for I cannot bring myself there. Make room for spiritual rest by bringing me before

Thee as one of the lowest sheep. I am glad to rest there, if only I may be of *Thy* flock."

The Rest of Tranquility

A third thing that prevents sheep from lying down to rest is the painful bite of insects. Keller writes, "Sheep, especially in the summer, can be driven to absolute distraction by nasal flies, bot flies, warble flies and ticks. When tormented by these pests it is literally impossible for them to lie down and rest. Instead they are up and on their feet, stamping their legs, shaking their heads, ready to rush off into the bush for relief from the pests."[8] The shepherd must help ward off these insects by applying oil to the sheep's head.[9]

Jehovah's sheep are also preyed on by pests that prevent spiritual rest. Although true believers strive against worldliness, the world often comes back to live within them, much to their annoyance. It encroaches upon their souls through many disguises. Like Lot, the sheep can become entangled with the world even as its filth vexes their righteous souls (2 Peter 2:7). Various temptations can be such spiritual pests that the sheep cannot lie down to rest. Some of God's sheep struggle with doubts concerning doctrinal truths, while others battle the temptation of a particular sin or fear that they will one day commit a gross sin. The greatest pest, however, is *self*. Like the apostle Paul God's sheep often discover that "what I hate, that do I," so that they cry out, "O wretched man that I am! who shall deliver me?" (Romans 7:15, 24).

The divine Shepherd provides something far better than insect repellent for relief from tormentors. He dips His flock in *the oil of the Spirit*, who cleanses, sanctifies, heals, comforts, and transforms the flock, working faith in their souls and uniting them to the Great Shepherd. Christ shares with His sheep the oil of gladness and joy that God has poured out on Him through the Spirit (Psalm 45:7; Isaiah 61:1–3). The Spirit's work gives them relief, especially when He takes the things of Christ and shows them to the flock (John 16:13–14). That allows them by faith to place their feet on the neck of the world, on temptations, and even on self. In this way too, the way is opened to true spiritual rest.

The Rest of Sufficiency

Finally, hungry sheep will not lie down to rest. Keller writes, "A hungry, ill-fed sheep is ever on its feet, on the move, searching for another scanty mouthful of forage to try and satisfy its gnawing hunger. Such sheep are not contented, they do not thrive."[10] Only when sheep have sufficient food to fill their hungry bellies can they lie down to rest.

Given the semi-arid climate of Israel, it is challenging for a shepherd to find good pasture for his flock. It demands careful forethought and constant effort. Bailey recounts how he was near the summit of Jabal Sannin (elev. 8,600 ft.) in Lebanon, where, he says, "I had an interesting conversation with an experienced shepherd (with his large flock) who described to me in fascinating detail the various options and the numerous decisions he was obliged to make each day as he sought forage and water for his more than one hundred sheep."[11]

The Good Shepherd leads His sheep to good pasture. He is the door through which they enter into salvation and go out to find the pasture of life, even abundant life (John 10:1–11). Jesus Christ is Himself the pasture of His people, for He is *the living Word of God*. To provide that cost Him more than planning and hard labor—it cost Him the bloody sweat of crucifixion and death. He is the pasture land of eternal satisfaction for His own. As the true meat and drink of life eternal, Christ feeds and nourishes hungry and thirsty souls with His crucified body and shed blood. His sheep find in Him everything they need for time and eternity. He is the Bread of Life (John 6:35). He is the Father's house in which there is bread enough and to spare. He is the focus, the centerpiece, the delight, and the all-in-all of His flock.

He also gives *the written Word of God* as pasture for His flock. The living Word (Christ) and the written Word (the Bible) are inseparably associated with each other. Christ is the great message of all the Holy Scriptures (Luke 24:27, 44; Acts 3:18, 21; 2 Timothy 3:14-16). The Scriptures reveal Jesus Christ as the righteousness of sinners and the Lord and Savior of all who call on His name (Romans 1:16-17; 10:12-15).

God's people love Scripture and honor it as the Word of God (Psalm 119:97) for it is their life, their food, their pasture. It is their bread when they are hungry (Isaiah 55:1-3, 10), their honey when they are faint (Psalm 19:10), their milk when they are babes (1 Corinthians 3:2), and their strong meat when they are men (Hebrews 5:12-14). They are brought by faith and through grace to "receive with meekness the engrafted word" (James 1:21), to keep this Word (John 17:6), and to continue in this Word (John 8:31).

God's house becomes their home where they feed in the green pastures of the Word of God with its ordinances for the worship of God. In the Old Testament, God gave Himself to His people in His special presence in the temple, though He also heard every prayer whispered in the Israelites' private homes. Psalm 87:2-3 says, "The LORD loveth the gates of Zion more than all the dwellings of Jacob. Glorious things are spoken of thee, O city of God." In the New Testament, Christ indwelt every believer by the Holy Spirit, but promised His special presence whenever the church gathers in His name (Matthew 18:20). In the congregation, the sheep hear their Shepherd's voice speaking to them through the reading and the preaching of the Word.

In addition to the Holy Spirit, the ministry of the Word is the principal benefit or gift of the Great Shepherd's ascension (Ephesians 4:10-11). It is a standing pledge to the church that Christ is now "in the presence of God for us" (Hebrews 9:24). Therefore it pleases Him to put special honor upon the preaching of "Christ crucified, unto the Jews a stumbling block, and unto the Greeks foolishness; but unto them which are called, both Jews and Greeks, Christ the power of God, and the wisdom of God" (1 Corinthians 1:23, 24). Oh, what a blessing it is to find rest for the soul in God's preached Word! In the house of God, Jehovah's flock meets their God and shepherding King. There Christ rests and dwells, "for the LORD hath chosen Zion; he hath desired it for his habitation." He promises to "abundantly bless her provision" and to "satisfy her poor with bread ... and her saints shall shout aloud for joy" (Psalm 132:13, 15, 16).

There, like sheep lying down in green pastures, the Lord's flock experiences divine rest. There the Shepherd provides spiritual *safety* from the predatory fears of sin, Satan, death, and judgment. He gives them spiritual *harmony* with one another so that they dwell together in humility and peace. He blesses them with spiritual *tranquility* as the oil of the Spirit soothes the pricking irritations of temptation and self. He feeds them with the spiritual *sufficiency* of His own fullness offered in His Word, the Holy Scriptures. Have you experienced this rest?

Arise, O Lord, our God, arise
And enter now into Thy rest
O let this house be Thy abode,
Forever with Thy presence blest.

I will abundantly provide
For Zion's good, the Lord hath said;
I will supply her daily need
And satisfy her poor with bread.

Salvation shall adorn her priests,
Her saints shall shout with joy divine,
Messiah's pow'r shall be revealed,
His glory in His Church shall shine.[12]

Enjoying Divine Rest by Faith

Jesus Christ is not only the Redeemer who purchases salvation for His flock, but He is also the King who applies that salvation to His flock. "He maketh me to lie down," David says. Jehovah provides salvation based on Christ's objective work of grace for His sheep. However, the Shepherd also works subjectively in His sheep, and this work appears in their experience and activity. *God* did the work, but *David* had to lie down.

Likewise, we must experience not only how the Lord provides the four conditions necessary for spiritual rest, but also the application of true rest to our souls. If we are one of Jehovah's sheep, the divine means that are instrumental to embrace spiritual rest must be exercised within our souls, enabling us to confess, "He maketh me to lie down in green pastures." This is the exercise of true, saving faith.

True faith is *of* the Lord and its only object *is* the Lord. Faith is essential for every aspect of spiritual life. It is the captain of all spiritual graces. George Swinnock (1627–1673) wrote, "Call forth that commander-in-chief; and then the private soldiers, the other graces, will all follow."[13] Christ honors faith the most, because faith honors Christ the most. Faith focuses upon Christ, believes in Him, trusts Him, and leans upon Him. True faith lies down in the finished work of Christ, confessing by its very exercise both self-deficiency and divine sufficiency. Oh, for grace to *abide* in the pastures of the living and written Word by faith!

In the exercise of faith the Holy Spirit offers to meet all the needs of His people in the Lamb of God, applying to them the written Word of God so that they are enabled to rest in the living Word. Through faith, they come to see that Christ is the answer to all the problems that burden their souls.

Are they *sinners*? Christ who knew no sin became sin for His people to redeem them from it (2 Corinthians 5:21).

Are they *law-breakers*? Christ is the law-keeper (Matthew 5:17).

Are they *separated from God*? Christ was forsaken of His Father as Judge so that they might never be forsaken of Him (Matthew 27:46).

Are they *unrighteous*? Christ is the all-righteous One, having a perfect robe of righteousness through His active and passive obedience to the will of God (Isaiah 61:10).

Are they *cursed*? Christ died the accursed death as curse-bearer of His elect (Galatians 3:13).

Are they under divine *wrath*? Christ is the peace-maker (Isaiah 53:5).

Are they *enemies of God*? In Christ "mercy and truth are met together; righteousness and peace have kissed each other" (Psalm 85:10).

Are they *foolish*? Christ is wisdom (Proverbs 8).

Are they *filthy*? Christ is "holy, harmless, undefiled" (Hebrews 7:26).

Are they *tempted*? Christ was "in all points tempted like as we are, yet without sin" (Hebrews 4:15).

Are they spiritually *poor*? Christ, who was rich, became poor so that through His poverty they might become rich (2 Corinthians 8:9).

Are they in spiritual *bondage*? In Christ there is liberty, for "if the Son therefore shall make you free, ye shall be free indeed" (John 8:36).

Are they *weak*? Christ is their strength (1 Samuel 15:29).

Are they *in need of prayer*? Christ is the praying High Priest, sitting at the right hand of the Father, who never ceases to make intercession for His people (Romans 8:34).

Are they *restless*? Christ, who by Himself purged our sins, is now sitting on His throne of rest, causing His people to rest in Him as the Priest who has paid everything, as the Prophet who teaches everything they need to learn, and as the King who rules over everything on their behalf.

There is no end to it. The green pastures of God's living and written Word can never become parched or overgrazed as long as we receive this Word in faith. The Word of God reveals Christ's person, natures, states, and offices as a medicine cabinet out of which the Holy Spirit administers healing for every disease that may afflict Jehovah's sheep.

By teaching that faith is the instrument through which God provides these rich spiritual blessings for His flock, we do not imply that the life of faith is easy or can have everything it desires. Far from it, for true faith can only receive what God gives. Faith does not labor to deserve anything from God. Faith is only the hand by which we receive God's gift in Jesus Christ. Christ's merit alone saves sinners.

Ever since the fall of mankind, we have fought to be our own shepherds, to find our own rest, and to be our own Lord. God's grace breaks this stubborn pride, making us dependent upon Him. Only then can we find true rest. By faith, we come to Christ and learn the reality of His promise: "Come unto me, all ye that labour and are heavy laden, and I will give you rest. Take my yoke upon you, and learn of me; for I am meek and lowly in heart: and ye shall find rest unto your souls. For my yoke is easy, and my burden is light" (Matthew 11:28–30).

The Holy Spirit works this rest in the souls of God's people. This rest increases in God and decreases in self-righteousness, self-reliance, and self-idolatry. It is spiritual rest, not a rest dependent on earthly circumstances or goods. As Luther said, the Spirit gives the believer "spiritual eyes" so that he knows "what is the best and noblest thing on earth," not visible splendor, power, and wealth, but "that the Lord is his Shepherd and that he is in His pasture and in His care, that is, that he has God's Word."[14] This rest leads them to sing in hope,

Thou wilt stretch forth Thy mighty arm
To save me when my foes alarm;
The work Thou hast for me begun
Shall by Thy grace be fully done;
Forever mercy dwells with Thee;
O Lord, my Maker, think on me.[15]

As the faith of God's people increases, it flowers and bears fruit in full assurance of faith. The Spirit applies the work of Christ deeply to the conscience. There is a difference between justification by faith, and the assurance of grace and salvation.[16] The first is an objective reality for all believers; the latter is a rich privilege which we must seek in growing experience.

United to Christ, believers can say with Asa even in days of conflict, "Help us, O LORD our God; for we rest on thee" (2 Chronicles 14:11). Yet this rest can attain greater stability and personal application. It has been said, "The heart of religion lies in its personal pronouns."[17] God's sheep thus learn to say, "*I* know whom *I* have believed" (2 Timothy 1:12); "*My* redeemer liveth" (Job 19:25); "*I* live by the faith of the Son of God, who loved *me*, and gave himself for *me*" (Galatians 2:20).

Spiritual rest in God becomes the flock's rich possession only as a fruit of justification. "Being justified by faith we have peace with God through our Lord Jesus Christ" (Romans 5:1). The guilt of sin is removed in its condemning power. The law of God no longer curses us with its impossible demand for perfection, for Christ has fulfilled its precepts and carried its curse (Galatians 3:13; 4:4). Conscience, once accusing, now rests quietly in Christ. "There is therefore now no condemnation to them which are in Christ Jesus" (Romans 8:1).

In Christ, God becomes a glorious resting ground instead of a cause for terror. Has God's *justice* become your strong fortress, knowing that Christ satisfied justice for you? Do you rest in God's *eternal truthfulness*, praying, "Fulfill this word unto Thy servant upon which Thou hast caused me to hope; O Lord, do as Thou hast said"? Are you conscious of your sin and are you being led to rest in the *mercy* of God which alone can blot it out? Burdened with guilt, have you found a resting place in sovereign, divine *grace*? Overwhelmed with affliction, have you been brought to rest in the *omnipotence* of Jehovah? Bound up with your own foolishness, do you rest in the *wisdom* of God? Has the Lord enabled you to rest in His *immutability* as a sure anchor in the troubled sea of life? Despite your unfaithfulness, are you resting in God's *faithfulness* whose promise is as good as His fulfillment?

The gospel gives us rest from our enemies. Satan's accusing head is crushed in Christ. The believer receives courage in Christ as his crucified, exalted King to resist the devil and put him to flight. Having died with Christ and been raised with Him, the Christian finds some rest even from self; the old nature can no longer have the upper hand, though the conflict continues until death.

At peace with God and in victory over his enemies, the redeemed sinner gains new strength to submit to the will of God, praying, "Thy will be done." Whatever the Lord does is best. The assured Christian wants to do God's will because it is *His* will. This gives believers great liberty in prayer. The Lord does not hesitate to hand them the keys of the storehouse of divine grace, saying to them what He did to the Canaanite woman: "O woman, great is thy faith; be it unto thee even as thou wilt" (Matthew 15:28). Indeed, they may then experience more rest in the furnace of affliction than with the king in his palace (Daniel 3:24), knowing that "many are the afflictions of the righteous, but the LORD delivereth him out of them all" (Psalm 34:19). They learn the secret of Psalm 37:7, "Rest in the LORD and wait patiently for Him."

All the lions that once terrified them are chained. They see Jesus holding the keys to death and hell (Revelation 1:18). They commit themselves to His hands for time and eternity. Sin itself is defeated and has lost its power to dominate them.

Oh, blessed is the rest that a sinner experiences in salvation! Secure in the possession of everlasting good, he may say, "'Return unto thy rest, O my soul, for the LORD hath dealt bountifully with thee' (Psalm 116:7). He maketh me to lie down in green pastures. Till the pastures of God wither and the river of life fails, my soul cannot lack anything, for the LORD is my Shepherd." This is a blessed foretaste of heaven.

Resting in the Love of the Triune God

The exercise of faith in Christ brings God's sheep to "boldness and access of confidence" (Ephesians 3:12) to the triune God. After describing the peace-making work of Christ, Paul writes, "For through him we both have access by one Spirit unto the Father" (Ephesians 2:18). There is an experiential resting in God by coming to know Him personally in His three divine persons. Paul desired this blessing for all believers: "The grace of the Lord Jesus Christ, and the love of God, and the communion of the Holy Ghost, be with you all" (2 Corinthians 13:14). Augustine taught that the Trinity is the true object of our enjoyment beyond anything that this world can offer.[18] By grace, we come to know the love and grace of each divine person, and in return our love and joy overflow.

The child of God has the privilege of knowing the Second Person of the Holy Trinity as his Elder Brother (Romans 8:29), as a merciful and faithful High Priest (Hebrews 4:15-16), and as his advocate with the Father (1 John 2:1). The believer can become personally acquainted with Immanuel Himself. He can know Christ as "a friend that sticketh closer than a brother" (Proverbs 18:24). Christ's gifts and benefits are wonderful, but His person is "altogether lovely" (Song of Solomon 5:16). Blessed are they who cannot only say, "He gave me peace," but also "He is my peace." This conviction strengthened the early Christians as they faced martyrdom; they inscribed on the walls of the catacombs, "In Christ, in peace."

What a wonder it is to be admitted into the circle of Christ's personal friends! He brings us to rest in Himself with the very rest which He enjoys with His Father. He rests in grateful submission in the Father's sovereign decree of electing love. He rests in the blessed contemplation of all that is delivered unto Him by the Father as the fruit of His work as Mediator. He rests in the completion of His work that the Father gave Him to do in this world (Hebrews 4:10). He rests in the full knowledge that He has of the Father and the Father of Him, and in the incomprehensible love between them. He rests in the very heart of His Father as the only-begotten Son (John 1:18). As we come to know Him better, we increasingly rest in His rest.

To know the Son is also to know the Father (John 14:9). Christ brings His friends and brothers to know the First Person of the Holy Trinity. He opens up for them the experiential enjoyment of their adoption into the household of God. The Father makes their adoption real by the Spirit of the Son, who witnesses with their spirits that they are children of God, leading them to cry out, "Abba, Father!" (Romans 8:15; Galatians 4:6). Through the last Adam, the Father restores the relationship they lost in the first Adam. Justification removes condemnation from a sinner and places him in a status of righteousness in God's courtroom. However, adoption goes further; it brings him to the table of God's household as one of His dear children.

Blessed are the prodigals who experience not only repentance and confession but are also received into the arms of a loving Father. In mercy the Father sees them a great way off, has compassion on them, runs to them, embraces them, and kisses them (Luke 15:20). Instead of being servants, they are restored to sonship; instead of filthy rags, they are given the best robe, a ring for their fingers, and shoes for the feet; and instead of the death they deserve, they partake of the feast of fattened calf. Blessed are they who know what it means to rest in the green pastures of God's fatherly heart. They have access to His throne of grace, which is the richest blessing in the whole world. They may tell the Father everything. No need is too small. No sin is too great. When they ask for bread, He will not give them a stone. "As a father pitieth his children, so the LORD pitieth them that fear him" (Psalm 103:13).

Finally, true children of God may rest in the Holy Spirit, the Third Person of the Trinity. At Pentecost, the disciples were allowed to embrace and rest in the triune God. Through Christ, they received reconciliation with God and adoption by the Father. As the "promise of the Father," they also received an experiential knowledge of the Holy

Spirit. Jesus became their Elder Brother, God became their Father, and the Holy Ghost came to dwell with them and work in them, in His offices as comforter, sealer, and intercessor (John 14:16; Ephesians 1:13; Romans 8:26). By the Spirit's dwelling in them, Christ's resurrection life dwelled in them, and the Father and the Son made their home with them (John 14:17, 19, 23). Richard Sibbes wrote that the Spirit "knits us to the Father and the Son ... because all the communion we have with God is by the Holy Ghost."[19] Resting in the Spirit, we find ourselves resting with the Son in the heart of the Father.

Yet all resting this side of the grave is a mere shadow of the perfect, eternal, and heavenly rest to come. Moments of rest that are "unspeakable and full of glory" here on earth (1 Peter 1:8) are but a foretaste of the river of pleasure flowing out of the throne of God (Revelation 22:1). Rest on earth from the guilt and dominion of sin foreshadows eternal rest from the pollution of sin. Here on earth, children of God are pilgrims passing through a wilderness, but soon they will arrive at the Father's house, where all their sorrows shall cease and they shall enter eternal rest.

In the mountains of Scotland a steep trail finally leads to a breathtaking mountain pass called Glencoe. At the top of the pass a stone is engraved with these words, "Rest, and be thankful." Sheep of the Lord's flock, the summit of the narrow way will be won. Here, though we are not weary *of* our Shepherd's service, we are often weary *in* His service. But the day will come when we shall look back at the way of life with true thankfulness as we view the wisdom of every little winding turn in the steep ascent by which we were led. Here in this world our sense of rest in God is feeble at best, but "when that which is perfect is come, then that which is in part shall be done away ... then shall I know even as also I am known" (1 Corinthians 13:10, 12). Finally, we will know perfect, eternal rest!

6

The Shepherd's Refreshment

He leadeth me beside the still waters.
—Psalm 23:2b

Approximately 70 percent of the human body is composed of water. Water is thus necessary for physical health. It is necessary to maintain normal body metabolism, for if the body does not have enough water, dehydration will result, causing weakness and even death. Fortunately, our Creator has supplied us with thirst to make us aware of water deficiency. Thirst tells us that our body needs to have its water supply replenished.

Everyone, whether young or old, has at some time been thirsty. Because of our fall in Adam, we deserve to thirst forever. All of us have earned the portion of the rich man in hell who lifted up his eyes and begged for one drop of water to cool his tongue (Luke 16:24). Hell is the place of eternal thirst, merited by every son and daughter of Adam (Isaiah 65:13).

I once witnessed my dad experiencing this powerfully. When I visited him following heart surgery, I found him crying. When I asked why, he told me that a nurse had just come in to moisten his lips. "It felt so good and was so humbling," he said, "because I couldn't help but think of the rich man in Luke 16 who didn't have a drop of water to cool his tongue." Have you ever been grateful for a drop of water?

It should be a wonder to us that we can receive something to drink in this life when we are thirsty. By nature, however, we take God's blessings for granted. Whether it is water, coffee, or milk, we drink everything as if it is our right. The awareness of thirst, the ability to swallow, the desire to drink, and every drop of water from the faucet ultimately comes from the Lord alone.

In Middle Eastern countries, barren and stony land makes thirst more prevalent. For the Bedouin, nothing is more dreaded than being caught without water on a desert journey. Travelers through deserts have frequently confessed that they would have been willing to give up everything they possessed for only a few drops of water. The agony of thirst is even greater than that of hunger.

The physical body is not the only thing that gets thirsty. Our fallen, human soul also thirsts for nourishment. Each created soul thirsts to fill the void left from paradise when we departed from the Lord. Jeremiah 2:13 says, "For my people have committed two evils; they have forsaken me the fountain of living waters, and hewed them out cisterns, broken cisterns, that can hold no water." By nature we try to fill the emptiness within with self-love, seeking to find satisfaction in anything apart from the true God of Scripture.

There is no end to the list of substitutes for God that we use to try to quench our thirsty souls. By nature we drink deeply from the wells of this world, only to turn away unsatisfied. Worldly companions, worldly fashions, worldly entertainment, worldly lusts, worldly music, worldly literature, worldly customs, and worldly places leave the soul unrefreshed.

We also try to suppress the thirst of our immortal souls with physical pursuits and activities. We feverishly participate in sports. We plan travel to exotic places. We seek adventures or indulge in social activities. We take up hobbies or engage in community efforts. We pursue academic careers. We turn to the arts, to culture, to literature, to human relationships, and to daily work. But when all is said and done, we still find ourselves thirsty and unfulfilled.

In the midst of this thirsting world, God's sheep say along with the psalmist, "He leadeth me beside the still waters." Jehovah's sheep do not lack divine refreshment. Their Shepherd leads them to refreshing waters where He quenches their spiritual thirst.

The Shepherd Leading to Refreshing Waters

Amid the chaos of a confused society that has little fear of God, Jesus Christ the Great Shepherd comes to proclaim that He offers living water to quench their thirst. As John 7:37-38 says, "Jesus stood and cried, saying, If any man thirst, let him come unto me, and drink. He that believeth on me, as the scripture hath said, out of his belly shall flow rivers of living water." Christ knows that the soul of man can never be satisfied with any substitute for God, so He offers the living water of divine refreshment.

But sinners refuse the Shepherd's offer of everlasting life. They try to refresh themselves with other means. In doing so, they are as foolish as sheep. When sheep are thirsty they become restless and set out in search of water. If they are not led to water that is clean and pure, they will drink from polluted potholes. Fallen man goes a step further by intentionally turning away from the pure water of God to drink filthy, infested water polluted by sin.

From his experience as a shepherd, Phillip Keller writes:

They remind me very much of a bunch of sheep I watched one day which were being led down to a magnificent mountain stream. The snow-fed waters were flowing pure and clear and crystal clean between lovely banks of trees. But on the way several stubborn ewes and their lambs stopped, instead, to drink from small, dirty, muddy pools beside the trail. The water was filthy and polluted not only with the churned up mud from passing sheep but even with the manure and urine of previous flocks that had passed that way. Still these stubborn sheep were quite sure it was the best drink available. The water itself was filthy and unfit for them. Much more, it was obviously contaminated with nematodes [roundworms] and liver fluke eggs that would eventually riddle them with internal parasites and disease of destructive impact.[1]

We are all like sheep. Satan whispers to us that small drinks from sin-polluted waters will not hurt us but are sweet (Proverbs 9:17-18). We drink forbidden water just as Adam ate forbidden fruit. When we feel no cramps or pain, we conclude that the water did not contaminate us. We hear Satan say, "Casual church attendance, hypocrisy, the neglect of the means of grace, a lack of weighing eternal realities, a little lie, or an unbiblical compromise—these things, and thousands more—will not really hurt you, for ye shall not surely die." But John 8:44 warns, "When he [Satan] speaketh a lie, he speaketh of his own: for he is a liar, and the father of it."

Who is leading you in your quest for satisfaction? Either Satan is leading you to drink polluted, muddy water that destroys your soul, or else Jesus Christ is leading you to pure streams of divine refreshment. To spiritually drink of the Jehovah-Shepherd's still waters is the portion of His flock. Christ promised the woman at the well, "Whosoever drinketh of this water shall thirst again: but whosoever drinketh of the water that I shall give him shall never thirst; but the water that I shall give him shall be in him a well of water springing up into everlasting life" (John 4:13-14). If you have tasted one drop of Christ's pure, clean, sweet water, you will be dissatisfied with anything else.

Are you partaking of the polluted rivers of this world, or have you tasted the water of the divine river, "the streams whereof shall make glad the city of God" (Psalm 46:4)? Those who have tasted God's goodness will trust Him (Psalm 34:8) and thirst for more (Psalm 63:1-5). They have discovered the spiritual refreshment of the Father's consolations, of Christ's graces, and of the Holy Spirit's inward workings. Their thirst for God moves them to separate from the world, for they have discovered that the joys of Christ are real and lasting, whereas the pleasures of sin lead to destruction. Even in the midst of conflict, they seek what they need in communion with God. Like David, they say, "Why art thou cast down, O my soul? And why art thou disquieted within me? Hope thou in God: for I shall yet praise him, who is the health of my countenance, and my God" (Psalm 42:11). When they do not have this living water, they thirst. Christ's sheep long to drink deeper from the well that is "God my exceeding joy" (Psalm 43:4).

All spiritual life that has a true beginning will yield rich fruit and finish in glory. The smallest in grace are just as much the Great Shepherd's possession as the most advanced. Christ allowed Himself to be killed in the doorway of His flock to redeem and deliver *all* His sheep: the smallest lamb as well as the oldest ewe or ram. He is the entire flock's Alpha and Omega. He leads all of His own to divine refreshment.

We can find this river of life by faith through Christ *alone* (Acts 4:12). Only of Him could the Father say, "I am well pleased" (Matthew 17:5). Our religion, our righteousness, and our humility cannot move the heart of the Father towards mercy. Rather, the Father in His own eternal initiative elected the Son to bring about reconciliation between the sinner and Himself. Christ is the unique Shepherd, who not only laid down His life, but also took it up again to bring His sheep to abundant, eternal life (John 10:10, 18, 28). He delights to lead His flock beside the still waters of salvation. He is their Way, their Truth, and their Life (John 14:6).

The Shepherd Leading to Quiet Waters

"He leadeth me beside the *still* waters," David said. The word *still* implies refreshing, peaceful, and pure water. Thus the Shepherd not only keeps His sheep from the muddy waters of this world but also from noisy, rushing mountain streams. Even burning thirst will hardly persuade a sheep to drink from turbulent water. It is terrified by a raging stream. Its fear is well-grounded, for a sheep is helpless in water. If it steps into fast-moving water, the sheep is likely to drown. Its coat acts as a sponge and becomes so saturated that the animal is quickly dragged to the bottom of the stream.

By contrast, still waters are "waters of rest." This *rest* is the same word used to describe Israel's entering into their inheritance by God's grace (Psalm 95:11), and God's dwelling among them by His gracious presence in the sanctuary (Psalm 132:8, 14). This truth contains a rich spiritual lesson. Since the fall of man broke the covenant of works, all of man's efforts to return to the Garden of Eden have been thwarted by the flaming sword of God's wrath (Genesis 3:24). The law cannot save us. A religion of merit and works will destroy the foolish and terrify those of sensitive conscience, much as rushing water will intimidate sheep. Christ leads His sheep to the quiet waters of gospel peace. He says, "Come unto me, all ye that labour and are heavy laden, and I will give you rest" (Matthew 11:28).

Pure, still water—the only kind fit for sheep to drink—is hard to find in Middle Eastern lands. Regions like these go for months with little rain. There are ways, however, that a shepherd can provide this water. First, very early in the morning a shepherd leads his flock to green pasture to allow them to drink from dew-drenched grass. Keller writes, "Dew is a clear, clean, pure source of water. And there is no more resplendent picture of still waters than the silver droplets of the dew hanging heavy on leaves and grass at break of day."[2] If the weather is not too hot, sheep can live off early morning dew for months at a stretch. But the shepherd must search carefully to find such pastures in the wilderness, then diligently lead the sheep some distance to feed and water in them.

Second, the shepherd supplies drinking troughs for his sheep. Shepherds have tediously built deep wells and cisterns from which to water their flocks. Both the construction of the well and the drawing up of the water are hard work for the shepherd. But the sheep eagerly wait as their shepherd draws up one bucket at a time from the deep well.[3]

Third, Eastern shepherds provide pure drinking water for their flock by damming up small streams. They literally "still" the water by using rocks and sod from the bank to construct a little dam across a swiftly moving stream. Gradually a pool of water collects behind the dam. The sheep then move forward without fear, drink from the pool, and are refreshed.

The provision of pure, refreshing water hinges on the work of the flock's shepherd. This reflects the work of Jesus Christ, the Good Shepherd. Through His perfect obedience He brings His people not to the rushing waters of God's wrath but to the quiet waters of God's grace. He cried out in succession on Calvary's cross, "I thirst," and "It is finished" (John 19:28, 30). He thirsted so that His flock might drink forever of His love. He suffered and died as the Substitute for sinners to satisfy God's justice for sin. Therefore He is "as the dew" for His people (Hosea 14:5), "as rivers of water in a dry place" (Isaiah 32:2). Are you with joy drawing water out of the wells of salvation (Isaiah 26:3) to quench your thirst for God?

As sheep learn to listen, recognize, trust, and respond to the voice of their shepherd, so the Lord's flock is spiritually tuned to their Master's call. Christ said, "The sheep hear his voice; and he calleth his own sheep by name, and leadeth them out. And when he putteth forth his own sheep, he goeth before them, and the sheep follow him: for they know his voice" (John 10:3–4).

Have you heard the voice of the Good Shepherd? Once inside the narrow gate of salvation, God's sheep cannot help but follow the voice of their Master. They are drawn by irresistible love. His call is too powerful to resist. His voice speaks with too much authority, with too much compassion, and with too much promise of peace and plenty to let it go unheeded. Jehovah's sheep must confess, "His voice draws me and compels me to follow Him. His voice speaks power, peace and stability to my soul. It leads me and inclines me to follow Him to refreshing waters."

When Christ leads His sheep with His voice, something miraculous takes place. Conquered from within, the sheep become willing to follow Christ as their Shepherd and are led to refreshing waters.

Not all belief in Jesus is a thirsting, following, and drinking faith. Thomas Shepard warned against "a fruitless faith" in Christ, which does not receive life from Him, and so, "like a bucket without a bottom," fails to draw up the water of life.[4] This is a dead faith (James 2:17) that cannot save. It hears the invitation, "Ho, every one that thirsteth, come ye to the waters" (Isaiah 55:1), but the words are foreign to them.

The Lord's sheep yearn for His communion and favor, His righteousness and salvation, His forgiveness and pardon, and His sanctification and application. "As the hart panteth after the water brooks, so panteth my soul after thee, O God" (Psalm 42:1). They cry, "I must drink or perish. Give me the thirst-quenching Savior, or else I die."

The Lord will not leave His flock's thirst unquenched. When Jehovah's sheep are parched and dry, the Great Shepherd picks them up, folds them in His cloak, holds them close to His beating heart, and carries them to refreshing waters. He opens their eyes to see springs in the desert. In response they cry out in amazement with Hagar, "Thou God seest me" (Genesis 16:13).

For thirsty souls He fulfills His Word: "When the poor and needy seek water, and there is none, and their tongue faileth for thirst, I the LORD will hear them, I the God of Israel will not forsake them. I will open rivers in high places, and fountains in the midst of the valleys: I will make the wilderness a pool of water, and the dry land springs of water" (Isaiah 41:17–18). He makes the psalmist's confession true: "He leadeth me beside the still waters." And the sheep sing in response,

> The Lord my Shepherd holds me
> Within His tender care,
> And with His flock He folds me,
> No want shall find me there.
>
> In pastures green He feeds me,
> With plenty I am blest;
> By quiet streams He leads me
> And makes me safely rest.[5]

The Shepherd Quenching the Thirst of His Sheep

God's people not only seek Him, but find and experience Him. Then the sheep of Christ enjoy God Himself and His sovereign love as the eternal fountain of salvation. God enables them to embrace the *electing love* of the Father revealed in His perfections, the *redeeming love* of the Son revealed in His fullness, and the *applying love* of the Spirit revealed in His operations. In this triune love the Great Shepherd quenches the thirst of His sheep.

The Lord's sheep find an ocean of refreshment in God the Father's divine sovereignty to rule, grace to save, wisdom to direct, power to protect, holiness to sanctify, justice to acquit, goodness to pity, and faithfulness to preserve. They savor the boundlessness, endlessness, and unchangeableness of the living God! Faith finds great springs of refreshment in the simple words, "I will be thy God."

They also experience God the Son in His loving fullness. "And of his fulness," said the apostle of love, "have all we received, grace for grace" (John 1:16). Their thirst is quenched as they view by faith the fullness of His redemption through His active and passive obedience. Unspeakable fullness lies in His person, names, natures, states, and offices. There is fullness of knowledge and wisdom in Him as Prophet, fullness of righteousness and peace in Him as Priest, and fullness of power and justice in Him as King.

Christ is everything to believers. He has fullness of grace as Surety to pay all their debts. He has fullness of skill as Physician to heal all their diseases. He has fullness of the spiritual treasury of grace as Intercessor to supply all their needs. Outside of Christ there is no life or refreshment, but in Him there is everything that sinners need. Because He thirsted upon the cross to purchase their forgiveness, He can now quench the thirst of His people. Every drop of spiritual life flows from this Mediator.

And they possess God the Holy Spirit in His loving operations. He is the Comforter who brings consolation in and through Jesus Christ. Therefore, His gracious labor is sometimes compared to:

- *wind*, for He stirs up dormant graces with zeal (Song of Solomon 4:16)

- *water*, for He cleanses the polluted heart with holiness (John 3:5)

- *fire*, for He warms the frozen heart with love (Matthew 3:11)

- *oil*, for He softens the hardened heart with joy (Psalm 45:7).

The Spirit quenches the thirst of Jehovah's flock by applying to them what they have in Christ, in ever increasing measure.

Indeed, the Lord is able to refresh His sheep with the promises of

Scripture. They learn that sickness, supported with a divine promise, is better than health. Poverty, enriched with a divine promise, is better than wealth. Prison, illumined with a divine promise, is better than a palace. Even death, transformed with a divine promise, is better than life. Walking by faith in God's Word and the Spirit rather than by reasoning and sight quenches the soul's thirst.

The richness of the Holy Spirit's refreshment is communicated by the plural word in our text "he leadeth me beside the still *waters*." This suggests the great variety and abundance of the Spirit's graces for the believer. The Spirit meets the believer in every place, supplying his every need. These graces comfort him at every turning point. They strengthen him for every duty. They are like a river fed by hundreds of brooks and streams. The Spirit leads the Christian every step in his earthly journey through misery, deliverance, and gratitude. The Spirit applies Jesus Christ to the soul in every dimension of His blessed person and work. As a result, we may confess with the psalmist, "My mouth shall shew forth thy righteousness and thy salvation all the day; for I know not the numbers thereof" (Psalm 71:15).

God's people experience the Spirit's graces as waters that never fail. Many natural streams only flow in winter or spring. In summer when water is most needed, many channels run dry. However, the Lord's "still waters" are full even in drought, for they are fed from beneath His eternal throne. When the world's streams run dry, the streams of grace are most ample and ever flowing for the sheep. "The LORD," says Isaiah, "shall guide thee continually, and satisfy thy soul in drought, and make fat thy bones: and thou shalt be like a watered garden, and like a spring of water whose waters fail not" (Isaiah 58:11). The river of divine waters will graciously flow from everlasting to everlasting.

Yet our deepest drink from the divine river is but a sip compared to what we shall receive in eternity. Revelation 7:16-17 promises, "They shall hunger no more, neither thirst anymore; neither shall the sun light on them, nor any heat. For the Lamb which is in the midst of the throne shall feed them, and shall lead them unto living fountains of waters: and God shall wipe away all tears from their eyes."

Dear believers, are you following your Shepherd to the waters of divine refreshment? Do you desire to know Christ and to experience a returning to the father-heart of God? Do you yearn to be conformed to the image of His Son? Do you seek to be rid of your pollution by the cleansing water of His sanctifying Spirit? Do you yearn for a closer walk with God? If you thirst for freedom from bondage to sin, you must recognize your wretchedness and pray for the deliverance of your soul and body from death. Then follow Christ as He leads you forward, for these longings and thirstings are from Him.

Robert Murray M'Cheyne said, "Those that are Christ's follow him." He explained,

- They follow him in bearing His cross.

- They follow him in His love.

- They follow him in His prayerfulness.

- They follow him in His holiness. [6]

Are you such a follower? Are you following your Shepherd in the paths of painful and costly obedience, of sacrificial love and service to others, of devoted petition and intercession in God's presence, and of separation from sin as one set apart for God?

"These are they who follow the Lamb whithersoever he goeth," says Revelation 14:4. God's sheep will follow Him to eternal bliss. Stilled by grace, they will say with David, "The LORD is my shepherd, I shall not want. He maketh me to lie down in green pastures: he leadeth me beside the still waters."

Part 3

Psalm 23:3
*"He restoreth my soul: he leadeth me in the paths of righteousness
for his name's sake."*

7

The Shepherd's Restoration for the Diseased and Downcast

He restoreth my soul.
—Psalm 23:3a

The Hebrew word translated "restoreth" in our text has a rich, though humble, meaning. It signifies reviving, retrieving, recovering, rescuing, strengthening, and even converting. "He restoreth my soul" is thus both a joyous and humble confession. David rejoices in his Shepherd's ability to restore, and he humbles himself for his constant need of such restoration. Jesus Christ is the all-sufficient and ever faithful Savior-Shepherd for our sinful, weak, and sometimes weary soul. Restoration humbles us because it reveals our lack of spiritual health. It also reveals the sin remaining in the nature of every converted person. However, the elect are called, renewed, washed, and clothed in Christ. These are the wonders of grace that God has wrought in their souls.

You should sorrow when you rebel against the sovereign God whose holy providence has continually upheld you. You grieve Him and resist Him despite His costly proofs of love for you. The flawed returns you offer to God are viewed against the backdrop of His continual faithfulness and loving kindness. As the Lord says in Micah 6:3, "O my people, what have I done unto thee? And wherein have I wearied thee? Testify against me." Testify, true believer, to what God has done for you compared to what you have done for Him. Has there ever been anything in your Great Shepherd's dealings or conduct that justifies turning your back on Him? On the contrary, He has been a fruitful garden, a pleasant land, and a fountain of living waters!

Boasting in your Great Shepherd and humbling yourself before Him is the only true religion on earth. As John the Baptist said, "He must increase and I must decrease" (John 3:30). "*He* restoreth *my* soul" implies that God must be exalted and man must be abased. That goal must be ours through all of life. In Luke 15 the shepherd and his friends rejoiced greatly over the restoration of one lost sheep, but God's true sheep continue to mourn over their sin (Jeremiah 31:18–19). Have you experienced the mixed joy and sorrow of divine restoration?

The parallels between literal sheep and God's spiritual flock in needing restoration are instructive. In referring to shepherding skills, we may speak of restoring diseased sheep, downcast sheep, and wandering sheep. In this chapter, we will consider the first two kinds of divine restoration.

The Shepherd's Restoration for the Diseased

The phrase *restore the soul* can also mean reviving someone's life and strength, as in providing them with food to avoid starvation (Lamentations 1:11, 19). Unless the Shepherd restores our soul through repentance and saving faith in Christ, mankind has no hope. The word *restore* can be translated "turn," "turn again" (Psalm 80:3), or "return" (Isaiah 55:7), reminding us that God's sheep experience true conversion as a "turning about." Christ turns them from darkness to light, from Satan to God (Acts 26:18). God accomplishes this through His Word (Psalm 19:7) and by His Spirit. In the preaching of the gospel and by the power of the Spirit, God moves His sheep to turn to Him from their idols and put their hope in His Son (1 Thessalonians 1:4-5, 9-10). Scripture associates turning to the Lord with spiritual healing (2 Chronicles 7:14; Isaiah 6:10; Jeremiah 3:22; Hosea 6:1).

Sheep are subject to a host of illnesses and diseases. The Shepherd who revives His sheep so they do not die suggests our profound need as sheep. Our fall in Adam is far more serious than a sickness that needs to be treated. We are not in danger of *being lost* because of the fall, but *were lost* in the fall. The fall resulted not merely in our *dying condition* but our *dead state*. By nature we are dead in trespasses and sins; only God can make us alive (Ephesians 2:1, 5). We need supernatural healing, indeed, a resurrection from death.

Although our depravity is more than sickness, it inevitably includes soul-sickness. Our fall subjects us to innumerable spiritual disorders. Isaiah aptly summarizes our condition: "The whole head is sick, and the whole heart faint. From the sole of the foot even unto the head there is no soundness in it; but wounds, and bruises, and putrefying sores: they have not been closed, neither bound up, neither mollified with ointment" (Isaiah 1:5-6). We have become so deathly sick that our sinful nature blinds us to our need for regeneration and recovery. Our greatest misery is that we do not know, see, or feel our misery. "They that be whole need not a physician, but they that are sick" (Matthew 9:12).

Only the sovereign Physician, the Shepherd Jesus Christ, can effectively diagnose and heal the spiritual diseases of sinners. We deserve the punishment of death (Romans 6:23): spiritual death, physical death, and eternal death. The Heidelberg Catechism queries, "Is there no way by which we may escape that punishment, and be again received into favor?" Its answer begins, "God will have His justice satisfied."[1] Therefore, only the death of Christ can save sinners, for He died as propitiation for our sin to satisfy the demands of God's justice and to deliver us from His wrath. Sinners are justified through faith in Christ's atoning blood (Romans 3:24–26).

Furthermore, Christ alone can apply what He has purchased, so that salvation becomes personally effective. As the man at the pool of Bethesda saw the waters of healing "troubled" or stirred many times during thirty-eight years but could not bring himself to them for healing (John 5:2–7), so the Lord's diseased flock cannot be restored or healed without the help and ministrations of the Savior-Shepherd. They need a Savior who is a Physician not only to free them from the guilt of sin (justification), but also to deliver them from the dominion, power, and love of sin (sanctification). They need Christ Jesus.

Heaven's healing regimen is unique. The Physician-Shepherd, who suffered death and shed His blood to raise His patients from death, applies the power of His blood to heal all the diseases of His sheep. He uses His blood-bought righteousness to heal their disease of self-righteousness. He uses His submission to God to heal their disease of rebellion. His humility heals their disease of pride. His self-denial heals their self-love, and His heavenly-mindedness heals their worldliness. His weeping heals their indifference. His suffering heals their lukewarm hearts. His heavenly power heals their hellish unbelief.

With Christ as Healer, God's treatment for His sheep cannot fail. Christ never misdiagnoses the ailment, applies the wrong medicine, or misjudges the dosage. He performs all His labors without money and without price, having paid the cost of His medicine once and for all with the shedding of His own blood. How well He knows all the symptoms, inclinations, infirmities, and complaints of His sin-bound, disease-prone flock!

Sometimes Christ's restorative labors are painful, especially when He touches our sore places and insists on probing the depth of our wounds. Like sheep we struggle against His healing hands. At times He even wounds us out of sovereign love to promote our healing. As Hosea 6:1 says, "Come, and let us return unto the LORD: for he hath torn, and he will heal us; he hath smitten, and he will bind us up." All of the Lord's flock will be taught His paradoxical way of restorative healing: the way forward is often backward, the way to exaltation is through humiliation, the way to the crown is by way of the cross.

Lesson by lesson and healing by healing, the Lord's sheep are brought to confess Christ alone as their divine Restorer. By faith they learn to see that if Christ were ever to cease making intercession on their behalf in the courts of heaven, they would be lost forever. Dying to all of their own attempts to restore themselves, they embrace the resurrected Lord, who holds in His hands the keys of hell, death, the grave, sin, Satan, and their own spiritual health. Their only hope lies in Him as exalted Shepherd of shepherds, Physician of physicians, and Lord of lords.

All the Lord's sheep will one day be placed without spot or wrinkle at His right hand. Healed of all disease and imperfection, no inhabitant of the heavenly Jerusalem will say, "I am sick." Healing will no longer be necessary, for the Healer will be all-in-all. Without diseases, infirmities, weaknesses, and sins, His sheep will live to reimburse their Physician with thank offerings of unending praise and crowns cast before His throne (Revelation 4:10).

Go to Christ for the healing of your soul. Labor to rid yourself of your own tonics and physicians, heeding the Lord's admonition: "In vain shalt thou use many medicines for thou shalt not be cured" (Jeremiah 46:11). Christ is the last physician to whom you and I will by nature go to for healing. Refusing to submit to free grace, we are like Naaman, who rejected God's way of restoration, saying, "Are not Abana and Pharpar, rivers of Damascus, better than all the waters of Israel? May I not wash in them and be clean?" (2 Kings 5:12).

Do you need healing? Is your cry, "Lord, be merciful unto me: heal my soul; for I have sinned against thee" (Psalm 41:4)? Or, do you think you can live as if there were no need for salvation, no deadly disease, no angry Judge, no offended justice, no condemning conscience, no punishing law, and no profound fall in Adam? Are you so deathly sick that you are blind to your desperate need for the Shepherd's healing?

The sheep of Christ who have submitted to the Shepherd's healing ministrations, have the joy of hearing Him say, "Be of good comfort: thy faith hath made thee whole; go in peace" (Luke 8:48). By faith they are justified from the guilt of all sin, made right with God, and restored to a place in His household and family.

The Shepherd's Restoration for the Downcast

Sheep who lose their footing and are thrown on their backs also need restoration.[2] Shepherds speak of such sheep as being "cast" or "cast down." The animal lies helpless on the ground and cannot right itself. A sheep can be cast down by carelessly lying down on soft ground. Rolling onto its side or back with its feet off the ground, it is unable to get up. A sheep is also in danger of being cast down when its fleece grows long and becomes matted with dirt and burrs, or the animal becomes obese.

Being cast down can terrify a poor sheep and leave it vulnerable to predators. Lying upside down also causes gases to build up in the first compartment of the sheep's four-stage stomach, eventually cutting off blood circulation to its legs. A cast sheep can die in a matter of hours, or, more commonly, a day or two. Thus a shepherd knows that if one of his sheep is missing, he must find it quickly.

The condition of being cast down mirrors the dangerous spiritual state into which believers can fall. They can lose heart, begin to despair, and feel quite hopeless. Each aspect of how a sheep becomes cast down and how a shepherd restores it illuminates the ways the Lord shepherds His sheep.

Causes of Spiritual Casting Down

The three ways in which sheep are cast down find parallels in the Lord's spiritual flock. First, *careless sheep* represent those who lie down on ground too soft to support their assurance of salvation and thus lose their spiritual footing in the gospel of peace. People of God carelessly cast themselves down when they rest only on the hollow ground of their former experiences of grace. They rest more on their faith than on Christ. They attempt to draw life, strength, and comfort from their own believing rather than from Him in whom they believe.

They cast themselves down when they heed Satan's ways, when sin works within them unchecked, and when their failures lead to a loss of assurance. They are cast down when they contemplate the future through the foggy spectacles of human reasoning rather than through the powerful telescope of God's Word. They cast themselves down when they say their prayers but never truly lift up their hearts to the prayer-hearing God. Sadly, even as children of God, we too often embody the picture of careless and cast down sheep.

"With thee is the fountain of life," wrote the psalmist (Psalm 36:9), but we all too often prefer to drink from cisterns of our own making. We rely on our repentance, prayer, faith, and humility, or on other sheep of God, or on the privileges of the Lord's house. But we rest carelessly if we do not rest in Christ Jesus, sitting at the right hand of the Father. He is the only true Fountain of our salvation. Oh, flock of God, turn away from everything but Christ as your foundation and diligently seek Him alone. Pray with David, "O my soul ... hope thou in God: for I shall yet praise him, who is the health of my countenance, and my God" (Psalm 42:11). God in Christ is the answer for your depressed, downcast soul.

Return to Him, backsliding children. And do not be careless in how you return. Do not forget Hosea's complaint concerning Israel: "They return, but not to the Most High" (Hosea 7:16). Seek the Lord Jesus as the only answer to your sins and need.

Second, the *burdened sheep* with wool that is heavy and caked with dirt teaches us that God's spiritual flock needs divine restoration when cast down under unnecessary spiritual burdens. Every idol is a burden to carry, whereas God's grace carries us (Isaiah 46:1–4). The heaviest burdens are self-righteousness and legalism (Matthew 23:4). Christ gives us rest when we submit to His yoke, take up our crosses, deny ourselves, and follow Him in the way of life (Matthew 11:28–30; 16:24–25). We must then be willing for Christ to shear us of excess burdens, for Scripture says: "let us lay aside every weight, and the sin which doth so easily beset us" (Hebrews 12:1).

The casting down of a burdened sheep also warns God's flock to flee the weight of pride. Pride lifts the heart above God. Pride opposes the law of God, power of God, and will of God. When the devil cannot stop a valuable and sound endeavor, he labors to make its author proud of it. Death is the last enemy, but pride is the last sin that will be destroyed in us. "Pride," quipped George Swinnock, "is the shirt of the soul, put on first and put off last."[3]

Rather let us cry aloud, "Lord, if pride has made angels devils, grant me rather the humility that makes men like angels! Teach me, Lord, who and what I am in Thy sight. Teach me my sinfulness and nothingness. Humble me, O God. Grant me freedom to cast away my burdensome pride and find my freedom in Christ alone."

Third, *obese sheep* represent a warning to those of the Lord's flock who turn from the diet and discipline of their Shepherd to the ways of the world. They graze upon the food of man instead of the Word of God. Lacking the discipline of the Holy Spirit, their spiritual life grows puffed up, flabby, and weak with worldliness. Obese sheep often try to dominate the rest of the flock, pushing and trampling them, much to the provoking of the Shepherd (Ezekiel 34:16–21). They grasp for the crown instead of taking up the cross. Like other downcast sheep, they soon find themselves struggling hopelessly to get back on their spiritual feet, and despair of God's mercy, knowing that they deserve only the sentence of death.

As vultures hover over fallen sheep in anticipation of their death, bitter enemies such as Satan, the world, sin, and a guilty conscience hover over God's downcast sheep. Yet, impossible though it seems, God's sheep will not stay down. Despite their carelessly placed confidence, burdensome pride, and bloated worldliness, Jehovah's cast-down sheep will not die. "He restoreth my soul," David says. He does not say, "He restored," meaning past deliverances, but "restoreth," in anticipation of more grace. There is always hope in God (Psalm 42:11).

Christ's Restoration of His Downcast Sheep

Christ is the Shepherd who neither slumbers nor sleeps (Psalm 121:4). He watches over His sheep at all times, counting them by number lest even one be missing. No one will pluck these sheep out of His hand nor out of His Father's hand (John 10:28–29).

Christ's watchfulness, diligence, and tenderness over His sheep are wondrous. He is truly the Good Shepherd. Phillip Keller writes about how he as a shepherd restored one careless sheep:

Again and again I would spend hours searching for a single sheep that was missing. Then more often than not I would see it at a distance, down on its back, lying helpless. At once I would start to run toward it—hurrying as fast as I could—for every minute was critical. Within me there was a mingled sense of fear and joy: fear it might be too late; joy that it was found at all.

As soon as I reached the cast ewe my very first impulse was to pick it up. Tenderly I would roll the sheep over on its side .... Then straddling the sheep with my legs I would hold her erect, rubbing her limbs to restore the circulation to her legs. This often took quite a little time. When the sheep started to walk again she often just stumbled, staggered, and collapsed in a heap once more.

All the time I worked on the cast sheep I would talk to it gently
.... always couched in language that combined tenderness and
rebuke, compassion and correction.

Little by little the sheep would regain its equilibrium. It would
start to walk steadily and surely. By and by it would dash away to
rejoin the others, set free from its fears and frustrations, given
another chance to live a little longer.[4]

God's people experience restoration of their souls through Christ.
First, Christ remedies the sheep cast down by its carelessness and
misplaced confidence by making it stand upon His grace. Child of
God, have you ever been restored like a careless, cast-down sheep?
Have you been cut off from all hope, then seen your Master coming to
you over the mountains and skipping upon the hills (Song of Solomon
2:8)? While laboring over you with tenderness through His Word
and providence, has not His voice spoken loving rebukes and asked
restorative questions, such as, "Simon, son of Jonas, lovest thou me
more than these" (John 21:15)? Have you not felt His sure, guiding,
everlasting arms around you, despite your repeated failures and falls?
Can you acknowledge His patience as opposed to your impatience?
Did He not firmly but lovingly lead you back to find life, safety, and
firm footing in Himself alone?

Everything apart from Christ brings you down and upon your back.
All ground but Christ is unable to support you in life. When Christ
puts you back on your feet, you learn again "to seek for our purification
and salvation without ourselves,"[5] through Christ alone, by faith in
Him alone, based on His Word alone.

Back on your feet, you may have experienced three emotions: holy
wonder that your life has again been spared, holy joy to stand again
on a good foundation, and holy fear lest you cast yourself down again.
Seek grace to retain all three, especially holy fear. "The best way never
to fall is ever to fear," wrote William Jenkyn.[6] "Wherefore let him that

thinketh he standeth take heed lest he fall," says 1 Corinthians 10:12. Remember, you must distrust yourself, but never distrust your Master. Keep up your courage, floundering sheep, for though you may often stumble, your perfect Shepherd will always be with you to restore you.

Second, casting down by the weight of the excess "wool" of self is remedied through *the shearing away of pride*. To shear a sheep clean is not a pleasant process for either sheep or shepherd. For shepherds it is hard and dirty work, and for sheep it is an alarming experience. Resisting, kicking, and struggling only add to a sheep's distress and may cause bleeding. Yet for the sake of the sheep, shearing must be done.

Through joyful submission to Christ's discipline, His sheep find life, for when the shearing is done, both sheep and owner are the better for it. Shearing gives the sheep freedom from their hot, heavy coats. Through shearing the shepherd also exposes his unique mark on his flock, which comforts both Him and the sheep by showing that they belong to one another.

True believer, you are acquainted with restoration via spiritual shearing. When dealing with your old life, with "the old man and his deeds" (Colossians 3:9), periodically the Holy Spirit takes in hand the keen cutting edge of God's Word, confirming Hebrews 4:12, which says, "For the word of God is quick, and powerful, and sharper than any two-edged sword, piercing even to the dividing asunder of soul and spirit, and of the joints and marrow, and is a discerner of the thoughts and intents of the heart."

Soul-shearing is unpleasant business for God's sheep. You kick and protest before you submit to the Lord's necessary work. However, the Great Shepherd proves strongest in the end, and by the transforming power of His grace makes you willing to find your life by losing it. You are set free from much of the weight and dirt of your sinful pride and selfishness, and are brought into the "glorious liberty of the children of God" (Romans 8:21). That is freedom indeed!

Christians should pray often for the Lord to shear away their pride, self-righteousness, and self-sufficiency. Consider the following prayer against pride:

O eternal God, merciful and glorious, Thou art exalted far above all heavens. Thy throne, O God, is glory, and Thy scepter is righteousness.

Thou, O God, who givest grace to the humble, do something also for the proud man. Make me humble and obedience. Take from me the spirit of pride and haughtiness, ambition and self-flattery.

O teach me to love to be concealed, and little esteemed. Let me be truly humble, and heartily ashamed of my sin and folly. Teach me to bear reproaches evenly, for I have deserved them; to refuse all honors done unto me, because I have not deserved them; to return all to Thee, for it is Thine alone; to suffer reproof thankfully, to amend all my thoughts speedily; and do Thou invest my soul with the humble robe of my meek Master and Savior Jesus.

And when I have humbly, patiently, charitably, and diligently served Thee, change this robe into the shining garment of immortality, my confusion into glory, my folly to perfect knowledge, my weaknesses and dishonors to the strength and beauties of the sons of God.

In the meantime, use what means Thou pleasest to conform me to the image of Thy holy Son; that I may be gentle to others, and severe to myself: that I may sit down in the lowest place; striving to go before my brother in nothing, but in doing him and Thee honor.

Grant this for Jesus Christ's sake, who humbled Himself to the death and shame of the cross, and is now exalted unto glory.

Unto Him, with Thee, O Father, be glory and praise forever and ever. Amen.[7]

Finally, the Great Shepherd restores the flabby, obese sheep by the *discipline of feeding on the Word and subjection to the rod of chastisement.* Just as a shepherd carefully rations his sheep's food,[8] so the Lord Jesus brings His sheep back to feed upon His written Word, and upon Himself as the living Word, rather than on the counsel, commandments, or personalities of men. He persuades the backslider to cast away the husks he once pined for, and invites him to feast again upon the wholesome and nourishing Bread from heaven, to be enjoyed only in the Father's house.

Restoration often involves the rod of chastisement, as we read in Hebrews 12:11, "Now no chastening for the present seemeth to be joyous, but grievous; nevertheless afterward it yieldeth the peaceable fruit of righteousness unto them which are exercised thereby." In the original language *exercised* has the root meaning of "to be stripped naked." It refers to the custom of the Greeks to perform rigorous exercise while nearly naked so their trainers could see their muscles and their flabby parts. Through strenuous exercise, hard wrestling, and well-aimed blows, training masters developed their students into masterpieces of physical fitness.

True believer, the Lord is your Master Trainer, before whom "all things are naked and opened unto the eyes of Him with whom we have to do" (Hebrews 4:13). He coaches and corrects you, leading you through afflictions. If your Master was exercised in the narrow way to Jerusalem, will not His disciples be likewise tutored? Unlike His sufferings, however, your chastening does not merit salvation. Yet a fruitful badge of your adoption as a child of God is to be truly "exercised thereby," for He scourges every son He receives (Hebrews 12:6).

Chastening is inseparable from belonging to Him, so receive it willingly. It is for your benefit, for Christ knows your fat places and your weak places, and He exercises you accordingly. He chastened Jacob through his lying sons, David through a sword that never departed from his house, Paul through his thorn in the flesh, and John through banishment on Patmos. Though God chastens you at times, "nevertheless afterward" it shall yield profitable fruit. Your Master will not destroy you by chastening you excessively, but will only firm you and fit you to be partakers of His holiness.

The Great Shepherd will try your faith, test the foundation of your hope, prove your love, strain your patience, and exercise every other spiritual grace in you. He will teach you through hard ways that there is more evil in one drop of sin than in an ocean of affliction. Yet be assured that He knows precisely what He is doing with you and exactly how much you can endure (1 Corinthians 10:13). By following Him in self-denying, burden-bearing, and cross-carrying paths, you will grow in grace, enabling you to abide more faithfully at the side of your Shepherd.

8

The Shepherd's Restoration for the Wandering Sheep

He restoreth my soul.
—Psalm 23:3a

In the last chapter, we considered how the Lord Jesus Christ restores His sheep from the mortal disease of their fall in Adam, and from their condition of being cast down through misplaced trust, self-righteousness, pride, and worldliness. Another kind of sheep that needs the Lord's gracious restoration is the wandering sheep. This represents the backsliding Christian who develops a pattern of not repenting in some area of life and as a result grows weak in faith and obedience.[1]

David's words tell us of the Shepherd's grace to this sinful sheep. "He restoreth my soul," could be translated, "He brings me back," which echoes our Lord's parable of the lost sheep (Luke 15:3–7). The form of the Hebrew verb used here implies that the divine Shepherd causes

His sheep to repent and turn back.[2] Crying out in their helplessness, the sheep are rescued by their loving Lord.

In this chapter we will consider why the Lord's sheep wander away from Him, how this wandering develops into backsliding, and what the Shepherd does to bring wandering sheep back to Himself and the flock.

The Causes of Wandering from the Shepherd

Sheep wander for three reasons: failure to keep an eye on the shepherd, following other sheep into wrong paths, and stubbornly taking the way of their own choosing.

First, a sheep wanders when it *forgets to keep its eyes fixed on the shepherd*. Putting its head down to taste a juicy tuft of grass, then moving to another and yet another, a sheep may eventually raises its head and discover that the shepherd and flock are nowhere in sight. Suddenly it is afraid, for it lacks an intuitive sense of direction and thus has no ability to retrace its steps.

The image of sheep distracted by lush green grass reminds us that nibbling at the poisonous weeds of the world is not always what draws Christians away from Christ. Certainly, love of the world hinders a believer's fellowship with the Lord. However, Christians may also be hindered by their preoccupation with good and lawful things. Earning a living, furnishing a home, recreational pastimes, and many other things can become distractions to the soul. Even our duties as Christians can become a snare to us if they are not done for the Lord, with our eyes fixed on Him. These activities are only means of seeking the ultimate goal of communion with the Shepherd. Our victory is union with Christ. Anything that draws sheep away from their Shepherd will defeat them.

Christians always need to be conscious of their Lord. They need His grace and guidance daily, hourly, and moment by moment. The sheep of the Lord must ever watch and pray, lest they enter into temptation.

You too can become so absorbed in activities intended to further the kingdom of God that you discover the absence of your Master only when you are forced to stop and rest. Martha of Bethany was distracted with much serving and resented her sister, Mary, for ignoring that as she sat at Jesus' feet. But Christ said to her, "Martha, Martha, thou art careful and troubled about many things: but one thing is needful: and Mary hath chosen that good part, which shall not be taken away from her" (Luke 10:41-42). Martha's duties in the kitchen were helpful, but what she did on other days kept her from enjoying the special presence of her Master. Like Mary, Martha needed to be at the feet of Jesus.

Examine yourselves. Have you become distracted in much serving? Are you guarding the Lord's Day and daily times of meditation and prayer or giving them up because of the busyness of daily life? Have you allowed good things to crowd out the One who is best?

Second, a sheep wanders when it *follows other sheep instead of the Shepherd*. Sheep enjoy being with one another and will often follow each other even into danger. The blessing of friendship for the Lord's flock is unequivocally stated by the apostle John: "We know that we have passed from death unto life, because we love the brethren" (1 John 3:14). But Satan seeks to pervert good things for evil purposes. He strives to turn love for the saints into misplaced reliance on fellow sheep rather than the Shepherd. As long as God's children follow the Master, they may also follow one another. But when they begin to follow each other away from the narrow path of salvation, they wander from their Master.

It was a blessing for people to follow John the Baptist, but a far greater blessing to follow Christ after John identified Jesus as the Lamb of God (John 1:36-39). When the Lord Jesus asked people, "What seek ye?" they answered, "Rabbi, where dwellest thou?" They wanted to be with Him. The best fellowship with the saints takes place when we follow Christ together.

Do you know what it is to abide in Christ? Does your heart beat to follow the Shepherd habitually, dependently, lovingly, and gladly? Or is your heart drawn to other Christians, even if they lead you in a way contrary to the Word of Christ? The love of honor among men is an enemy to faith in Christ (John 5:44). Do not give yourself to its influence. Bow before the will of Christ alone.

Third, a sheep wanders when it *stubbornly chooses its own path.* At times a sheep will go anywhere and take any path except the one the shepherd has chosen. A stubborn sheep will choose brown pasture rather than green pasture. It will force its way through small openings even if the result is torn wool and bleeding wounds. It goes about as if seeking its own destruction. The further a sheep goes its own way, the more it becomes bewildered and frustrated. As it becomes aware that it is lost, a sheep will begin to utter piteous cries of distress that attract wild, devouring beasts. The sheep would be destroyed if the shepherd did not rescue it.

By nature, human beings are also perpetual wanderers. Isaiah 53:6 says, "All we like sheep have gone astray; we have turned each one to his own way." We pursue any route but the narrow way to everlasting life. We pick any pasture but the green grass of God's Holy Word. And we wriggle our way through the Lord's boundary fences and hedges of His commandments, heedless that our foolish goal is to escape our loving Shepherd's presence and care.

The condition of God's people is somber when their carnal nature gets the upper hand in their inward conflicts. "My sheep wandered through all the mountains and upon every high hill," says the Lord through the prophet Ezekiel (Ezekiel 34:6). God has planted spiritual life in the regenerate so that they may live by faith, but they must still live in the flesh (Galatians 2:20). So while on earth they struggle with earthly corruptions, weaknesses, and assaults of the flesh. Satan is ready to attack them at any moment, and the world constantly tempts them to wander off God's path.

Though God's true flock is renewed in the spirit of their minds (Ephesians 4:23), they still carry corruption with them, which inclines them to turn away from the living God. Apart from God's grace, the most enlightened and advanced believer will go astray. Scripture contains many examples of fallen saints such as Abraham, David, and Simon Peter to warn us that the godliest Christian carries the seeds of wickedness in his heart. The Heidelberg Catechism rightly speaks of "that depravity which always cleaves to us."[3]

The Lord's flock is not content when they wander away from their Shepherd. They delight to do their Lord's will (Romans 7:22). However, though they recognize the fearful consequences of departing from the living God, they discover that they are unable to bring themselves back to God. Just as they were once saved by grace, so they must continue to be saved by grace.

The Road to Backsliding

Sheep of God's flock that go back to their old ways fear that they will grow continually worse until they are completely lost. Caught in the downward spiral of backsliding, they mournfully search for the cause of their relapse. They ask, "Lord, where and how did all this wandering begin?" In mercy, the Lord opens their eyes to the dreadful process that led them away from Him. He restores them to the flock by leading them back to the fold. Then He shows them how they strayed from Him. Their first step in the wrong direction was their neglect of *secret prayer*. Formerly, they looked forward to times of prayer. They longed to be alone with the Lord, to speak with Him and to pour out their hearts before Him.

But gradually their prayer life began to diminish. Even before they were aware of it, their prayers became mere formality rather than "the offering up of their desires unto God."[4] Their love and urgency to pray cooled. Before long they dropped their morning prayer, feeling it was no longer necessary to begin the new day with God. Other prayers were shortened, then omitted as well. Wandering thoughts multiplied. Intercessions for husband, wife, children, church, and nation became infrequent. When God in grace opens the eyes of these wandering sheep, they soon realize that their prayers lack sincerity and passion.

Without that awakening, wandering may increase even to the diminishing of all *the means of grace*. Church attendance is not neglected but is not wholehearted. The public means of grace are substituted for a close and secret walk with God; the body is present but the heart is not engaged. Backslidden sheep may read the Bible regularly, but not with the spiritual relish of former days. As the Bible becomes dry to them, their eyes also become dry, empty of tears that once flowed in repentance and gratitude.

The center of all the means of grace, Jesus Christ, seems distant for believers who revert to their old ways. He who was their life, the source of their sanctification, the spring of their joy, the theme of their song, the glorious person upon whom their eyes rested, and the mark towards which they were pressing, now withdraws the sense of His presence. Unfortunately, instead of blaming themselves, wandering sheep are more inclined to blame the Lord, or their pastors and the church they belong to for the Shepherd's absence.

The next step is that *inner corruptions* begin to multiply. These wandering sheep no longer pray, "Search me O God, and know my heart: try me, and know my thoughts: and see if there be any wicked way in me, and lead me in the way everlasting" (Psalm 139:23-24). They find excuses for their lack of enthusiasm or pretend that it still exists. Gradually these sheep become more interested in merely speaking the language of Christianity than in experiencing the life of Christianity. When they do talk of the Lord's ways, self creeps in. With their mouth they speak of God's free grace, but deep in their heart they exalt themselves. Lowliness of mind yields to spiritual pride.

They begin to live a double life. Secret sins multiply. Temptations thought to be in the grave are resurrected with even more power than before. These sheep may confess their sin but not to repent. They regret their sin but do not zealously wage war against it. Self-examination becomes less frequent, less thorough, and less prayerful for those who wander from their Shepherd. Although God's children will never go back to live with the world, the world often comes back to live with them.

Backsliding can go so far that even *brotherly love* seems to dissipate. Communion of the saints becomes a seemingly unnecessary practice. Backslidden sheep are convinced that they can travel the narrow path of salvation to glory on their own without other believers. God's people become strangers instead of fellow pilgrims.

Conflicts, troubles, disputes, and self-exaltations develop as a result of backsliding. Instead of covering the faults of their brethren, these backsliders often take the opportunity to talk against others and defend their own name. Instead of running with others, they run against them. Instead of considering others better than themselves, they despise God's work in others.

Are you caught in this deadly spiral downwards? If so, does it break your heart? The pathway out of backsliding begins with godly sorrow that leads to repentance.

The Shepherd Bringing Back His Wandering Sheep

The Shepherd's first remedy for wandering sheep is repentance. It is critical to bear in mind that repentance is the gift of Jesus Christ. By His humiliation, Christ merited repentance for His flock. He "bare our sins in his own body on the tree, that we, being dead to sins, should live unto righteousness: by whose stripes ye were healed. For ye were as sheep going astray; but are now returned unto the Shepherd and Bishop of your souls" (1 Peter 2:24–25). Christ did not wander from the pathway of obedience. He walked steadfastly in His Father's will to His very death on the cross (Philippians 2:8). He obeyed God's eternal purpose, fulfilling the covenant of salvation in which the Father had engaged Him before time began.

In His state of exaltation, Christ offers this gift of repentance. Acts 5:31 says, "Him hath God exalted with his right hand to be a Prince and a Saviour, for to give repentance to Israel, and forgiveness of sins." Christ keeps His sheep saved by the divine love, power, and wisdom He exercises at the right hand of the Father. Through Christ, God grants "repentance unto life" to the elect of nations (Acts 11:18). By Christ's mighty hand, the preaching of the gospel turns many back to the Lord (Acts 11:21). As His grace works repentance in them, wandering sheep turn back to their Shepherd. They discover that in love He has sought them out and rescued them from the peril into which their wandering hearts have led them.

Christ kept Peter's faith from utterly failing even as Peter denied his Lord, and promised his repentance (Luke 22:31–32). Christ broke Peter's backsliding heart with a single look of love (Luke 22:61–62). Christ both humbled and restored Peter by His threefold questioning, *Do you love me?* (John 21:15–17). Years later, Peter declared that believers "are kept by the power of God through faith unto salvation" (1 Peter 1:5). He knew that keeping power by experience. Is this also your experience and hope?

What is this repentance by which the Shepherd brings back wandering sheep? Thomas Watson defines biblical repentance as a medicine consisting of six ingredients: sight of sin, sorrow for sin, confession of sin, shame for sin, hatred for sin, and turning from sin.[5]

(1) *Sight of Sin.* The first grace you must seek as a backslider is a Spirit-worked enlightenment about your condition. Repentance and returning cannot take place without receiving spiritual eyes to see the grievous ugliness of your backsliding. David saw his sins and cried out, "I acknowledge my transgressions: and my sin is ever before me. Against thee, thee only, have I sinned, and done this evil in thy sight:

that thou mightest be justified when thou speakest, and be clear when thou judgest" (Psalm 51:3-4). The Spirit enabled David to see his sin as an offense against God and His righteousness in condemning it as sin.

For backsliding believers, repentance must be coupled with remembrance. To the church of Ephesus the Lord wrote, "Nevertheless I have somewhat against thee, because thou hast left thy first love. Remember therefore from whence thou art fallen" (Revelation 2:4-5). The Spirit plants the remembrance of former spiritual blessings in the hearts of believers, saying, "Remember from whence thou art fallen." Remember your former sorrow over sin and conviction of guilt. Remember taking refuge in Christ. Remember your first love for Christ, His people, and His Word. By remembering this former love, backsliders are awakened to the evil of their coldness and corruption.

(2) *Sorrow for Sin.* Repentance also rends the heart with mourning over sin (Joel 2:12). Paul rejoiced when the saints in Corinth turned from their sinful backsliding, writing, "Now I rejoice, not that ye were made sorry, but that ye sorrowed to repentance: for ye were made sorry after a godly manner, that ye might receive damage by us in nothing. For godly sorrow worketh repentance to salvation not to be repented of: but the sorrow of the world worketh death" (2 Corinthians 7:9-10). Watson said, "A woman may as well expect to have a child without pangs as one can have repentance without sorrow."[6]

Paul distinguished between worldly sorrow and godly sorrow, saying godly sorrow is to be "grieved according to God." Many people feel bad when they suffer the consequences of sin for themselves, their families, and other people. That is not the godly sorrow of true repentance, which is "a sincere sorrow of heart that we have provoked God by our sins," as the Heidelberg Catechism says.[7]

True sorrow for sin focuses on God rather than the sinner. It moves the repentant one to say, "I have provoked God by violating His commandments, trampling upon His law, scorning His majesty, despising His attributes, destroying His image, and acting as a friend to His enemies." The believer who has wandered but is now returning grieves over sinning against a holy God, a suffering Savior, and an indwelling Spirit.

(3) *Confession of Sin.* A mark of the true children of God as opposed to self-deceived hypocrites is that "we confess our sins," trusting that "he is faithful and just to forgive us our sins, and to cleanse us from all unrighteousness" (1 John 1:9). This confession is necessary to restore our fellowship with God (v. 7), for the Lord says, "I will go and return to my place, till they acknowledge their offence, and seek my face" (Hosea 5:15).

True sorrow cannot be covered up. It can only pour out its heart before God in owning its transgressions (Psalm 51). In true confession, all things are spread out before the Lord while deeply conscious that He knows them far better than they know themselves. As the psalmist says, "I acknowledged my sin unto thee, and mine iniquity have I not hid. I said, I will confess my transgressions unto the LORD; and thou forgavest the iniquity of my sin" (Psalm 32:5).

(4) *Shame for Sin.* True repentance bows to sin's deserved punishment (Jeremiah 31:19). It tramples sin in the dirt and reveals sin's moral filth. The returning backslider is humbled by the way his sins have defiled him. The prodigal son confessed, "Father, I have sinned against heaven, and in thy sight, and am no more worthy to be called thy son" (Luke 15:21).

Someone might object, saying, "How can he feel shame? Isn't he forgiven? Isn't the repentant believer washed by the blood of Christ?" It is true that no repentance is possible without the Spirit's revelation of Christ's grace. We cannot walk in God's holy light and fellowship with Him unless "the blood of Jesus Christ his Son cleanseth us from all sin" (1 John 1:7). When a believer sins, Scripture directs him to

Christ, our righteous Advocate in heaven, whose propitiation turns away God's wrath (1 John 2:1–2).

However, Christ's cleansing blood also humbles us, for we realize afresh the horror of what our sins cost Him on the cross. God's atoning grace releases us from guilt and punishment, but it also increases our humility and moves us to close our mouths in shame (Ezekiel 16:63; 36:31–32). It makes us cry out, "How could I sin against such divine love?"

(5) *Hatred for Sin.* Repentance from backsliding renews love for God. And love for God inflames returning sinners to hate all that is against God. The essence of sin is hating God (Romans 8:7). How then can we turn back to God without hating sin? "Ye that love the LORD, hate evil" (Psalm 97:10). If we claim to return to God with love, but do not hate our sins, our love is hypocritical (Romans 12:9).

The cross of Christ is the most awful exhibition of God's hatred of sin as well as the richest manifestation of His readiness to pardon it. Pardon is written in every drop of Calvary's blood. Yet blood-bought forgiveness inspires holy fear (Psalm 130:4). It moves us to tremble at the awesome justice of God, for the cross declares that God is just (Romans 3:26). The fear of God moves us to hate all that He hates. Christ, our divine Wisdom, says, "The fear of the LORD is to hate evil" (Proverbs 8:13). Thus, Watson wrote, "A true penitent is a sin-loather …. Heaven is never longed for till sin be loathed."[8]

(6) *Turning from Sin.* As noted before, "He restoreth my soul," can be translated, "He causes me to turn" in a new direction. Fleeing from sin back to our God and Savior is a mark of true repentance. It means a practical cutting off of sin and its occasions in one's life. Counterfeit repentance goes no further than outward reformation. True repentance fights to cut off sin not only in its fruits but right down to its roots.

The practical effects of turning from sin back to God must be evident in every area formerly polluted by backsliding. Prayer must be reinstated as a holy habit. Access to Jehovah's throne and vital communion with Him must be pursued as a privilege and a mercy. The soul must lay its lamentations, confessions, praises, and earnest desires at the foot of the Lord's mercy seat.

The restored backslider must also treasure and use the means of grace. Thereby the soul receives renewed freedom to carry its guilt to divine blood, its corruption to divine grace, its afflictions to divine providence, its impossibilities to divine omniscience, and its love to the divine heart.

The Bible once again becomes a precious treasure. Renewal causes an inward softening that leads to meekness and contrition. The soul is once more attracted to "things which are not seen" (2 Corinthians 4:18), to eternal realities that deaden the lure of sin and the world and the shadows of time and sense. The preached Word does not rattle dead bones but breathes life and vigor into the soldiers of the Lord. Self-worship is sacrificed to the heartfelt worship of the triune God.

Awakened from spiritual slumber, the eyes of the soul once more turn to Christ, who is radiant in His beauty and draws near to His beloved sheep. Oh, what a wonder that He should come once more to His wandering sheep! How the soul rejoices in His longsuffering and goodness, His kind and tender forbearance, and His wondrous grace and mercy! The sheep admires and adores its Shepherd. It is convinced anew of the immense value of His precious blood and righteousness, and the sweetness of His love.

What is the condition of your soul? Are you a stranger to the experience presented in the simple words, "He restoreth my soul"? Oh, friend, your need is urgent and your case is desperate. Pray like the wrestling Jacob: "I will not let thee go, except thou bless me" (Genesis 32:26). Remember that no case is too hard for the Lord. However vile, no sinner whose only plea is the precious blood of Christ is ever cast out of His presence. Place your sin before God as a holy challenge for divine power and as a plea for the extension of divine mercy. Listen to David's pleading petition: "For thy name's sake, O LORD, pardon mine iniquity; for it is great" (Psalm 25:11). Seek God's all-sufficient, all-availing grace.

Are you a believer who has received God's sovereign grace, yet are not presently in the right place before God? Cease your wandering and return to your Shepherd. Do not rest until you experience the sweet beating of His heart. Arise, beg, and agonize for the outpouring of the Spirit upon your soul. Give up lifeless religion, form without power, prayer without communion, confession without brokenness, and zeal without love. Seek grace with perseverance, believing that you might be filled with the Spirit's saving graces. Seek grace to live afresh for God. Let this be your prayer at the footstool of mercy: "O Lord, revive Thy work. Quicken me, O Lord. Restore unto me the joy of Thy salvation! 'Come down like rain upon the mown grass: as showers that water the earth'" (Psalm 72:6).

Finally, are you a child of God who can humbly testify that you are not backsliding? If so, guard your soul. Remember that you are still in a state of imperfection and infirmity. No matter how spiritual your present condition is, you are not beyond the reach of the enemy. Yet, true believer, be of good courage. Paul said, "He which hath begun a good work in you will perform it to the day of Jesus Christ" (Philippians 1:6). The Lord who saved you now keeps you by His power. Follow Him, keep your eyes on Him, and He will lead you safely to the Father's house!

Unrighteousness Uncovered and Righteousness Imputed

He leadeth me in the paths of righteousness for his name's sake.
—Psalm 23:3b

To be righteous generally means to be upright and virtuous, to faithfully walk in the path of duty, and to act with integrity. The term *righteousness* covers every aspect of life. Righteousness involves our relationships with God, our neighbors, and ourselves. It calls for faithfulness and truth in every aspect of every relationship. Righteousness establishes numerous standards, laws, norms, and rules for religious, marital, domestic, ecclesiastical, vocational, societal, and international life.

In Psalm 23, David speaks of righteousness in regard to the relationship between God and man. Before we can become righteous in relationships with other people, we must be justified or made right with God through sovereign grace.

No term is more central to Scripture's message of the critical relationship between Creator and creature than *righteousness*. Righteousness is essential to understanding man's natural state of original righteousness in Paradise, his state of unrighteousness after his tragic fall, his restoration to a state of grace by faith through the righteousness of his substitute, the God-man, Jesus Christ, and his eternally state of everlasting righteousness.[1]

In Paradise, a perfect relationship existed between the triune Creator and man, who was the crown and masterpiece of all creation. No sin, trouble, sorrow, pain, conflict, or misunderstanding prevented our first parents from enjoying sweet communion with the Most High. Adam and Eve daily walked with God in pure friendship and untarnished fellowship.

Man's original state of righteousness was neither *imputed* nor *acquired*, but *inherent*. His entire being was subordinated to God without a single inclination toward evil in reason, will, or affection. As prophet, priest, and king, Adam was dedicated to God. He not only was capable of doing the will of God but delighted in it. He fully met the demands of God's righteousness.

When Adam fell into sin, however, he exchanged his perfect righteousness for voluntary unrighteousness. Abandoning righteousness and obedience, Adam—and we his offspring—became totally depraved. Our nature now totally defiles us. The law demands love, but we have become haters of God and of one another (Romans 1:30; Titus 3:3). Adam and Eve brought no love with them out of Paradise, not even natural love or social justice. Such gifts flow only out of common grace, granted to mankind out of divine goodness. Common grace will restrain sin and preserve the world until God's last sheep is safely gathered into everlasting life.

The Great Shepherd leads His sheep in the paths of righteousness. In this chapter we will consider how He does so, first in uncovering our unrighteousness, and second in imputing Christ's righteousness to us. Other dimensions of righteousness will be considered in the next chapter.

Revealing Our Unrighteousness

The depth of human depravity is unfathomable. As Jeremiah 17:9 says, "The heart is deceitful above all things, and desperately wicked: who can know it?" But as sinners, we refuse to acknowledge the truth of our total depravity. Like Adam and Eve, we busy ourselves with sewing fig leaves together to cover our sin instead of confessing and forsaking it.

By nature our life is nothing but a futile attempt to carve for ourselves a path of self-righteousness. Traveling along destruction's path, we are foes of the first word of our text: "*He* leadeth me in the paths of righteousness." We want to be our own leader, shepherd, savior, master, and guide. We are loath to acknowledge God as God (Romans 1:21), and we join others in rejecting Christ, saying, "We will not have this man to reign over us" (Luke 18:14). We think we can do better for ourselves than Christ can. Bypassing our broken covenant with God, our deep fall in Adam, and our daily stream of foul transgressions, we expect God to walk with us on our terms in the pathways of self-reformation, self-religion, self-righteousness, and self-effort. Acting as if we had never sinned nor fallen, we present ourselves before God as Cain did, thinking that we deserve life and His favor.

When the Lord begins to lead sheep in *His* paths of divine righteousness, His first work is to uncover the barrenness of all other paths of righteousness. As a good shepherd, the Lord does a thorough rather than a hurried work. He may allow His sheep to wander at some length in fruitless paths prior to bringing them back and guiding them along the path of true righteousness. The Shepherd painstakingly handles His sheep even as they bleat, "we are able" (Matthew 20:22), while choosing their own paths of self-righteousness. To bring them to His blessed path, the Shepherd must first show His sheep the futility of finding a righteousness of their own in good works, in their efforts at self-reformation, and even in their admissions of unworthiness.

Christ Overthrows Our Self-Righteous Standing on the Law

The first path God makes barren for His people is that of righteousness according to the law. When the Holy Spirit begins to work in the heart of a sinner, sin is viewed in a new light. The sinner begins to see sin as God sees it. He sees that his righteousness is in fact unrighteousness. Desiring to become righteous in God's sight, a convicted sinner labors to obey God's law perfectly and to live a holy life. He vows to live such a godly life that the Lord will notice and forgive. He says, "What good thing shall I do, that I may have eternal life?" (Matthew 19:16).

His attempt to establish his own righteousness may seem to prosper for a while, though it never reaches its goal of perfection. In the effort to reform himself in every respect, the sinner may wage a relentless battle against sin. But he fails to see that this war is one he cannot win, and his sin remains a debt he can never repay.

Try as he might, his attempt to reform himself is short-lived as the goal more than exceeds the grasp. As he looks into his own heart, he begins to see the sinfulness of his motives, thoughts, and actions. As he meditates upon the law, he begins to see the *spirituality* of the law, the *demand* of the law, the *curse* of the law, the *punishment* of the law, and the *inflexibility* of the law. He begins to despair of achieving righteousness by obeying the law. He trembles when he hears, "Cursed is every one that continueth not in all things which are written in the book of the law to do them" (Galatians 3:10).

When the sinfulness of sin and the curse of the law become real to the sinner, he begins to see the righteousness of God revealed in the law. The darkness of sin becomes blacker when placed before the backdrop of God's pure and spotless perfections. Holiness and justice are no longer just words but daily and condemning realities. The sinner learns that the living God can have no communion with sin, cannot even look upon iniquity, and is perfect and holy in all His ways (Habakkuk 1:13). Brought to a standstill before the perfections of God, the sinner's conscience is further burdened when the Spirit places before him all the sins of his past life (Psalm 50:21). Sin and guilt are evident on every page of his history. With David he confesses, "Innumerable evils have compassed me about: mine iniquities have taken hold on me, so that I am not able to look up; they are more than the hairs of my head: therefore my heart faileth me" (Psalm 40:12).

The longer a sinner persists in self-righteous striving, the more he becomes a mystery to himself. The more he fights for righteousness, the more unrighteous he becomes. He parts with some beloved sins, yet finds other sins bothering him, for sinful motives stain all his efforts. His attempts to conform to the demands of the law end in failure until he cries out, "The bed is shorter than that a man can stretch himself on it: and the covering narrower than that he can wrap himself in it" (Isaiah 28:20). The law becomes a sentence of death (Romans 7:10). Yet this sinner may not yet be willing to submit to God's righteousness through Christ (Romans 10:3–4).

Christ Overthrows Our Self-Righteous Standing on Repentance

The sinner may resort to a second path: righteousness by repentance. He offers up penitent prayers, penitent sighs, penitent tears, and penitent humility as a sacrifice on God's altar. He cries to God, "Why have I fasted, and thou dost not see? Why have I afflicted my soul, and thou dost not know?" (Isaiah 58:3).

The Spirit's enlightening, however, reveals penitent prayers to be soiled with pride and self-centeredness. The repentance of a double-minded man merits nothing but divine displeasure. His pleas and tears are ineffective. His humility cannot be deep enough to satisfy the standards of God's holy justice. The Holy Spirit uncovers the sinner's true condition. The sinner discovers that he cannot shut out nor can he stop the flow of sin from within. His heart is nothing but a fountain of unrighteousness (Genesis 6:5). The sinner faces the horrible reality of Jeremiah 13:23: "Can the Ethiopian change his skin or the leopard his spots? Then may ye also do good, that are accustomed to do evil."

The sinner also discovers his unity with fallen Adam. Adam's fall is his fall, and Adam's guilt his condemnation (Romans 5:12–19). Unrighteousness, sin, and guilt are not only his portion, but they define who and what he is. He is in darkness, and he is darkness (Ephesians 5:8) to the core of his being (Ephesians 4:18). In the light of God's truth, his acts of righteousness are as "filthy rags" (Isaiah 64:6). His prayers are an abomination (Proverbs 28:9).

God bars this pathway of achieving self-righteousness with a flaming sword. This way seems right to many people but it only leads to death. Christ commands repentance (Mark 1:15), but repentance cannot be our righteousness before a holy God, and there is little true repentance until we see that.

Christ Overthrows Our Self-Righteous Standing on Unworthiness

Amazingly, sinners bent on justifying themselves may actually try to turn their sense of unworthiness into righteousness before God. If the works of legalism and the piety of penitence fail to win God's favor, they may take the path of self-righteous unworthiness. They think that if they feel their guilt and shame enough, God will show them mercy. They view humility as a platform when it is really pride.

Our sense of unworthiness is no basis for God to bless us. Our poverty does not cause God to show mercy to us, for we willfully plunged ourselves into the abyss of misery and deprived ourselves of God's gifts. Christ shows the sinner that God would be perfectly righteous to leave us in sin and wretchedness. We cannot humiliate ourselves enough to excuse the damnation we deserve. God's mercy is free; its sole cause is God, who determined from eternity to glorify His name through the salvation of sinners, whom He knows by name. Salvation is not of man, not even of his need and unworthiness; it is from God, through God, and to God's glory (Romans 9:16).

Justice must be satisfied against sin, however. Works of the law, repentance, and unworthiness cannot accomplish that. Realizing this, the sinner is brought to the spiritual intersection of impossibility and necessity. Though God's way varies for each sheep of the flock, each comes to acknowledge, "I *cannot* save myself, but I *must* be saved." The sinner can make no claim on God. Fears of damnation may wash over him like mighty waves. Yet as Christ's grace pursues him, he finds his only hope in God's mercy. Like blind Bartimaeus, the sinner pleads for mercy, for without sovereign grace he will perish.

Imputing Christ's Righteousness

Those who look for a way of salvation outside themselves are eager to hear the good news of Jesus Christ. They find hope in texts such as 1 Timothy 1:15, "This is a faithful saying, and worthy of all acceptation, that Christ Jesus came into the world to save sinners; of whom I am chief." The Lord leads them to say, "Give me Jesus, or else I die."

Augustus Toplady expresses the sinner's inward condition once he sees himself in the light of God's law and the holy gospel:

> Not the labor of my hands,
> Can fulfill Thy law's demands;
> Could my zeal no respite know,
> Could my tears for ever flow,
> All for sin could not atone;
> Thou must save and Thou alone.[2]

The moment of surrender is the moment of victory as God by His Word reveals Jesus Christ in all His fullness, perfection, and sweetness as the Way, the Truth, and the Life (John 14:6). He merits, possesses, gives, and sustains life for His believing sheep.

In Christ's active and passive obedience, the soul beholds a clear and simple solution to all his questions about how to be right with God. Christ's active obedience as a man "born under the law" fulfills all the law's demands for perfect conformity to God's revealed will (Galatians 4:4). Christ's passive obedience as the righteous One who was "made a curse for us" on the cross fulfills all the law's demands for the punishment of sin (Galatians 3:10, 13). In this great exchange He took our guilt and gave His perfect obedience: "For he hath made him to be sin for us, who knew no sin; that we might be made the righteousness of God in him" (2 Corinthians 5:21).

Jesus Christ is "the LORD our Righteousness" (Jeremiah 23:6). His righteousness alone is acceptable to the Father. In Christ "mercy and truth are met together; righteousness and peace have kissed each other" (Psalm 85:10). The righteousness of Christ causes the believer to exclaim with David, "I will go in the strength of the Lord God: I will make mention of thy righteousness, even of thine only" (Psalm 71:16).

Christ and His righteousness become the believer's all-in-all. With holy amazement at the sinner's former blindness and Christ's present fullness, nothing is left but to cry as a bride: "My beloved is white and ruddy, the chiefest among ten thousand" (Song of Solomon 5:10). The justified sinner experiences the fulfillment of the promise in Malachi 4:2 as he sees "the Sun of righteousness arise with healing in his wings." So the sinner is set free to skip and leap for joy like a young calf.

John Bunyan struggled for a long time with guilt and fear over his sin until the Lord revealed to him the righteousness of Jesus Christ for sinners. Bunyan wrote,

> One day, as I was passing in the field ... this sentence fell upon my soul: *Your Righteousness is in heaven*; and I thought withal, I saw with the eyes of my soul, Jesus Christ at God's right hand, there, I say, was my righteousness; so that wherever I was, or whatever I was a-doing, God could not say of me, "He wants [lacks] my righteousness," for that was just before Him. I also

saw, moreover, that it was not my good frame of heart that made my righteousness better, nor yet my bad frame that made my righteousness worse; for my righteousness was Jesus Christ himself, "the same yesterday, today, and for ever" (Hebrews 13:8). Now did my chains fall off my legs, indeed, I was loosed from my afflictions and irons, my temptations also fled away .... Now I went also home rejoicing for the grace and love of God .... I lived, for some time, very sweetly at peace with God through Christ. O I thought Christ! Christ! There was nothing but Christ that was before my eyes.[3]

Salvation, which is impossible for fallen man, is more than possible in Christ. This revelation gives life to faith, hope, and love for the sinner. The heavy yoke of Moses is replaced with the easy yoke of Christ. The future appears secure, desirable, and rewarding. The believer is moved to sing with David:

How blest is he whose trespass hath freely been forgiv'n,
Whose sin is wholly covered before the sight of heav'n.
Blest he to whom Jehovah imputeth not his sin,
Who hath a guileless spirit,
Whose heart is true within.[4]

And with Augustus Toplady:

Rock of Ages, cleft for me;
Let me hide myself in Thee;
Let the water and the blood,
From Thy riven side which flowed,
Be of sin the double cure,
Cleanse me from its guilt and power

Nothing in my hand I bring;
Simply to Thy cross I cling;
Naked, come to Thee for dress;
Helpless, look to Thee for grace;

Foul, I to the fountain fly;
Wash me Savior, or I die.[5]

How can the righteousness of Christ justify a sinner? Justification is a judicial term. It is the act of God's free grace wherein He pardons all our sins and accepts us as righteous in His sight because of the righteousness of Christ that is imputed to us.

Justification has various aspects in God's plan of salvation:

- Christ is the Lamb slain from before the foundation of the world (with respect to God's eternal decree, Revelation 13:8) on behalf of His elect (1 Peter 1:2, 19–20). That decree, however, must be worked out in history by Christ and in the believer.

- Christ died on the cross for our offenses, and in His resurrection was raised for our justification collectively (Romans 4:25).

- In the moment of the sinner's regeneration and faith in Christ, justification becomes an objective reality to God, who translates the elect sinner from the state of condemnation and death into the state of life and reconciliation with God (Galatians 2:16).

- By the Spirit's internal witness, the believer is justified in his own conscience resulting in enlarged measures of personal assurance of grace and salvation (Romans 8:15–16). That transpires when the triune God impresses upon the believer a sense of pardon for all his transgressions and the right to eternal life.

- Justification or vindication of the redeemed is made public when the Lord Jesus Christ comes again on the clouds of heaven to judge the living and the dead.

Justifying faith declares, "I have seen Christ taking upon Himself the avenging wrath of God against all the sins of His people, in Gethsemane where He cried out to God with tears, and on Golgotha where He made His soul an offering for sin. I have seen that Christ has satisfied divine justice, and purchased perfect righteousness for His people. By His active and passive obedience, sinners are reconciled to God, stand justified in His sight, and are given a title to their heavenly inheritance." The justified sinner now can sing with John Kent:

> Without a seam this garment's wove
> Bequeath'd in everlasting love;
> Ere time began, design'd to be
> A royal robe to cover thee.[6]

A believer's greatest joy is to know that his name is written in heaven. Because of Christ the Savior, God writes "paid in full" across all the accounts of the past, present, and future sins of His sheep. He casts their sin behind Him into the sea of eternal forgetfulness, so that these prophecies becomes true: "He hath not beheld iniquity in Jacob, neither hath he seen perverseness in Israel" (Numbers 23:21). "As I have sworn that the waters of Noah should no more go over the earth; so have I sworn that I would not be wroth with thee, nor rebuke thee" (Isaiah 54:9). "Son, be of good cheer; thy sins be forgiven thee" (Matthew 9:2).

Like the burden carried by Bunyan's Christian, the burden of sin rolls off the backs of sinners into the empty sepulcher of the risen Lord, never to be seen again. The guilt of sin will never return to condemn them. They now have freedom to walk like the lame man who was healed by Jesus. They may leap up and praise God in His temple. They may confess with Thomas, "My Lord and my God" (John 20:28). They may rejoice with Job, "I know that my Redeemer liveth" (Job 19:25).

They experience what is written in Isaiah 61:3 and can say, "I have received beauty for ashes, the oil of joy for mourning, the garment of praise for heaviness; that I might be called a tree of righteousness, the planting of the Lord, that He might be glorified." Their filthy garments are stripped away and washed in the robes of Christ's righteousness. As Zechariah 3:4 says, "Behold, I have caused thy iniquity to pass from thee, and I will clothe thee with change of raiment." Liberty and boldness in the faith becomes their portion. They are free indeed.

Children of God, should we not treasure such great blessings? Let us labor "to make our calling and election sure" (2 Peter 1:10). While the Lord is free to give or withhold our assurance of justification, we must hunger for it, seek it, and guard it by walking closely with God and making diligent use of the means of grace. We must set our hearts on Christ alone so that we can say with the Heidelberg Catechism, "I am righteous in Christ, before God, and an heir of eternal life."[7]

If you are a believer but you lack full assurance, fly to God's promises, reflect on God's work in your own soul, and wait on the Lord! Listen to the words of the psalmist: "Be of good courage, and he shall strengthen thine heart: wait, I say, on the LORD" (Psalm 27:14). Believe that Christ, the greater Boaz, will "not be in rest, until he has finished the thing this day" (Ruth 3:18). Do not rest until the triune God is the foundation of your salvation and the center of your life, enabling you to boast in your Redeemer with the bride who exclaimed: "He brought me to the banqueting house, and his banner over me was love" (Song of Solomon 2:4). Until then, trust that He who has drawn you to Himself will not forsake you along the way. Say to your soul, "He leadeth me in the paths of righteousness."

If you are unconverted, listen to the good news of the righteousness of Jesus Christ that has been presented to you. It is a righteousness fit for an unrighteous sinner. Consider seriously the consequences of rejecting God's calling to believe on the only Name given among men under heaven by which we must be saved (Acts 4:12). The fault of refusing to do so will be yours, not God's or Adam's. The gospel allows no excuse for failing to respond. How can you dare to stand before a holy God in your own unrighteousness? The Lord can accept nothing from you or from any other sinner. You dislike a religion that says you are nothing, for you want to *have* something, *be* something, and *do* something. You are not willing to receive Christ as everything.

But the Lord's patience will not last forever. An almost Christian will not stand in the Day of Judgment. Half-hearted divine righteousness cannot be merged with half-hearted self-righteousness; the attempt to join them will bring only cause eternal condemnation. Do not wait any longer. Stake your eternity on Christ alone as "The LORD our righteousness" (Jeremiah 23:6).

10

The Shepherd's Righteousness to Sanctify and Preserve

He leadeth me in the paths of righteousness for his name's sake.
—Psalm 23:3b

C hristian, the main character in John Bunyan's *Pilgrim's Progress*, did not lose the burden of his sin when he first began his walk with the Lord by passing through the strait gate, but neither did he have to wait until the end of his journey. Rather, he was delivered of his sin when he looked upon Christ's cross. That was when his burden rolled off his back and fell into the empty tomb. Have you ever wondered why Bunyan told the story that way?

Many people today might think the pilgrim would lose his burden as soon as he passed through the strait gate. They would fault Bunyan for putting Christian's release from sin too late in the story. However, Bunyan wisely delayed that release, showing that some people may be born again and yet not experience the consciousness of justification until they walk with God for a time. What Christian experiences at the cross is justification from the guilt of all his sin. At the same time, he receives a roll with a seal upon it, to be given back when he reaches the gates of the Celestial City. Christian is granted justification and assurance of faith at the same time. For some of God's people, however, assurance of faith is a more gradual process.

Others might fault Bunyan for putting relief from sin too early in the story, arguing that Christians do not experience deliverance and assurance of salvation until they have walked with God a very long time. Some do not experience this assurance at all in this life. However, Bunyan understood that it is normal for ordinary Christians to experience assurance in varying degrees as they journey toward heaven. I believe that Bunyan placed the scene relatively early to teach an important lesson.

Bunyan shows there is more to vital Christianity than the experience of justification. The flock of God needs to learn from the Lord to dip faith's bucket deeper into the well of salvation. The flock will then experience that justification is only the beginning of divine fullness and grace that flow to us from the fountain of life, Jesus Christ. No bride would be content to remain forever engaged to her future husband, much less be satisfied with only signing the marriage license. She yearns to live with her beloved. Likewise, for God's people, the end point of their relationship must not be in coming to faith in Christ and their first experience of being justified. They must yearn to walk with Christ in holiness and perseverance until they see Him face to face in glory.

Bunyan teaches us the importance of sanctification, as well as its indispensable connection with justification. By writing that most of Christian's journey occurs after he is delivered from sin at the cross, Bunyan emphasizes the completeness of God's work in saving His elect. God's paths of righteousness include more than calling, regeneration, and justification. The life of sanctification inevitably follows. This is a life not only of joy and peace. Bunyan says sanctification includes conflict and peace, surrender and victory, death and life. Justification leads to sanctification, and sanctification leads to perseverance in the faith.

Righteousness Imparted to Sanctify Jehovah's Sheep

After rejoicing in the Shepherd's restoration of His sheep through conversion and continual repentance, David describes how the Good Shepherd leads the restored flock in the paths they had formerly deserted, "the paths of righteousness." He leads them in the right ways.

Sheep need to be led for two reasons. First, because of the inhospitable terrain in Israel. Halvor Ronning writes, "On the steep slopes of the Judean hillsides are myriads of parallel paths permanently etched by centuries of foot traffic by sheep and goat searching for one blade of grass to munch on. In this setting, it is comfortable to know that the Lord is able, even in dry inhospitable desert terrain with a multitude of circling confusing paths, to lead His sheep on the right path to the restful waters and grassy patches."[1]

Second, sheep need to be led because of themselves. Keller writes, "If left to themselves, they will follow the same trails until they become ruts; graze the same hills until they turn to desert wastes; pollute their own ground until it is corrupt with disease and parasites."[2] He goes on to explain that shepherds must thus lead their flocks in a carefully determined plan of movement from one field to another, lest the sheep destroy the land, even to the point of tearing grass roots out of the ground. The progress of the flock to fresh pasture is a great joy to the sheep.[3]

In the same way, the Good Shepherd leads his repentant sheep by a route planned for their good, though it often seems barren and circuitous to His sheep. The process of Christ leading His own in the daily pursuit of righteousness is called sanctification. The Westminster Shorter Catechism gives us a good definition of this process. It says,

"Sanctification is a work of God's free grace, whereby we are renewed in the whole man after the image of God, and are enabled more and more to die unto sin, and live unto righteousness" (see Ephesians 4:22–24).[4] The Heidelberg Catechism offers us further insight, saying that the mortification or "putting to death" of sanctification consists of "a sincere sorrow of heart that we have provoked God by our sins, and more and more to hate and flee from them" (see Romans 8:13). The quickening or renewed life consists of "a sincere joy of heart in God, through Christ, and with love and delight to live according to the will of God in all good works" (see Romans 6:10; Galatians 2:20).[5]

How is sanctification related to justification? Justification and sanctification have much in common. (1) Both proceed from free grace and are rooted in the sovereign good pleasure of the triune God (Ephesians 1:4; 1 Peter 1:2). (2) Both are made possible only by Jesus Christ acting on behalf of the elect through union with Him (John 15:5; 1 Corinthians 1:30). (3) The elect, consequently, are the only recipients of justification and sanctification (Romans 8:30), which are inseparable. (4) Both are necessary for salvation and begin from the moment of regeneration (1 Corinthians 6:9–11).

Despite their similarities, however, there are important distinctions between justification and sanctification. (1) Justification is an objective change in one's status before God (Romans 4:5), while sanctification is a subjective change within the person's soul (Romans 6:13–17). (2) Justification declares the sinner righteous and holy in Christ (Philippians 3:9) on the basis of Christ's work and obedience for the sinner (Romans 5:19), while sanctification makes the sinner righteous and holy as a fruit flowing from union with Christ (Philippians 1:11). In sanctification we bear fruit in our obedience because of God's work of grace within us (Philippians 2:12–13). (3) Justification takes away the legal guilt of sin (Romans 4:7; 8:33–34), while sanctification takes away the pollution of sin in the sinner's heart and life (2 Corinthians 7:1). (4) Justification is a complete and perfect act and takes place only once (Romans 8:1), while sanctification is a daily process, which is not perfected until the final breath of God's child (Romans 8:4, 13). (5) Justification gives God's people the title for heaven in Christ (Romans 5:1–2), while sanctification makes them suitable for heaven so that they may enjoy God's holy presence there (Revelation 21:27; 22:1).

As the Shepherd leads His sheep in the paths of righteousness, he calls His sheep to avoid the dangers of four errors regarding sanctification. The first error is the antinomian teaching that says sanctification is nonessential. Once after I preached a sermon on justification and sanctification, a person politely informed me that the second half of my sermon was unnecessary because if we are justified, we do not need to be sanctified! But Scripture plainly tells us that without inward holiness no man is able to see the Lord (Matthew 5:8; Hebrews 12:14). John Owen said that there is no imagination that stupefies mankind more than this error: "that persons not purified, not sanctified, not made holy in their life, should afterwards be taken into that state of blessedness which consists of the enjoyment of God," for "neither can such persons enjoy God, nor would God be a reward to them." Owen said, "Holiness is indeed perfected in heaven: but the beginning of it is invariably confined to this world."[6] William Gurnall similarly wrote, "Say not thou hast royal blood in thy veins, and art begotten of God, except thou canst prove thy pedigree by this heroic spirit, to dare to be holy in spite of men and devils."[7]

Second, sanctification is distorted into heresy when it is made an end in itself instead of a means of pursuing Christ. Ephesians 2:8–9 tells us, "For by grace are ye saved through faith; and that not of yourselves: it is the gift of God: not of works, lest any man should boast." Sanctification can never be our justification. Furthermore, sanctification is always the result of God's sovereign grace acting through our union with Christ: "For we are his workmanship, created in Christ Jesus unto good works, which God hath before ordained that we should walk in them" (Ephesians 2:10). Gurnall counsels us to "prize Christ's grace" within us as a bride cherishes her husband's portrait drawn by his own hand but is never so foolish as to love the picture more than the husband. Do not set *Christ within you* against *Christ outside of you*, for only what Christ did outside of us in perfect obedience can be the foundation of our forgiveness and comfort.[8]

Third, we must avoid the error of turning sanctification into fatalism by viewing man as a robot moved by external forces. Though the sanctification of Christians is not ours originally, it is ours inherently. The Spirit infuses the principle of holiness into our souls as a fruit of Christ's righteousness. Therefore, it is not surprising that Scripture speaks more than a hundred times of man humbling, converting, and sanctifying himself. The Canons of Dort guard against this error when teaching this about conversion: "The will thus renewed, is not only actuated and influenced by God, but in consequence of this influence, becomes itself active. Wherefore also, man is himself rightly said to believe and repent, by virtue of that grace received."[9] God not only gives grace, but causes His people to exercise the graces that He gives them.

Fourth, we must avoid all notions that justification is God's work but sanctification is the work of His people by their free will. God in Christ is the Author, Sustainer, and Finisher of His people's salvation. "*He leadeth me in the paths of righteousness*," David says. Paul wrote that Christ "is made unto us wisdom, and righteousness, *and sanctification, and redemption*" (1 Corinthians 1:30). When God's flock understands this correctly, they greatly rejoice over this truth, for sanctification is really nothing more than holiness, and they have no ability to make or keep themselves holy apart from Christ. They cannot conquer one sinful thought or give themselves one pure desire. Their only hope as they "work out" their salvation is that "it is God which worketh in you both to will and to do of his good pleasure," by the same power with which He rose the "highly exalted" Christ from the dead to sit in the highest place (Philippians 2:9–13; see Ephesians 1:19–23).

Sanctification undercuts self-confidence. No matter what others think of God's people, as they grow they remain dissatisfied with themselves, their religion, their prayers, their worship, and even their preaching if they are ministers of God. The more holy they and their labors are, the more unholy they view themselves and their labors. Remember the confessions of Daniel and Paul (Daniel 9; Romans 7). Witness the confessions of church history's holiest saints—Augustine, Luther, Calvin, Rutherford, Whitefield, and many more.

For example, after preaching on one occasion, Thomas Shepard (1605–1649) was deeply distressed by his spiritual weakness and grieved that he lacked "light, and life, and affection," and "was not a burning and shining light."[10] On another occasion after preaching, he saw the pride of his heart and was moved to ask whether he had "pleased man," instead of seeking to do good and glorify God.[11] On his deathbed, Shepard exclaimed, "O my sinful heart! O my often-crucified but never wholly mortified sinfulness! O my life-long damage and my daily shame! O my indwelling and so besetting sins, your evil corruption is over now!"[12]

Though fed at the King's table, God's people in themselves can only limp along the path toward eternity. There is no end to the holiest believer's infirmities that cry out for further sanctification, such as vileness in affections, power in unbelief, perverseness in will, and rebellion in walk. The saints need daily grace to grow in holiness. Thus, their hope is, "*He* leadeth me in the paths of righteousness."

Sheep of God, you must learn to trust the Shepherd's ways. Seek grace to confess, "O Lord, I know that the way of man is not in himself: it is not in man that walketh to direct his steps. Thy ways are far above mine. Thou great Shepherd of sheep, lead me on the right ways. Lead me forward with Thy Word and Spirit according to my present need in spite of myself and my opposition. Establish Thou my goings."

God's sheep must not complain when their Shepherd leads them on hard paths, for those paths lead to righteousness. As Gurnall wrote,

"God would not rub so hard if it were not to fetch out the dirt that is ingrained in our natures. God loves purity so well that he would rather see a hole than a spot in his child's garments."[13] Oh, if only you could believe that God's "rubbings" are always signs of covenant love! He guides you through low valleys of disappointments, trials, chastening, and impossible challenges for your good. Learn to confess, "I know, O LORD, that thy judgments are right, and that thou in faithfulness hast afflicted me" (Psalm 119:75). At times you may say with Jacob, "All these things are against me" (Genesis 42:36). Let that prompt you to exercise faith in the promise that God will cause all things to "work together for good to them that love him" (Romans 8:28). Look to Jesus Christ, for He has traveled all your pathways before you, sanctifying them with His bloody footsteps. Trust this Shepherd, for He leads you in paths of righteousness.[14]

Righteousness Established to Preserve Jehovah's Sheep

"He leadeth me in the paths of righteousness for his name's sake," David writes. The name of the Lord is His glory (Exodus 33:18-19; Psalm 148:13; Isaiah 48:11).[15] Why does the Lord continue to lead His sheep despite all their wanderings? Scripture says, "For his name's sake." Shepard writes, "And so sin abounds, but grace abounds. Why should this be so? For his name's sake …. I have marveled at God's dealings with his people; they depart, and stay long, and care not for returning again; in that time a mighty power teaches, humbles, brings back, when they never thought of it. O, the reason is, God will have his name."[16]

In every age, God's redeemed people know and love nothing so much as God's name (Isaiah 56:6). The name of the Lord is their sure hope for time and eternity. God revealed his name to Moses in Exodus 3:14 as "I AM THAT I AM," and later as "The LORD, the LORD God, merciful and gracious, longsuffering, and abundant in goodness and truth, keeping mercy for thousands, forgiving iniquity and transgression and sin, and that will by no means clear the guilty" (Exodus 34:6-7a).

God's name is as glorious as Himself (Psalm 52:9; Isaiah 30:27). God is inseparable from His name; therefore, God will have His name listened to, understood, received, appropriated, rested on, trusted in, feared, loved, adored, desired, believed in, and glorified by all His sheep. From Paradise onward, the Bible places great significance in the giving of names (Genesis 2:19–20). A name can be cut off (Joshua 7:9), destroyed (Deuteronomy 7:24), taken away (Numbers 27:4), blotted out (2 Kings 14:27), or left to rot (Proverbs 10:7). We highly value our own names; we rise up in anger against those who criticize or ridicule our names.

Earthly names are faint reflections of the exalted name of God, which holds the sum total of Jehovah's being, triune personhood, and glorious attributes. Even the Lord's works which extend outside of Himself—His creation, providence, and redemption—are inseparable from His name and reputation. God's sovereign name is involved in all that He does.

The foundation of all God's works is His name. Scripture speaks of His acting for the sake of His glory, the sake of His covenant, and the sake of His promises, but the common denominator of all is *for His name's sake* (Psalms 25:11; 31:3; 79:9; 106:8; 109:21; 143:11; Jeremiah 14:7, 21; 1 John 2:12). The Lord seeks the glory of His name in His general providence over all creation, His special providence over angels and men, and His very special, saving providence over the elect. As Scripture says: "Therefore say unto the house of Israel, thus saith the LORD God; I do not this for your sakes, O house of Israel, but for mine holy name's sake" (Ezekiel 36:22). "I, even I, am he that blotteth out thy transgressions for mine own sake" (Isaiah 43:25). Nothing a sinner does before or after regeneration motivates God to convert or preserve His chosen flock. Saving grace flows from the sovereign good pleasure of His eternal will to exalt His great name.

Whether it is salvation thought by the Father, bought by the Son, or wrought by the Spirit, all flows forth from the Lord's name. Therefore, the Lord's righteousness guarantees the preservation of His sheep. The Father engraved the names of His beloved children on His heart with unconditional love. He has chosen and predestined them for adoption (Ephesians 1:4–5). He has promised that no one can snatch them out of His hand (John 10:29). His very name *Father* is at stake in the salvation of His people, for He has intertwined their names with His.

Jesus Christ voluntarily took the office of Mediator for the elect, suffering for their sins and dying their death to satisfy divine justice on their behalf. His name *Redeemer* stands or falls with the life and well-being of His elect, for the Father gave them to Him and charged Him to lose not one (John 6:39).

The Holy Spirit willingly gave Himself to dwell in the hearts of the elect among Adam's fallen children, becoming within them a fountain that springs up to eternal life (John 4:14). He sealed them, not just for a time, but all the way to the day of redemption, for He is the down payment of their inheritance (Ephesians 1:13–14; 4:30). For the sake of His name as *Comforter*, the Spirit will abide with them forever (John 14:16).

Therefore, the Lord says, "O house of Jacob, for my name's sake will I defer mine anger, and for my praise will I refrain for thee, that I cut thee not off .... For mine own sake, even for mine own sake, will I do it: for how should my name be polluted? And I will not give my glory to another" (Isaiah 48:9, 11).

Oh, child of God, "for his name's sake" teaches you that not only has righteousness been imputed to you in Christ, but also that the name of the Father, the name of the Son, and the name of the Spirit offer a foundation of righteousness to secure and preserve you. The perseverance of the saints is grounded upon the solid rock of God's name.

If you are a believer in Christ, take up God's names in your prayers. Say to Him, "For thy name's sake, O LORD, pardon mine iniquity; for it is great" (Psalm 25:11). Learn to claim the divine names of your Great Shepherd as your confidence and hope. Is His name *wonderful*? Call upon Him to work wonders of His power and grace to mature you. Is His name *Counselor*? Pray to Him for His perfect wisdom to lead you in the right paths. Is His name *mighty God*? Ask Him to give you His strength in the midst of your weakness. Is His name *everlasting Father*? Invoke His tenderness that He would deal with you even in discipline. Is His name *Prince of peace*? Claim Him as your peace, and pray that His peace would rule your heart and mind in Christ Jesus.

For His name's sake God will not deliver the soul of His elect to the multitude of the wicked, nor forget the congregation of His poor forever (Psalm 74:19). If His name did not secure your preservation, weak and wounded believer, would you not have been consumed long ago by inner and outer enemies? Except for Him who is Lord of the sea and its waves, eternal destruction would be your portion (Psalm 20:5).

Someone might ask, "How can it glorify God's name to save a wandering sheep like me? Though I love the Lord, I have sinned so much against God's grace. Surely it would honor Him more to cast me away forever." In answer, we may say that God is greatly glorified by saving the worst of sinners. As John Newton wrote, "In one sense we are well suited to answer his purpose; for if we were not vile and worthless beyond expression, the exceeding riches of his grace would not have been so gloriously displayed. His glory shines more in redeeming one sinner, than in preserving a thousand angels."[17]

Even if you are spiritually hospitalized rather than enjoying the tents of feasting, for His name's sake you will not die. Zion is indestructible because God has anointed His Son as King upon its holy hill (Psalm 2:6). The invisible church is a living tabernacle never to be taken down. As Isaiah 33:20 says, "not one of the stakes thereof shall ever be removed, neither shall any of the cords thereof be broken."

Though their sins may have been paid for at the cross (Isaiah 40:2), soldiers of the Lord of hosts walking in the paths of righteousness may still be attacked. Ultimate victory will be theirs, however, for "ye are Christ's; and Christ is God's" (1 Corinthians 3:23). Skirmishes may be lost, but the war is theirs to win. When conscious that Christ is their General above, the Holy Spirit their General within, the angels their allies encamped roundabout, and they are outfitted with the whole armor of God, these soldiers in faith triumphantly proclaim: "If God be for us, who shall be against us?" (Romans 8:31).

Rather than the damaging, destroying, and damning inheritance they have earned and feared, Christ's sheep will be led "for His name's sake" to heavenly inheritances of glory. His righteousness exceeds their sinfulness. With such a Shepherd and Friend you have no reason to fear any evil. Trials will turn into mercies; sorrows will give place to joys; losses will be resolved into gains. In the words of Ezekiel, you may "dwell securely in the wilderness, and sleep in the woods" (Ezekiel 34:25). And when the bright morning of heaven finally breaks and you attain the sunlit uplands of the everlasting hills, the righteousness of grace will be exchanged for the righteousness of glory. The Chief Shepherd of Israel, your eternal inheritance, will come forward to greet you with this promise: "I will write upon him the name of my God, and the name of the city of my God, which is new Jerusalem, which cometh down out of heaven from my God: and I will write upon him my new name" (Revelation 3:12).

Forever you will shout, "Hallowed be thy name!" Your greatest happiness in eternity will be to praise His name, your greatest freedom to serve His name, your greatest honor to be a subject of His name, and your greatest peace to forever rest in His name.

So hold high the name of your God, as well as the beauty, fullness, reality, and eternal nature of your inheritance! Far too often you sit in earthly places, forgetting that you will one day sit perpetually in heavenly places in Christ Jesus (Ephesians 2:6). Confess with Paul, "Our light affliction, which is but for a moment, worketh for us a far more exceeding and eternal weight of glory; while we look not at the things which are seen, but at the things which are not seen: for the things which are seen are temporal; but the things which are not seen are eternal" (2 Corinthians 4:17–18). One moment of God-centered glory in heaven will cause you to dismiss all earthly costs and pains as nothing. And in that day, you will join with the redeemed of all nations to sing praise to the name of the One who saved you, crying out, "Who shall not fear thee, O Lord, and *glorify thy name?*" (Revelation 15:4).

.

Part 4

Psalm 23:4
"Yea, though I walk through the valley of the shadow of death,
I will fear no evil: for thou art with me;
thy rod and thy staff they comfort me."

11

The Shepherd's Protection and Spiritual Growth

Yea, though I walk through the valley of the shadow of death,
I will fear no evil: for thou art with me.
—Psalm 23:4a

A shepherd in Israel leads his sheep to different pastures at various times of the year. They must graze at lower altitudes in the winter when the heights are too cold, while in the heat of summer the flock can be taken to higher altitudes.[1] Thus with the change of seasons comes the necessity of travel and transition. Here in Psalm 23 we also see evidences of change. These sheep must pass through valleys that they would not otherwise visit. Verses 4 and 5 describe dangers and difficulties that are only implied in the first half of the psalm.

Furthermore, the language of the psalm shifts from speaking of God in the third person, *He*, to speaking directly to God in the second person, *Thou.* Passing through the dangerous wilderness of trials, the presence of the Shepherd becomes more precious to His sheep. Just as a child at play in a room will run to you when lightning flashes and thunder booms, so God's spiritual children cling to their Shepherd when the sky darkens and storms come. In this way, the valley of the shadow of death becomes the valley of His presence.

David understood this from his experience as a shepherd. Many times he led his father's flock along such paths. Phillip Keller writes, "He knew from firsthand experience about all the difficulties and dangers, as well as the delights, of the treks into high country …. all the dangers of rampaging rivers in flood; avalanches; rock slides; poisonous plants; the ravages of predators that raid the flock or the awesome storms."[2] As an experienced and caring shepherd, David knew how to lead his sheep through such dangers. Under the inspiration of the Holy Spirit, this experience became to him a precious symbol of the Lord's protection of His people. "Yea, though I walk through the valley of the shadow of death, I will fear no evil: for thou art with me."

David not only wrote that he was in the valley, but that he *walked through it* in purposeful motion. God's protection is neither stagnant nor merely defensive. Rather the sheep progress and grow under the Shepherd's guidance as the very factors that threaten life and well-being become opportunities for positive change. We learn that divine wisdom protects us, even as it promotes spiritual growth through the experiences of darkness, difficulty, and death. Each dimension of this experience is implied in the phrase, *the valley of the shadow of death.*

Spiritual Growth under the Shepherd's Protection in Darkness

David makes progress in spiritual growth while walking through valleys of death-shadows. *Shadow of death* can also be translated as "deep shadow" or "deep gloom." The kind of valley that David alludes to here is a narrow, rocky gorge. A Middle Eastern shepherd described one such "valley of the shadow of death" in these words: "The path plunges downward ... into a deep and narrow gorge of sheer precipices overhung by frowning Sphinx-like battlements of rocks, which almost touch overhead. Its side walls rise like the stone walls of a great cathedral .... The valley is about five miles long, yet it is not more than twelve feet at the widest section of the base."[3] For most of the day, the low parts of such valleys remain in the shade. This is a symbol of the great distress, dark affliction, heavy trials, and imminent danger that the believer experiences. David also refers to such valleys in Psalm 44:19, "Thou hast sore broken us in the place of dragons, and covered us with the shadow of death," and again in Psalm 107:14, "He brought them out of darkness and the shadow of death, and brake their bands in sunder."

Temporal calamities such as illness, accidents, broken homes, and business failures, as well as spiritual conflicts such as sins of the heart, enticements of the world, and assaults of the devil, may all be dark valleys for the Lord's sheep. God has not promised to exempt His flock from tribulation in this world, so his sheep should not think it strange when fiery trials test them (1 Peter 4:12). Their Shepherd calls them to deny themselves, take up their cross, and follow Him (Matthew 16:24). They are warned from the beginning that they may enter heaven's kingdom only after much tribulation (Acts 14:22). John Preston said, "If you mean to follow Christ, look for a rainy day. It may be it is a fair morning, but yet we know not what the evening will be .... Shall a man go to sea and not look for storms? Shall a soldier go into wars, and not look for enemies?"[4]

Nonbelievers may endure troubles without much complaint, but the Christian receives them from the redemptive hand of God and seeks grace to embrace them for spiritual profit. God's people receive both sunshine and storms as gifts of their Savior. Richard Sibbes wrote, "God hath rejoicing days for His people, as well as mourning days; fair weather as well as foul; and all to help them forward in the way to heaven."[5]

Witness Job. Stripped of his children and possessions, Job confessed, "Naked came I out of my mother's womb, and naked shall I return thither: the LORD gave, and the LORD hath taken away; blessed be the name of the LORD" (Job 1:21). His wife urged Job to curse God and die as her husband scraped at the stinking boils that erupted from his skin. Society despised him and his friends nagged at him to confess the great sin he must have committed to merit such trials. But from his ash heap, Job declared, "Shall we receive good at the hand of God, and shall we not receive evil?" (Job 2:10).

God's church has also endured suffering through the ages. Under heavy trials, God's people grow in sanctification and other graces as they realize more fully their sinfulness in the hidden intentions of their hearts. God tests their faith through such trials. Abraham's faith was tested when he was told to sacrifice his only son, Isaac. David, after being anointed as the next king of Israel, was tested for sixteen years as he was pursued by the murderous King Saul. Through such trials God cuts believers off from all hope in themselves or other people. They must lose their life to find it. As Romans 8:36 says: "for thy sake we are killed all the day long; we are accounted as sheep for the slaughter." Over time, believers learn to boast in their weaknesses, knowing that God's power is made perfect in their weakness (2 Corinthians 12:10).

Their zeal to follow Christ grows as they confess with the apostle Paul, "Not as though I had already attained, either were already perfect: but I follow after, if that I may apprehend that for which also I am apprehended of Christ Jesus" (Philippians 3:12). They sense the very heartbeat of spiritual growth as they look to Christ for all things and are filled with His Spirit. In these spiritual exercises, they ask less, "Why am I suffering?" and pray more, "How can I grow through this trial to be closer to Christ and more like Him?" The valley of darkness, which they once dreaded, becomes the place of learning "thou art with me." They sing,

Jehovah is my strength and tower,
He is my happiness and song;
He saved me in the trying hour,
Hence shall my mouth His praise prolong.[6]

Spiritual Growth under the Shepherd's Protection in Difficulty

A walk through the valley of the shadow of death is not easy. Rather it is like a hard trek up a rough trail. The Hebrew word for "valley" indicates a chasm or deep ravine with steep sides and a narrow floor. It is a difficult and dangerous path for the sheep. To quote again from Keller's experience as a shepherd, "The actual path, on the solid rock, is so narrow that in places the sheep can hardly turn around in case of danger …. In places gullies seven and eight feet have been washed."[7]

Traveling such paths is hard work, but it is the only way to heaven. Though salvation's merit is not based on works, salvation's path involves heavy spiritual labor and many difficulties for the true Christian (Philippians 2:12). Sin, Satan, and the world oppose God's sheep. Philip Henry said, "Our journey is uphill, with a dead body upon our backs, the devil doing what he can to pull us down."[8]

Christians yearn to abide in mountain-top experiences of intimacy with God. Like Peter, they would build tabernacles on the mount of Christ's transfiguration (Luke 9:33). But they forget that the only way to higher ground is through dark and dangerous valleys. Holiness demands personal discipline and sustained effort. Paul said to Timothy, "Exercise thyself rather unto godliness" (1 Timothy 4:7). Holiness is by unmerited grace but is not lazy, indifferent grace. Sanctification demands exertion and endurance. Holiness calls for commitment, diligence, practice, and repentance. Jonathan Edwards resolved, "Never to give over, nor in the least to slacken, my fight with my corruptions, however unsuccessful I may be."[9]

The way forward in the Christian life is hindered by remaining sin; progress therefore requires the agony of inner conflict with our worldly nature. We must kill the sin in us as we are led by the Holy Spirit. Romans 8:13 says, "For if ye live after the flesh, ye shall die: but if ye through the Spirit do mortify the deeds of the body, ye shall live. For as many as are led by the Spirit of God, they are the sons of God." That does not lessen our work. John Owen said, "He works in us and with us, not against us or without us; so that his assistance is an encouragement as to the facilitating of the work, and no occasion of neglect as to the work itself."[10]

God's children love holiness, but they shrink from the paths of hardship. Those paths are chosen for them. So when the believer asks, "Why do I walk through the valley of the shadow of death?" he finds the answer in the previous verse: "he leadeth me in the paths of righteousness for his name's sake." That is not the route the sheep would choose, but the Shepherd leads them on it. The path of righteousness often winds through valleys of darkness and death. The Lord does not shepherd us in those ways to advance our earthly comfort and honor, but for "his name's sake." Too often, child of God, you forget that God is the end of all things and you exist for His glory. Every time you try to make God the means to your end, you will experience failure. Every time you make God and His glory your end and goal, you will experience joy.

God is your loving guide. If He can save you from dark valleys, He will do so, but not at the price of losing your holiness and diminishing His glory. No child of God is exempt from the school of suffering. Yet your Master will not desert you in the valleys but promises: "When thou passest through the waters, I will be with thee; and through the rivers, they shall not overflow thee: when thou walkest through the fire, thou shalt not be burned; neither shall the flame kindle upon thee, for I am the LORD thy God, the Holy One of Israel, thy Savior" (Isaiah 43:2-3).

Spiritual Growth under the Shepherd's Protection in Death

Finally, "the shadow of death" can refer to death itself. In Scripture, death refers to three kinds of separation. Physical death is the separation of soul from body (Matthew 10:28). Spiritual death is the separation of the soul from God (Ephesians 2:1; John 5:24; 1 John 3:14). And eternal death is the separation of both soul and body from God's favor forever in hell (Revelation 21:8).

No formal definition can express the horrifying reality of death. By nature we are blind to our present spiritual death and our fast-approaching eternal death. But physical death conveys an impression sufficient to convince us that death can better be felt than expressed. Unnatural before the fall, chosen in the fall (Genesis 2:17), and inevitable since the fall (Genesis 3:19), death is the awful, unspeakable payment for "the wages of sin" (Romans 6:23).

Most of us are escapists in the matter of death. We scrupulously avoid thoughts and conversations about our own death and the death of others. We substitute words or phrases for death, or hide it under flower-bedecked coffins. We refuse to confront the grim reality of death, despite knowing that every minute more than a hundred people die in the world. That's almost two per second.[11] We know that death is inevitable, but we act as if we will live forever. Scripture presses us to consider that "it is appointed unto men once to die, but after this the judgment" (Hebrews 9:27). Christians are not exempt from physical death. George Swinnock wrote, "A godly man is free from the sting, but not from the stroke, from the curse, but not from the cross, of death."[12] We should prepare ourselves for death, praying, "LORD, make me to know mine end, and the measure of my days, what it is; that I may know how frail I am" (Psalm 39:4), and "So teach us to number our days, that we may apply our hearts unto wisdom" (Psalm 90:12).

Death can be a painful process. It can also be terrifying, even for God's children. As they lay dying, their sins may rise against them, the devil may assault them, and God may not grant them a comforting sense of His presence. Yet Scripture offers believers great reasons to hope as they confront death. First, their living Lord has conquered death, so "Precious in the sight of the LORD is the death of his saints" (Psalm 116:15). Second, they are "carried by the angels into Abraham's bosom" (Luke 16:22). And third, their death ushers them into the Father's house to be at home with the Lord forever (2 Timothy 4:6; John 14:2; 2 Corinthians 5:8).

When Thomas Halyburton (1674–1712), a faithful Scottish minister and professor of theology, lay dying in bed at the age of thirty-eight, a friend asked him how he had rested the night before. He said, "Not well," he said, for he was in "a great conflict" as he was besieged by terrifying thoughts of God, and unable to see evidences of his own salvation clearly. Three days passed, and his struggle finally led him to hope. He said, "Here I am now, a man, a weak man, in the hands of the king of terrors, rejoicing in the hope of the glory that is to be revealed, and that by the death and resurrection of a despised Christ." Leaning on the arm of Jesus he said: "Come, sweet Lord Jesus, come and take me by the hand, that I stumble not in the dark valley of death." Three days later, Halyburton died. One of his last acts was to clap his hands in response to the question of whether he was hoping in the Lord.[13]

Whether a Christian's experience of death is severely trying or not, God can also transform it into a time of spiritual growth. Deathbeds can lead to growth in many divine graces, particularly the three jewels of faith, hope, and love. Too often, we assume that spiritual growth only happens in life's happy times. We forget that growth most often comes through conflict. On a dark deathbed, when battling satanic unbelief, past and present sins, and a host of other enemies, the Holy Spirit makes the believer utterly dependent upon God. He recognizes his debt to free grace in Christ. He sees his need for holy submission at Jehovah's throne. In godly humility, he hates his sin and acknowledges the curse of it; but he also trusts that all his sins are forgiven because of the passion and death of Christ. Consequently, he must walk by faith rather than by sight and wean himself from the world in preparation for heaven.

Seek more for spiritual growth than for spiritual joy in living and in dying, and you will receive much. If you struggle with doubts and temptations on your deathbed, do not let them terrify you. Just as John the Baptist wrestled with questions in prison but received Christ's glowing commendation (Luke 7:19–28), so we Christians may wrestle with great enemies in our dying. Yet we must press on to receive the Lord's crown. Happiness will never be found when sought as an end in itself, but rather will be received as a byproduct of growth in submission to the will of God. By this means, a believer learns that, "though I walk through the valley of the shadow of death, I will fear no evil."

Maintaining Hope in the Valley

God does not allow His sheep to wander aimlessly in the valley but helps them walk through it. Although the sheep learn precious lessons in the darkness, this valley is not their home but a passageway into the light. When their faith is weak, the sheep fear that they will die in the valley, but by faith they may confess that no evil is to be feared in the thickest shadows as long as the Master is near. Though a valley seems endless, the Lord will lead His people step by step.

For those without Christ, death, darkness, and difficulty foreshadow the wrath of God, which awaits them at the end of the valley. They will be plunged into the lake that burns with fire and brimstone, which is the second death (Revelation 21:8), and into the outer darkness where there is the weeping and gnashing of teeth (Matthew 25:30).

But for those who live and die in the Lord, all valleys, including death, are but passing shadow lands. For them the power and sting of death died when Christ died. That was buried with Him in the tomb, but did not rise with Him, for He "abolished death and brought life and immortality to light" (2 Timothy 1:10). For Christ's sake, all God's sheep will safely reach the end of every dark valley along the way to eternal life and glory.

These shadows are temporary, but your light is eternal, for "God is light and in him is no darkness at all" (1 John 1:5). Christians are "partakers of the inheritance of the saints in light," for God "hath delivered us from the power of darkness, and hath translated us into the kingdom of his dear Son" (Colossians 1:12–13). You must walk through this world's lonely and evil-infested valleys, but you are on the way to eternal rest. You have no reason to fear, for Christ has conquered death for you.

The question we should ask is not whether we must go through such valleys or how dark they will be. Rather, we should ask: Has the Lord made these valleys the paths of righteousness for me? Am I walking with Him in holiness? Am I growing in holiness, even in the darkness? On my journey am I looking to Christ and seeking His Spirit to guide me safely through? Furthermore, are valleys not only a blessing for me but also for others around me? Do the fruits of my life clearly reveal that God has blessed me as He blessed Abraham, saying "I will bless thee …. and thou shalt be a blessing" (Genesis 12:1–2)? In a word, am I growing in grace?

If you never experienced growth in grace you should ask whether you are spiritually alive. This is a most urgent question. Years are slipping by; time is flying. Graveyards are filling, and family ranks are thinning. Death and judgment are near to us all. Yet you dare to live as one asleep to your soul's needs! What form of suicide can be worse than this? Sinner, bow before the Lord before it is too late. As Ephesians 5:14 says: "Awake thou that sleepest, and arise from the dead, and Christ shall give thee light."

Perhaps you can see some signs that you are spiritually alive. You trust in Christ alone and sincerely love Him and His people. Yet you must admit that you have fallen back into sin instead of making progress in holiness. Resolve this very day that you will find the root of your low condition. Probe every corner of your soul. Read chapter 8 of this book again, and consider how you have wandered and how you must return. Ask the great Physician of souls, the Lord Jesus, to heal the sickness within you, whatever it may be. Ask for grace to pluck out the right eye of sin and temptation. Do not be content if your soul does not grow.

You may be a Christian but have difficulty seeing spiritual growth in yourself because you increasingly sense the fear of the Lord, the awareness of your sins, and the immensity of His holiness. That is a blessed condition. James Hervey said,

> Some go forward, even when they imagine quite the contrary. They grow more fat even when they cry out, "My leanness, my leanness, woe is me!" For what means their uneasiness under a state of barrenness? Whence come their increasing hunger and thirst after righteousness? Why do they pant ardently after an established interest in Christ's righteousness, and a more thorough conformity to His example? Surely because they have a large portion of the Spirit, who begets these inward groanings, and enlarges their holy desires.[14]

Hervey said Christians sometimes grow downward instead of upward. This paradoxical way of growing is painful, but richly rewarding. He said,

> God's people may be growing down in humility, when they are not growing upwards in faith, and hope, and love. They may strike their root deeper, even when they do not lift their branches higher. "O," says a poor creature, "instead of growing better, I grow worse!"... Indeed you have rather reason to bless God for opening your eyes, for giving you a knowledge of yourself.[15]

Growth in self-knowledge humbles the soul but strengthens the root of spiritual life even if the tree's branches are not yet bearing more fruit. Such growth increases our dependence on Christ as our wisdom, righteousness, sanctification, redemption, indeed, our all in all.

Maybe you are growing spiritually. By God's grace, you are bearing fruit by increasing in virtue, knowledge, self-control, patience, godliness, brotherly kindness, and love (2 Peter 1:5–7). Seeing such fruits growing in your life is a great encouragement. You are not what you should be and want to be, yet you are not what you used to be. If that is your condition, give thanks to God, acknowledging that all spiritual fruit comes through Jesus Christ by His Spirit (Galatians 5:22). Pray for more fruitfulness, knowing that you are called not just to bear fruit but to abound in much fruit (Philippians 1:9; 1 Thessalonians 4:1, 10). Keep pressing on! Follow your Shepherd through the dark valley, trusting that the path of obedience is the path of growth.

Christians should strive to grow in grace, for spiritual growth glorifies God. Our Lord Jesus said, "Herein is my Father glorified, that ye bear much fruit; so shall ye be my disciples" (John 15:8). Paul said we should pray for believers to be "filled with the fruits of righteousness, which are by Jesus Christ, unto the glory and praise of God" (Philippians 1:11).

Growth in grace is also the true beauty of a Christian life. A godly person's primary beauty is not in the outward appearance of body and clothes, but in the "hidden" beauty of the heart which lasts forever, "a meek and quiet spirit" (1 Peter 3:4). Faithful, honest, humble conduct in our calling shows the beauty of biblical truth to the world (Titus 2:1–10). We cannot grow too much in grace.

Spiritual growth is also the best proof of spiritual life and health. Just as life has a natural tendency towards motion, activity, and growth, so spiritual life cannot stand still (Psalm 1:3). Christianity is not a spectator sport to be watched from the stands. It is a race to be entered by faith and run by grace until we reach the finish line (Hebrews 12:1–2).

Meantime, we live in a constant state of conflict as we battle against sin (Galatians 5:17). If faith does not grow, unbelief will. We should aim to flourish in grace today, so that we may flourish in glory forever. Christ taught that faithfulness in the small things of this world leads to great rewards in the world to come (Luke 19:17).

Most importantly, growth in grace pleases God. Christ is a gardener who loves to see the plants in which He invests so much labor flourish and bear fruit (Song of Solomon 6:11). It pleases God when we trust Him, walk with Him, and do good to others (Hebrews 11:5–6; 13:16). Rather than grieving the Spirit by unrepentant sin and thus losing the fullness of His comfort and help (Ephesians 4:30), let us labor to please the God who so loved us that He gave His only Son for our sake. If He *died* for us, shall we not *live* for Him? Our Good Shepherd lays down His life for His sheep. He calls us by name. His sheep hear His voice and follow Him wherever He goes, even through the valley of the shadow of death.

12

The Shepherd's Protection and Spiritual Courage

I will fear no evil.
—Psalm 23:4b

Psalm 23 is intensely personal in its description of the relationship between a believer and the Lord. Though the believer is part of a larger flock, David speaks here as an individual sheep under the care of his Shepherd. The psalm begins: "The LORD is my shepherd; I shall not want." It closes with "*I* will dwell in the house of the LORD forever." And in between the psalmist says, "*I* will fear no evil: for thou art with me." Each time, the first person *I* declares David's confidence in the Lord.

No verse in the psalm is as bold as "I will fear no evil," for in it David asserts that he can face anything if God is with Him. Just four psalms later, we read, "The LORD is my light and my salvation; whom shall I fear? The LORD is the strength of my life; of whom shall I be afraid?

When the wicked, even mine enemies and my foes, came upon me to eat up my flesh, they stumbled and fell. Though an host should encamp against me, my heart shall not fear: though war should rise against me, in this will I be confident" (Psalm 27:1–3; see 3:6; 56:3–4). Proverbs also tells us, "The righteous are as bold as a lion" (Proverbs 28:1; see 1:33; 14:26). And Paul wrote to Timothy, "God hath not given us the spirit of fear; but of power, and of love, and of a sound mind" (2 Timothy 1:7).

Sheep are not by nature courageous. Yet the presence of their shepherd makes them brave. The divine protection of the great Shepherd also makes Christians confident as they follow their leader.

Wise and Godly Fearlessness

When considering spiritual courage, we must avoid the danger of misunderstanding the meaning of "I will fear no evil." That is especially true today when people confuse faith with presumption, and confidence with self-assertiveness. To understand the true nature of godly courage, let us clearly define the meaning of David's declaration.

First, David's words do not imply there is *no evil to fear*. He does not claim that the future will hold no evil. Rather, David confessed, "Many are the afflictions of the righteous" (Psalm 34:19). In Psalm 23, it is as if he is saying, "I am surrounded by evils in the valley of death's darkness, but I will not fear them, for no evil can truly do evil to me as long as I remain near my royal Shepherd."

In this present life, evil of one kind or another always exist, also for true believers. "In the world ye shall have tribulation," Christ told his apostles (John 16:33). Christ also said to Simon Peter, "Satan hath desired to have you, that he may sift you as wheat" (Luke 22:31; note that Christ addresses Peter in the plural as representative of all the disciples). The worst evil a believer faces is that which dwells within him. As Romans 7:21 says: "I find then a law, that, when I would do good, evil is present with me."

The world is often blind to evil, especially moral and spiritual evil. Evil is treated as a mere shadow. Dishonoring God and committing atrocities against others are rationalized away. The corruption of the human heart is whitewashed with good intentions. As a result, innumerable sinners blindly rush ahead along a path that eventually will plunge them into hell. By contrast, the Christian faces the reality of evil within as he struggles to overcome it.

Second, David's lack of fear does not imply *any sufficiency within self* to overcome the evils of everyday life. False courage builds on our will and ability, but true courage trusts only in God's will and power. As Psalm 27:14 says, "Wait on the LORD: be of good courage, and he shall strengthen thine heart: wait, I say, on the LORD." Martin Luther said it this way:

> Though my temptations were even more numerous and great, though my lot were even worse, and though I were already in the jaws of death, I will fear no evil. Not that I could assist myself through my own care, efforts, work, or help. Nor do I depend on my own wisdom, piety, royal power, or riches. Here all human help, counsel, comfort, and power are far too weak. This, however, alone avails me, that the Lord is with me.[1]

Sadly, the number of professing Christians who rely on their own strength is rising. Buoyed up by the false hope of human ability, many leaders today try to persuade us that Christians can expose themselves to every kind of temptation without fear of sin's pollution. Even conservative Christians encourage broad participation in wicked and immoral media so long as we can say it is done for the glory of God or to bring more souls to Christ. John Flavel (1628–1691) wrote, "By the fear of the Lord men depart from evil (Proverbs 16:6); by the fear of man they run themselves into evil (Proverbs 29:25)."[2] The true Christian is painfully aware of his weakness and flees from such evil, praying, "Lead me not into temptation."

True believers who trust in God are rooted in the very nature of God. Jeremiah 17:7–8 says, "Blessed is the man that trusteth in the LORD, and whose hope the LORD is. For he shall be as a tree planted by the waters, and that spreadeth out her roots by the river, and shall not see when heat cometh, but her leaf shall be green; and shall not be careful in the year of drought, neither shall cease from yielding fruit" (cf. Psalm 1). In waiting on the Lord, true faith courageously casts its every need on the protecting Shepherd.

Third, "I will fear no evil" does not imply that David intended to walk with *rash spiritual boldness*. The same David also wrote, "I will teach you the fear of the LORD…. Depart from evil, and do good" (Psalm 34:11, 14). He could claim to walk boldly without slavish fear but not without childlike fear. Slavish fear is rooted in our fallen state under the covenants of works, whereas childlike fear flows out of the eternal covenant of grace. Slavish fear is provoked by the consequences of sin, whereas childlike fear is prompted by a heartfelt desire to please God. At best, slavish fear produces a sinner whose eyes are blind to Christ, whereas childlike fear belongs to a converted sinner whose eyes are fixed on Christ.

Today, many Christians reject such distinctions. All fear is to be rejected as slavish or childlike. A shallow admission of having sinned, easy acceptance of Christ as Savior, and a life of carefree self-indulgence is the religion of today. With unholy, proud, and irreverent boldness, millions treat Holy God as if He were a mere man (Psalm 50:21–22).

However, David, with a vastly different boldness declares his desire to walk fearlessly through dark valleys by grace. His courage is a holy, humble, and reverent boldness that issues from childlike fear. It never forgets who God is or what self remains in him in its ragged imperfections. David follows the admonitions of the Epistle to the Hebrews, which call us to "come boldly unto the throne of grace that we may obtain mercy" through faith in Christ our High Priest, and to "serve God acceptably with reverence and godly fear: for our God is a consuming fire" (Hebrews 4:16; 12:28-29).

Finally, David did not imply that he would *never again fear evil*. He personally knew the fear that may grip believers and drive them along; witness him fleeing to the Philistines for "a full year and four months" to escape from Saul (1 Samuel 27:1-7). Isn't that what every true believer experiences? When faith is weak, every valley is a mountain, every cliff hides a cougar, and every storm threatens destruction. Rather, David confesses that he will not fear as long as he may say with boldness, "the LORD is my shepherd." When God enables the Christian to exercise faith in the Shepherd, fears fade and confidence grows.

The Courage of Faith

As our Shepherd works to break down all false courage and self-confidence in His sheep, He also labors to train them in the true courage of trusting in the Lord. He leads them into the valley of the shadow of death so that they learn to say, "I will fear no evil, for thou art with me." Let us consider in more detail how faith promotes courage in dark places.

Faith Focuses on the Shepherd's Wisdom

Faith produces courage in dark places as the sheep learn to trust that every valley is lovingly chosen by their personal Shepherd. The Shepherd not only has the power to spare His sheep from every danger, but He also has the wisdom to use such dangers for the good of their souls. Faith considers what God makes of trials. Ebenezer Erskine (1680-1754) wrote,

> Faith inspires with Christian courage in times of danger and trouble from the world, by viewing the inside of troubles for Christ, as well as the outside of them. When we walk by sense, and not by faith, we will soon be dispirited in a day of trouble and danger, and be ready to cry, "There is a lion in the way." ...

But now faith looks to the inside of troubles, and considers what God has made, and can still make these unto his people.[3]

Under God's hand, troubles and dangers become treasure chests that are rough wood and cold iron on the outside but full of gold within. The wounds of His piercing become opportunities for His healing medicine to flow into our hearts. The Lord can turn the house of suffering into the school of holiness (Psalm 119:71), or prisons into palaces of praise (Acts 16:24-25). Seeing all things in light of the character of their sovereign God, Jehovah's sheep can say, "Thy valleys are good. Thy lessons are good. I will fear no evil."

Faith also inspires spiritual fortitude in dark places by presenting God's glorious attributes to the soul. Walking in faith beside the Shepherd, our fears diminish. As Scripture says of Moses: "By faith he forsook Egypt, not fearing the wrath of the king: for he endured, as seeing him who is invisible" (Hebrews 11:27). When the soul's eye is opened, it sees the infinite majesty, greatness, excellence, power, holiness, and grace of the sovereign Lord. Faith that is focused on God steadies the soul under trial, and says, "I have set the LORD always before me: because he is at my right hand, I shall not be moved" (Psalm 16:8).

Christ leads His people to trust Him in all His offices. As Prophet, He grants them faith to see God's glory, even in the cross. As Priest, He grants faith that rests upon His offering as the perfect sacrifice for our sins, and intercedes for our eternal well-being. As King, He grants faith to surrender all of self, soul and body, into His hands as sovereign Lord.

Faith's spiritual courage enables the Lord's saints to be "more than conquerors," even when "accounted as sheep for the slaughter" in the valley of the shadow of death (Romans 8:36-37). They trust that they have a "house not made with hands, eternal in the heavens" (2 Corinthians 5:1), and are persuaded "that neither death, nor life, nor angels, nor principalities, nor powers, nor things present, nor things to come, nor height, nor depth, nor any other creature, shall be able to separate us from the love of God, which is in Christ Jesus our Lord" (Romans 8:38–39).

Faith Focuses on the Shepherd's Traveling with Us

Spiritual courage is multiplied in dark places when faith centers on Jesus Christ, and is assured that He will travel with His flock every step in the valley, from the city of destruction to the courts of heaven.

Christ *has already traveled* before His flock. From eternity He promised to come from sinless heaven to a sin-stained earth. He traveled every step from Bethlehem to Golgotha in perfect obedience, allowing the religious, political, educational, and social leaders of the day to condemn Him to death on the cross. He merited full salvation for His elect through His suffering as their Substitute. He hung in the valley of the shadow of death under the curse of God's abandonment (Matthew 27:45–46). He sanctified every step in the valley that His people are called to traverse.

There is no sorrow, apart from sin, which Jesus has not experienced. He confessed, "Reproach hath broken my heart, and I am full of heaviness" (Psalm 69:20). He cried out, "My soul is exceeding sorrowful, even unto death" (Matthew 26:38). Of Him alone could Paul testify, "We have not an high priest which cannot be touched with the feeling of our infirmities; but was in all points tempted like as we are, yet without sin" (Hebrews 4:15).

Child of God, behold your royal High Priest in death's gloomy valley. He was thorn-crowned, mocked, spat upon, rejected, and condemned to die. His body was nailed to Golgotha's accursed tree. Christ was pressed by the forces of hell and by the wrath of His Father. He bore the burden of the sins of His elect and journeyed forward in obedience to the Father's will. Such painful experiences enable Him to help His sheep as they trudge through their valleys. The Great Shepherd does not ask His sheep to tread any path that He has not already trodden.

He is an example for His sheep, but as their spiritual guide He also guarantees them safe passage. He submitted to beatings, mocking, scourging, and death during His thirty-three year travel in this life so that we might feel secure along our journeys with Him. Christ's love is so incomprehensibly great that He was willingly forsaken by God that we might never be forsaken by Him. Why then should we fear evil, when we have such a Savior?

Christ *is still traveling* with His flock. As the pillar of cloud and fire preceded Israel in their journey through the wilderness, Jesus Christ went before His flock. Though exalted to heaven in His human nature, "with respect to His Godhead, majesty, grace, and Spirit, He is at no time absent from us," says the Heidelberg Catechism.[4] He leads His sheep to show the way as well as to keep His eye on each individual believer. He names, feeds, and loves each sheep as if it were the only object of His care and regard. He is intimately acquainted with all of its valleys, journeys, circumstances, sorrows, and joys. True believer, He loves you as if you stood alone in the world, and He had no one but you on whom to lavish His blessings! Pointing to a sparrow, the Shepherd declared, "One of them shall not fall to the ground without your Father." He then said, "Fear ye not therefore, ye are of more value than many sparrows" (Matthew 10:29, 31).

Christ has traveled, is traveling, and *will go on traveling* before His flock. He has promised the church, "Lo, I am with you alway, even unto the end of the world" (Matthew 28:20). Why, then, do you still fear the future? Will Christ's faithfulness ever fail? Will He not go before you in spite of yourself? Has He not given you an inheritance that cannot be corrupted, defiled, or destroyed and is reserved in heaven for you (1 Peter 1:4)? Instead of fearing, seek grace to follow Christ in good courage, declaring:

> In God will I trust, though my counselors say,
> O flee as a bird to your mountain away;

The wicked are strong and the righteous are weak,
Foundations are shaken, yet God will I seek.

The Lord in His temple shall ever abide;
His throne is eternal, whatever betide.
The children of men He beholds from on high,
The wicked to punish, the righteous to try.[5]

With such courage you can confront any enemy. When you are threatened with a fiery furnace if you refuse to worship the golden images of this world, you can boldly confess with Daniel's three friends, "Our God whom we serve is able to deliver us from the burning fiery furnace, and he will deliver us out of thine hand, O king. But if not, be it known unto thee, O king, that we will not serve thy gods, nor worship the golden image which thou hast set up" (Daniel 3:16-18).

Courageous faith will not falter even at the risk of being thrown into a lion's den. In Daniel's day, a law was issued that forbade anyone to pray to any god but the king. But Daniel by faith went to his house, opened its windows, and praised God three times a day. As a result, He was thrown into the midst of ravenous lions, but he still trusted God. Like other heroes of faith, his actions testified, "if God be for us, who can be against us?" (Romans 8:31).

Seek a Courageous Faith and Its Benefits
Friends, strive for the grace of courageous faith, for it fills the soul with peace in the midst of danger (Psalm 32:6-7). Courageous faith takes risks and embraces hard service when the Lord calls. It walks on, undaunted by pursuing enemies, even when the Red Sea seems to cut off all escape (Exodus 14:13-15). Courageous faith teaches the soul to wield the weapon of "the sword of the Spirit, which is the Word of God" by the example and application of Christ (Ephesians 6:17; Matthew 4:1-11). By the blood of the Lamb, the soul gains victory over the strongest enemies: overcoming the world (1 John 5:4), resisting the

devil (Revelation 12:11), conquering death and the grave (1 Corinthians 15:55–57), and, above all, putting sin to death (Romans 8:13).

Courageous faith also includes other benefits. Faith sets Christ up high. It unites sinners and the Savior (Acts 16:31). It views the Savior's fullness with delight (John 15:1–8). It feeds the soul by partaking of the flesh and blood of the Son of God (John 6:54). Saving faith is an active grace, not dead orthodoxy (James 2:17, 19). The glorious sight of the Savior ignites faith to burn with love for God, His Word, and His people (Galatians 5:6). Faith cleanses the heart, producing fruit through a sanctifying holiness that pervades one's entire life (Acts 15:9). Faith produces a life pleasing to God (Hebrews 11:6). Flavel said, "All other graces, like birds in the nest, depend upon what faith brings in to them."[6] Courageous faith boldly sets its seal on the truth of God before a blind world (Daniel 6). It defies all oppressors of the truth (Acts 4:13), enables the persecuted church to obtain the grace to witness (Acts 4:23–31), and sweetly persuades sinners of personal salvation, planting within them the unshakable hope that they will be led by the Lord to a better day (Romans 5:10; Luke 12:8). Truly the Christian can say, "I live by the faith of the Son of God" (Galatians 2:20), for apart from faith, the righteous do not live (Habakkuk 2:4). By faith we say, "I will fear no evil."

Do you have this faith? If not, then do not rest until you know your sinfulness and put all your trust in Christ. If you are not sure, ask yourself the following questions to determine whether you have true saving faith:

- Is faith your soul's captain that leads all other graces of true Christianity? Does your faith feed the lamp of hope with oil, oblige love to work diligently, and bring sanctifying patience?

- Does faith produce spiritual war in you against unbelief? Does it produce in you the cry, "Lord, I believe; help thou mine unbelief" (Mark 9:24)?

- Does faith humble you, giving you eyes to see your corruption and emptiness as well as Christ's righteousness and fullness? Thomas Watson said that true justifying faith produces *self-renunciation*: "Repentance and faith are both humbling graces; by repentance a man abhors himself; by faith he goes out of himself," for the believer needs a righteousness he cannot find in himself.[7] Is that true of you?

- Does your faith rest upon the Word of God, so that if human judgment reasons that a promise cannot be fulfilled, faith replies, "It both can and will be, for I have God's Word on it"?

- Above all, has your faith driven you to Jesus Christ? Have you discovered that the promise is but the dish, while Christ is the food that faith feeds upon? Is your faith set upon Christ crucified and raised from the dead, upon Christ as both Savior and Lord? Does your faith put such a high value on Christ that you are willing to part with any worldly gold for this pearl of great price?

- Does your faith urge you to a life of love and good works toward other people? Can you testify with Martin Luther, "Faith gives me Christ, and love from faith gives me to my neighbor"?[8]

- Is faith bringing your soul into conformity with Christ, so that your life is a living testimony? Have you experienced what Thomas Watson wrote: "Looking on a bleeding Christ causes a soft bleeding heart; looking on a holy Christ causes sanctity of heart; looking on a humble Christ makes the soul humble"?[9]

- Does your faith produce in you what Paul called the "obedience of faith" (Romans 16:26)? Do you serve the Savior? Watson said, "Faith is not an idle grace; as it has an eye to see Christ, so it has a hand to work for him."[10]

Do you have faith in Christ, but it is so weak that you hardly dare to call it faith? Weak faith may nonetheless be true faith, just as a spark of fire is still fire. It is precious even though it is not as great as strong faith. It has the same Spirit as its Author and the same gospel as its instrument. It is not the strength of our faith that saves but its authenticity; nor is it the weakness of our faith that condemns, but the lack of faith. The weakest faith justifies as well as the faith of the most eminent saint, so long as they rest in Christ. Therefore, believer, take heart and remember that a weak faith may receive a strong Christ, may be fruitful in love and godly affections, and may grow in grace and become strong.

If you can honestly say that you have saving faith in Christ, be of good courage. Consider that the day we live in requires it. If Christ was courageous for you in the days of His sufferings, should you not be courageous for His cause in this day of abounding iniquity?

Consider that Christ commands His followers to be bold in Him, saying, "Stand fast in the faith, quit yourselves like men. Be strong in the Lord, and in the power of His might. Fight the good fight of faith. Be not afraid, neither be thou dismayed: for the LORD thy God is with thee whithersoever thou goest" (1 Corinthians 16:13; Ephesians 6:10; 1 Timothy 6:12; Joshua 1:9). The triune God is your "refuge and strength, a very present help in trouble" (Psalm 46:1). Your cause is good, for you are fighting for the honor of God, His precious, unchangeable truths, and the liberty with which Christ makes His people free (John 8:36).

Consider also that victory is certain for Christ's soldiers. Christ has already conquered death, and He has promised to give victory to all that are faithful after Him (Revelation 2:10). Your glorious Leader has already slain sin's Goliath; His nearing Judgment Day will soon shackle all the forces of evil for eternity (Revelation 20:10–15). Be courageous, for faith believes what we do not yet see, and its reward will be to see what we now believe.

If you are yet unconverted, you have every reason to fear, for you must find your own path through all of life's valleys, only to face eternal death in the end, if you don't repent of your sin and cast yourself by faith on the person and saving work of Jesus Christ. May God make you tremble before His Word and be led to believe in the Good Shepherd, Jesus Christ. And may He also grant His fearful children strength and courage, for the Lord our God is with you, to help you and to fight your battles (2 Chronicles 32:7, 8).

13

The Shepherd's Companionship

For thou art with me.

—Psalm 23:4c

When summoned to a trial for his beliefs, Martin Luther resolved to stand firm even if opposed by all the powers of hell, and as many devils waited for him as there were tiles on the rooftops.[1] Do you know what lies at the core of this kind of spiritual courage? The answer is Christ's companionship. As David wrote, "I will fear no evil: for thou art with me."

The Shepherd's protection through dark valleys promotes spiritual growth and fosters spiritual courage, but both are rooted in His companionship. "Thou art with me" is inherent in all the prayers and desires of true believers. Without this assurance, there would be no gospel and no salvation. To be with Christ enjoying God's favor is the best part of the gospel. His presence turns even the darkest valley into paradise. Christ is the delight of all the hopes of His people. His presence is better than life and His absence worse than death.

The Essence of the Shepherd's Companionship

As the essence of divine protection is divine companionship, so the essence of divine companionship is divine communion. By nature we are without God in the world, separated from Him by our sins (Ephesians 2:12). No heart can feel, and no tongue can express the awful wretchedness and ruin into which sin has cast us. In separating us from God, sin has severed us from the fountain of life, happiness, and holiness. We have fallen so far from our Creator that we cannot walk together, for we are not in agreement (Amos 3:3). Our fall in Adam has ruined us. It has made us love sin and hate God (Romans 1:30, 32; 8:7). It has filled us with pride, lust, and cruelty. Every thought and inclination of our natural minds and hearts seek to find pleasure and satisfaction in something abhorrent to the will of the living God.

Despite our sinfulness, God has used man's fall into sin and all its miserable consequences to reveal the glorious love of Christ. The bride of Christ fell into unfathomable depths of sin and misery, but she never fell out of His heart. Without the ugliness of sin we would never know the beauty of God's grace and mercy!

As the church's Head and Husband, Christ could not take His bride to Himself in all her filth and guilt. He had to first redeem her with His own blood and with sufferings that no one on earth or in heaven had ever before witnessed. When His Father hid His face from His Son, Jesus cried out in such agony that the earth quaked, rocks split, and the sun grew dark. But Christ's love was as strong as death, and He endured the cross to bear the sins of His bride on the tree. He suffered the penalty due to His bride's sin to reconcile her to God "in the body of his flesh, through death, to present her holy, and blameless and without fault in his sight" (Colossians 1:22). Having reconciled His bride unto God, Christ now visits members of His elect church with saving grace to "sanctify and cleanse it with the washing of water by the word," and will finally "present it to himself a glorious church, not having spot, or wrinkle, or any such thing" (Ephesians 5:26, 27).

Christ's companionship and communion, therefore, begin with regeneration. Before the mystery of the marriage union is made known, espousals are made and the first kiss of betrothed love is given (Jeremiah 2:2; 2 Corinthians 11:2; Song of Solomon 1:2). The celebration of marriage is yet to come (Revelation 19:7–9), but the original betrothal makes Christ and the church eternally one. In proposing to her, He promises to love His bride, cherish her, feed her, and to count her interests as His own, her honor as His honor, and her happiness as His happiness. Christ promised from eternity to be to her everything pertaining to her happiness, honor, perfection, and glory. He said, "And I will betroth thee unto me for ever; yea, I will betroth thee unto me in righteousness, and in judgment, and in lovingkindness, and in mercies. I will even betroth thee unto me in faithfulness: and thou shalt know the Lord" (Hosea 2:19–20). "For thy Maker is thine husband; the Lord of hosts is his name; and thy Redeemer the Holy One of Israel; the God of the whole earth shall he be called" (Isaiah 54:5). Thus there must be union before communion, regeneration before companionship, betrothal before possession, and membership before abiding in Christ and He in us.

This is the work of the Holy Spirit. The Spirit stirs sinners to feel their need of Christ. The Spirit quickens needy sinners to seek everything in Christ, to believe in Him unto everlasting life, and to live by faith in Him. By His witness to the person and work of Christ, the Spirit draws us to Christ and unites us with Himself. He makes the eternal wonder of the Immanuel principle, "God with us," a reality. Brought to faith in Christ by the Holy Spirit, the child of God can then say, "Thou art with me."

All these wonders of free grace are granted when God's people are enlightened by the Spirit. *Thou*, the thrice-holy God, "the high and lofty One that inhabiteth eternity" (Isaiah 6:3, 57:15), the eternal King of kings, condescends to dwell with *me*, a rebellious sinner. He "is of purer eyes than to behold evil, and canst not look on iniquity"

(Habakkuk 1:13). Before Him all nations of the earth are less than a piece of dust on the balances or a drop of water in a bucket (Isaiah 40:17). Yet God pursues sinners even though nothing in them could please, attract, or move Him. No good thing is in them because they have walked contrary to all God's commandments and rejected all His warnings and callings. Still, He dwells *with* us, blessing us with the Father's love from heaven, the Son's intercession from His place at God's right hand, and the Spirit's communion with us as members of Christ's body. What eternal and amazing grace that God through Christ has found a way to commune with sinful man! As David says, "Thou art with me."

In companionship and communion, the Holy Spirit wins the affection of the flock for the Shepherd. The sheep behold God's beloved Son as "the chiefest among ten thousand" and "altogether lovely" (Song of Solomon 5:10, 16) and love Him. They rejoice like the bridegroom in Song of Songs: "I am my beloved's, and my beloved is mine" (Song of Solomon 6:3).

Religion is empty without a living faith and love for Jesus Christ. Reading Scripture, hearing sermons, praying, meditating, and conversing with the saints of God becomes cold, heartless work when Jesus is not present. Only when we seek His face and experience His presence through the Word and Spirit will we experience joy in the worship of God as communion with Christ brings heaven to earth. We must seek the means of grace in the ordinances of worship, the reading of the Bible, the preaching of the Word, the power of prayer, and fellowship with other believers. But only Christ can infuse life and joy into those means of grace. Without Him, worship is dark and dreary, wandering thoughts, formality, and emptiness. At times God leaves us in this valley to show us what we are and what we cannot do without Him. He is our light, and without Him all is darkness. He is our life, and without Him all is death. He is the author and finisher of our faith, the substance of our hope, and the object of our love. All true faith flows from communion with God in Christ by His Spirit.

This inward sense of the blessedness of Christ's companionship and the misery of life without Him makes the sheep of Christ seek communion with Him. This fellowship implies mutual interest, mutual contact, and mutual participation. Communion is not one-sided but requires the sharing of life and affection. The foundation of communion with God is the blessed truth that the "the Lord Jesus Christ, ... being the eternal Son of God, became man, and so was, and continueth to be, God and man in two distinct natures, and one person, forever."[2] In Jacob's vision of a ladder, the foot of the ladder rested on earth while the top reached to heaven. Likewise, the human nature of Christ touches earth with its sorrows, while He in His divine nature now rules in heaven. Christ fulfills His office as the Mediator between God and man by bringing God's love down to us on earth, and lifting us up to heaven to behold His glory.

God was not obligated to share His divine love with us, for He is love from eternity to eternity. He exists in love with the three persons in the sacred Godhead. But it pleased Him to share this love with His chosen people, despite their unworthiness to receive it. The nature and delight of His love is to give, especially to His people, and all He asks of them is to love Him in return. So the heart of divine communion is delighting to love and be loved.

Have you experienced this mutual giving and receiving of love, the flowing together of two hearts? Are you familiar with the communion in which each party maintains its distinct identity yet is the object of affection and delight to the other?

What can God's people who have experienced His love give to Christ? Oh, child of God, you have your sins, your sorrows, your burdens, and your trials to give Him. You can also give Him the love that the Spirit works in your souls, making you willing to live for Christ. Therefore, fear no evil, as long as He is with you. David implies all this in his simple, yet profound words: "Thou art with me."

The Security of the Shepherd's Companionship

Christ's companionship also means safety and security for God's flock. "Thou art with me" guarantees divine protection, because the Shepherd walks with His sheep throughout life as their Savior and Lord. That means the following:

First, *Thou with me* guarantees a Shepherd who will fight for His sheep. This Shepherd will fight every roaring lion or beast that threatens them. Ironically, God's people discover that it often takes more courage to trust the Shepherd than to face a lion. They resist relying on divine strength and surrendering themselves to Him. By weakening their strength (Psalm 102:23), Christ teaches them that submission and surrender are the keys to victory. Christ as willing King then takes over their battle and fights their fight. God's people receive new strength by learning to depend on His divine companionship. Their King then teaches them how to fight, arrayed in armor from His storehouse of strength (Psalm 144:1; Ephesians 6:10). He confirms His own Word: "My grace is sufficient for thee: for my strength is made perfect in weakness" (2 Corinthians 12:9). As the invincible warrior, Christ the captain of our salvation will not fail to bring every one of His own to victory.

Second, *Thou art with me* guarantees the sheep that Christ is with them in the dark valleys. His companionship gives God's people courage in entering their valleys, in going through valleys, and in leaving their valleys. The long march of the living church through all generations reveals that God travels with His people through the shadows and into the light. If the world through sin is covered with a flood of waters, God will build an ark to preserve His infant church. If famine threatens the church with starvation, God will open the storehouses of Egypt to supply her need. If the sea blocks the church from moving ahead, Jehovah will open a passage through the Red Sea on which she will trod with dry feet. If the church suffers hunger in the desert, the God of her salvation will unlock the pantry of heaven and feed her with heavenly food. If the church is thirsty, streams of living water will pour forth from the rocks. By God's presence through Christ, all the church's foes will fall before her: Jordan's waves will roll backwards; Jericho's walls will give way; Canaan will surrender its stores of milk and honey. As Deuteronomy 33:29 exclaims, "Happy art thou, O Israel: who is like unto thee, O people saved by the LORD, the shield of thy help!"

A young boy was on board a ship that was being tossed mercilessly on the waves. Not a sailor or a passenger on board could hide his fear except for this boy, who appeared quite calm. Asked how he could be unafraid at such a time, he replied simply, "My father is the captain; he knows how to manage this ship." The believer may likewise trust his divine Helmsman. The ship of the elect cannot go down while Christ is at the helm.

Third, *Thou with me* guarantees that Christ died as our substitute and arose to give us life. Christ gave Himself to death in place of His church (Ephesians 5:25), and continues to quicken His church and keep her alive (Romans 8:34).

A poor miner had only one son. He often took the boy with him when he went to work in a deep mine. One evening he put his son into the basket to be drawn up from the mine. Half way up the narrow shaft, something cracked and the rope began to break. In an instant the father saw that the rope would not bear both he and his son, and the only chance of saving his boy was to sacrifice his own life. He said, "Lie still, my son, and you will soon be safe at the top." He then dropped out of the basket and was killed. The child reached the top in safety, thanks to his father's selfless devotion. Yet the love and devotion of Christ in dying for His sheep is even greater. Christ leaped into the depths of divine wrath that sinners deserved. He died not merely for sweet children but also for criminals, lawbreakers, and rebels of our fallen race. He redeemed a multitude of sons and daughters. And, unlike this heroic father, Christ rose from the dead to justify and sanctify His children forever.

Finally, *Thou art with me* guarantees that Christ will never forsake His people. God must cease to be God before He can cast away one soul that places its trust in Christ. The mountains may depart and the hills be removed, but His kindness will not depart from His sheep. Neither will the covenant of His peace be broken (Isaiah 54:10). "I will never leave thee, nor forsake thee" (Hebrews 13:5) is one of the most gracious promises that He makes to us.

The Canons of Dort also testify of this comforting truth:

> Thus, it is not in consequence of their own merits or strength, but of God's free mercy, that they do not totally fall from faith and grace, nor continue and perish finally in their backslidings; which, with respect to themselves, is not only possible, but would undoubtedly happen; but with respect to God, it is utterly impossible, since His counsel cannot be changed nor His promise fail, neither can the call according to His purpose be revoked, nor the merit, intercession and preservation of Christ be rendered ineffectual, nor the sealing of the Holy Spirit be frustrated or obliterated.[3]

God will remain forever with His people. Christ will remain with His church to the end of the world (Matthew 28:20). The government of this world will remain upon Christ's shoulders until Judgment Day (Isaiah 9:6), for from eternity to eternity His name is Immanuel—*God with us* (Matthew 1:23).

The Experience of the Shepherd's Companionship

Have you experienced companionship and communion with God? Have you met this Christ, who fights His people's battles, accompanies them through dark valleys, died as their Substitute, and now lives to give them life and will never forsake them? Can you say, "I trust the Lord has begun His good work in me through Jesus Christ? I have tasted something of His communion, I have encountered His power, and I have heard His voice speaking to me by His Word and Spirit. At times He has taken me by the hand and led me through the dark valley of sin, humiliation, and trial. I long for more times like this, even if they can only be found through suffering or sorrow."

Communion with God requires agreeing with what He says in the gospel (Amos 3:3). We must agree that we deserve damnation and are utterly unworthy of eternal life. We must agree that God is holy, righteous, wise, and good. We must give our amen to the sovereignty and beauty of God's grace in His salvation through Jesus Christ. Only if we find God to be a consuming fire outside of Christ but a friend closer than a brother in Christ, will we value God's companionship with us. Though a believer's faith may increase or decrease, the deepest and truest desire of his heart is to walk with God in love.

Blessed are the sheep who exercise their faith and can say, "I will fear no evil, for thou art with me." They honor Christ and cherish His protection as the source of their spiritual growth and courage, and have experienced companionship with Him. Though their sins grieve them, God's righteousness extends beyond them, for Jesus Christ, the Lord our Righteousness, sits on God's throne (Jeremiah 23:6). By grace believers fear no evil, knowing that Christ's name is at stake in their salvation. The Lord must save them for His own sake.

Perhaps you feel that such truths are far above you. You confess that you do not experience communion with Christ. Rather, you feel the lack of His companionship in the dark valleys of your life. Be encouraged; Christ delights to give grace to needy people. Indeed, He causes death to work in them so that life may work in them more.

Christ carries His weakest ones into safe places. Gerard Wisse once saw a shepherd carrying a bag that was moving. He stopped the shepherd and asked him what was in the sack. The shepherd opened the bag and showed three newborn lambs. "These little animals cannot as yet walk so far," said the shepherd. "They are unable to reach the fold, and therefore I have taken them in a bag." In the same way, the Lord Jesus tenderly carries the weakest lambs of His flock. Fear not, flock of God: "He shall gather the lambs with his arm, and carry them in his bosom" (Isaiah 40:11).

Children of God, whether you have little faith or great faith, your Shepherd will be with you and protect you through all your journeys.

Embracing the Shepherd's Companionship in the Valley of Death

The companionship of Christ is most precious when we walk through the shadow of death. David wrote, "Yea, though I walk through the valley of the shadow of death, I will fear no evil: for thou art with me." The valley of darkness and death is the way for believers to walk into the life and light of heaven. It is the entrance to uninterrupted spiritual companionship with the triune God, His angels, and His saints. It is the exodus of the soul from the house of bondage to the house of everlasting joy.

We must all walk through the valley of death. Are you prepared for this journey? Are you ready for that time when life comes to an end? Do you have the staff of promises close at hand, so that, like the aged Jacob, you may lean on that staff and confess, "I have waited for thy salvation, O God" (Genesis 49:18)? The greatest issue is not how we face this life but how we face eternity. Are we ready to appear before the judgment seat of Christ?

Death's dark valley may seem far away from you. You may not yet have had any startling warnings of mortality. The angel of death may have traveled his rounds without breaking into your family circle. Yet, death will come to you. It may be sudden and unexpected. It may be in your youth or in old age. Do not imagine that you will be more prepared for death as you get older. Rather, you may be more disinclined to believe death is near. Therefore, heed the warning, "today if ye will hear his voice, harden not your hearts" (Hebrews 4:7). Scripture warns us to flee from the wrath to come, and not once does it allow any person any excuse before the tribunal of God.

Some people appear to walk backwards to the grave so that they will not see it, only to be surprised when they fall in. Our dream of the present will be shattered if physical death leads us to eternal death in hell. It will be unspeakable agony never to have known the companionship of God. The psalmist says of the wicked, "Like sheep they are laid in the grave; death shall feed on them [literally, death will lead them to its pastures]; and the upright shall have dominion over them in the morning; and their beauty shall consume in the grave from their dwelling" (Psalm 49:14). Death drives the ungodly into the bleak and dreary pastures of eternal condemnation. Hell knows nothing of companionship with God.

It will be completely different, however, for the sheep that the Lord leads through the valley of death. Their Shepherd is also the Lamb who died for their sins. He walks with them through the darkest moments; even when they cannot see Him, He is by their side. Death for them will be the gateway to eternal life with Him in glory, where they will rejoice forever. Revelation 7:15-17 portrays their future:

> Therefore are they before the throne of God, and serve him day and night in his temple: and he that sitteth on the throne shall dwell among them. They shall hunger no more, neither thirst any more; neither shall the sun light on [strike] them, nor any heat. For the Lamb which is in the midst of the throne shall feed them, and shall lead them unto living fountains of waters: and God shall wipe away all tears from their eyes.

In the hope of everlasting joy in His presence *then*, Christians are empowered to say *now*, "Though I walk through the valley of the shadow of death, I will fear no evil, for thou art with me." Though our friends and loved ones may fall back at the approach of death, their Shepherd will walk with them to the last breath, and beyond. Therefore, they may be strong and courageous, fearing no evil.

Is Christ your Shepherd? Why would you die an eternal death instead of choosing life? Believe on the Lord Jesus Christ, and you will live with Him forever.

Hope in the Lord, ye waiting saints and He will well provide,
For mercy and redemption full and free with Him abide;
From sin and evil, mighty thought they seem,
His arm almighty will His saints redeem.[4]

14

The Shepherd's Comfort

Thy rod and thy staff they comfort me.
—Psalm 23:4d

The shepherd of old struggled with many difficulties. He was exposed to extreme heat and cold (Genesis 31:40). His food consisted primarily of what he could gather from the earth, such as the nuts and fruit of uncultivated trees and wild honey. He had to defend his flock from the attacks of wild beasts including lions, wolves, and bears (1 Samuel 17:34; Isaiah 31:4; Amos 3:12; John 10:12). He also faced the threat of wildfires and thieves who would kill him and steal his sheep (Job 1:16-17; John 10:8, 10).

The shepherd confronted these hardships with a minimum of equipment, especially when traveling with the flock to new pastures. He carried a small tent (Song of Solomon 1:8), a bag (1 Samuel 17:40), and two sticks (Zechariah 11:7). These wooden sticks are still used today by some shepherds in the Middle East and Africa.[1] David spoke of these sticks in Psalm 23:4, calling them "thy rod and thy staff." The rod is a club, perhaps two or three feet long with one end thick and heavy for striking, and the staff is a slender stick several feet long with a crook at one end for grasping and lifting.[2] The shepherd would carry the rod on his belt and lean on his staff as he walked with the sheep.[3] These tools were constantly with him and over time became, as it were, extensions of his arm.

In our psalm, David uses these tools of the shepherd to symbolize two aspects of the Lord's activity in caring for His sheep as the divine Shepherd. Together, His rod and staff bring comfort and security to the flock of God,

The Comfort of the Shepherd's Rod

The rod in the Bible often represents Christ's authority and strength. According to Isaiah 11:4, the Lord Jesus "shall smite the earth with the rod of his mouth." Christ will shatter the wicked among the nations "with a rod of iron" (Psalm 2:9), which is not made of iron but is a wooden club with pieces of iron embedded in its head.[4] The ancient Greek translation of Psalm 2, the Septuagint, literally says, "you will *shepherd* them with an iron rod" (see also Revelation 2:27; 12:5; 19:15). That may also be said of the scepter of Christ the King: "Thy throne, O God, is for ever and ever: the sceptre of thy kingdom is a right sceptre" (Psalm 45:6).

In Scripture, the shepherd's rod serves two main functions: it helps him defend the sheep and to count and examine them.

The Rod of Defense

The shepherd's rod is a deadly club. A Middle Eastern shepherd said, "One good blow from it will kill or cripple to utter disability almost any ferocious animal."[5] David knew the power of this weapon. He said to Saul, "Thy servant kept his father's sheep, and there came a lion, and a bear, and took a lamb out of the flock: and I went out after him, and smote him, and delivered it out of his mouth: and when he arose against me, I caught him by his beard, and smote him, and slew him" (1 Samuel 17:34–35). David had no sword, so he must have conquered the beasts with a rod. In the hand of a skillful shepherd, a rod can crush a venomous serpent before it can strike.[6]

Christ Jesus, the Good Shepherd, also uses His rod to defend His sheep. This protection calms the flock and gives them comfort. Faith says, "Thy defending rod comforts me." Oh, how glorious is Christ when He comes forth with the weapons of His eternal power to fight the serpent that would poison our souls and destroy the roaring lion that would tear us to pieces!

The rod of our Shepherd is "the rod of his mouth" and "the breath of his lips" (Isaiah 11:4), that is, His Word inspired and empowered by His Spirit. Christ Jesus uses His Word in the lives of His people to drive away their enemies. When His sheep are weary and defenseless today, King Jesus places the sword of the Word in their hands. He speaks, "It is written," and, "Thus saith the LORD," to their souls. This power enables their hands to fight against their foes. Strong in the Lord, they resist the devil and he must flee (Ephesians 6:10; James 4:7).

The Word of the Lord is mighty. "He sent his word, and healed them," declares the psalmist (Psalm 107:20). One word from the mouth of the risen Jesus motivated His disciples to come to Him, hold Him by the feet, and worship Him (Matthew 28:9). With heaven's stamp of authority, the Word of God becomes the believer's water, food, warmth, counselor, heritage, and rock of defense (Psalm 119:9; Luke 24:32; Psalm 119:24; Job 23:12; Galatians 6:16; John 8:31). It is a book of wisdom, a fountain of sweetness, a treasury of riches, a medicine for all diseases, a tune with perfect harmony, and a mirror of divine beauty. It is also a mighty rod the Shepherd uses to defend His people against all enemies.

The Word of God is inextricably bound up with Christ's mission to save His people. Christ promised His Father that He would keep His

Word though He must die as a sacrifice, for that Word was written in His heart (Psalm 40:7-8; Hebrews 10:5-10). Stepping out of the waters of baptism into the fire of trial, Christ countered every temptation with, "It is written," so that His people might know the power of this mighty rod (Matthew 4:1-11). Christ prayed in agony in Gethsemane, but He persevered in submitting His will to that of His Father, declaring that the Scriptures must be fulfilled (Matthew 26:54, 56). On Golgotha, He suffered and died with Scripture on His lips (Mark 15:34; Luke 23:46), and throughout the horror of His crucifixion, He often said He submitted to this, "that the scripture might be fulfilled" (John 19:24, 28, 36). By giving His life as the substitute for His people in fulfillment of God's Word, Christ earned the right to wield God's Word for their eternal defense against enemies.

Even now, while seated at the Father's right hand, Christ does not lay down the holy rod of the Word. As High Priest of the church, He pleads the Word in His intercession so that no accuser can condemn His flock or separate them from His love (Romans 8:34-39). He intercedes with the merits of His blood on the foundation of God's everlasting covenant. His priestly righteousness guarantees the promise, "No weapon that is formed against thee shall prosper; and every tongue that shall rise against thee in judgment thou shalt condemn" (Isaiah 54:17). As King, even in the darkest night, Christ lies at your door with the rod in His hand. He never sleeps or slumbers on His watch (Psalms 121:4; 139:12). He can destroy any enemy, no matter how strong. His flock can thus confess, "Lord, it is nothing for thee to help those who have no power" (2 Chronicles 14:11). In His royal hands, the Word of God has the power to cast down strongholds and everything else that exalts itself against the knowledge of God. He takes every thought captive to obey Him (2 Corinthians 10:4-5). The Shepherd defends His sheep and conquers all enemies, including sin, unbelief, Satan, the world, and death.

Child of God, are you comforted by knowing that no enemy will have dominion over your soul because of your Good Shepherd? When faith beholds Christ and His rod, the darkest valleys become places of great rejoicing. By faith, we must freely entrust our souls to this faithful Redeemer, making Him the custodian of us, soul and body, both in this world and the next. Believing that the hands once pierced by nails now wield the rod, we trust that we will never perish, for no one can snatch us out of His hand (John 10:28).

Though you are one of Christ's sheep, perhaps you lack boldness of faith. Yet weak faith cannot lessen the power of Christ's truth. The Shepherd's rod is strong to defend you. He who defended you yesterday will not cease to guard you today and tomorrow.

Scripture also says the flock passes "under the rod." When the shepherd brings his sheep into the fold in the evening, he holds out his rod so the sheep may only enter one-by-one, enabling him to count them (Leviticus 27:32; cf. Jeremiah 33:13). If any sheep are missing, the shepherd sounds the alarm and a search begins (Matthew 18:12).[7] This is also a time for the shepherd to examine each sheep.[8] Ezekiel used the passing of the sheep under the rod as a metaphor for God sorting out His true sheep from outsiders, just as He judged Israel in the wilderness (Ezekiel 20:33–37).[9] Ralph Alexander writes, "Only when a sheep passed under its shepherd's rod did it indicate that a sheep belonged to the shepherd."[10]

These shepherding customs are replete with spiritual applications. God's people must learn that they cannot pull the wool over their Shepherd's eyes (Psalm 44:20, 21). We may deceive our associates, relatives, and even ourselves, but as God informed Samuel, "The LORD seeth not as man seeth; for man looketh on the outward appearance, but the LORD looketh on the heart" (1 Samuel 16:7). And Hebrew 4:13 warns, "Neither is there any creature that is not manifest in his sight: but all things are naked and opened unto the eyes of him with whom we have to do."

Christ uses the rod of His powerful Word to search for and prove His people. They may shrink from this process, even though it is done for their welfare. They may try to present themselves as holy before allowing their Shepherd to examine them. They may grow weary of Christ's tests and trials in the valley of the shadow of death. Yet, the true sheep of Christ long to pass under Christ's rod to experience His searching and to know they are in His fold. Their Shepherd's exams enable them to bare their soul before the God whom they so deeply love. Thus David prayed, "Search me, O God, and know my heart: try me, and know my thoughts: and see if there is any wicked way in me, and lead me in the way everlasting" (Psalm 139:23–24).

God's people find comfort in being numbered and examined among the Lord's flock. They willingly pass under His rod, for their joy and hope is to belong to Him. The believer can confess with the Heidelberg Catechism,

What is thy only comfort in life and death?

That I with body and soul, both in life and death, am not my own, but belong unto my faithful Savior Jesus Christ; who, with His precious blood, hath fully satisfied for all my sins, and delivered me from all the power of the devil; and so preserves me that without the will of my heavenly Father, not a hair can fall from my head; yea, that all things must be subservient to my salvation, and therefore, by His Holy Spirit, He also assures me of eternal life, and makes me sincerely willing and ready, henceforth, to live unto Him.[11]

The comfort of all comforts is to be able to say by faith, "The Lord counts me as one of His. I am in the valley of the shadow of death, but I am one of the Lord's own purchased flock. I am undergoing heavy trials, but I am numbered with His redeemed."

We need no better comfort than that. When Jesus' disciples rejoiced because even the devils were subject to them, their Master said,

"Nevertheless, rejoice not in this, but rather rejoice because your names are written in heaven" (Luke 10:20). We may be weak in faith, small in grace, and sick with sin, but we may still belong to the Good Shepherd if He claims us as His own. Thus we are comforted by our Lord's words in John 6:39, "This is the Father's will which hath sent me, that of all which he hath given me I should lose nothing, but should raise it up again at the last day." We may be as inconsequential as the dust in the balance, as smoking flax, or as bruised reeds, but in the eye of the heavenly Father we are precious jewels. As sheep of the Good Shepherd, we will be guarded by Him to the end (Psalms 5:11; 79:13). Therefore, we may say, "Thy rod comforts me."

The Comfort of the Shepherd's Staff

Whereas the rod is used to strike predators, the staff guides the sheep along their journey. Phillip Keller writes, "In a sense the staff, more than any other item of his personal equipment, identifies the shepherd as a shepherd. No one in any other profession carries a shepherd's staff. It is uniquely an instrument used for the care and management of sheep—and only sheep. It will not do for cattle, horses or hogs."[12] The staff is a symbol of a shepherd's compassion for His sheep.

Just as with the rod, Christ uses His staff through His Word and Spirit. We must never attempt to separate the Word from the Spirit, for Word without Spirit does not impart life, and the Spirit without Word tends to promote mysticism, but when Word and Spirit are united, they offer truth, life, power, and comfort. Thus the Lord Jesus calls the Holy Spirit "the Spirit of truth" (John 14:17), and says that His words are "spirit and life" (John 6:63). The Spirit of Christ uses the Word to direct His sheep to keep them in the way of Christ.

Christ also called the Holy Spirit "another Comforter." The word for this in the original language is *Paracletos*, which means more than our English translation. It means someone we may call on to help us, whether by pleading our cause, instructing us, or abiding with us to comfort us. God's people receive the Holy Spirit as *Paraclete*, meaning Helper, Intercessor, Advocate, Comforter, and Counselor all rolled into one. As Christ is our Advocate in heaven (1 John 2:1), the Holy Ghost is the Advocate in our souls (Romans 8:26). Through Christ, the Holy Spirit turns impossibility into possibility and necessity into reality for His sheep. Christ promised: "He will dwell in us and sanctify us to be members of Christ, applying to us that which we have in Christ."[13] He also said, "He will guide you into all truth. He shall glorify me: for he shall receive of mine, and shall shew it unto you" (John 16:13-14). Christ's sheep need the comforting presence of the Spirit.

The Staff of Guidance

As a shepherd uses his staff to guide his sheep into the paths he chooses, Christ directs His flock through His Word and Spirit. We are not to determine our Shepherd's will by examining dreams, emotions, unusual happenings, fortune tellers, horoscopes, or putting the Lord to the test. Rather, we are to heed the following ordinary means by which the Shepherd leads His flock to discern His will.

First, the Shepherd guides His sheep by directing us to *read the Word*. That means we must read the Scriptures, hear the Word preached, meditate upon the Word, and obey the Word. The Bible is the rule of faith and life for the Christian. Everything in life, whether reason, emotion, experience, common sense, or science must adapt to Scripture, not Scripture to it. Jesus said in John 10:27, "My sheep hear my voice, and I know them, and they follow me."

The Bible is God's revealed will to fallen man, the infallible guide for every area of life. As 2 Timothy 16-17 says, "All Scripture is given by inspiration of God, and is profitable for doctrine, for reproof, for correction, for instruction in righteousness: that the man of God may be perfect, thoroughly furnished unto all good works." Thomas Watson said, "Read the Word as a book made by God himself .... It is the library of the Holy Ghost."[14] And Ezekiel Hopkins wrote, "The

Bible, therefore, is the statute-book of God's kingdom. Therein is comprised the whole body of the heavenly law, the perfect rules of a holy life, and the sure promises of a glorious one."[15]

Second, we must *pray for the Holy Spirit's assistance* in interpreting God's Word. Paul writes to the Corinthians, "the Spirit searcheth all things, yea, the deep things of God. For what man knoweth the things of a man, save the spirit of man which is in him? Even so the things of God knoweth no man, but the Spirit of God. Now we have received, not the spirit of the world, but the Spirit which is of God; that we might know the things that are freely given to us of God" (1 Corinthians 2:10-12). Within God's people, the Holy Spirit uses God's Word to teach them truth and discernment, to encourage them to pursue paths of righteousness, to rebuke them when they sin, to guide them in the paths of righteousness, and to apply the Word to specific situations.

Third, pray for God to fulfill the promises of His Word through His *works of providence* and enable you to do His will as the Spirit opens your eyes to see it. Do not assume God has denied your request if His answer is delayed, for God often hides His face for a time because His will may be to do even more than you asked. Also, be careful how you interpret providence. Obstacles and difficulties in your path do not necessarily mean that God frowns on your endeavor.

Above all, rely on God's revealed will in Scripture rather than on extraordinary providences. John Flavel acknowledged that in Scripture God sometimes revealed His will in extraordinary ways to men like Samuel and David, but he warned, "But now, all are tied up to the ordinary standing rule of the written Word, and must not expect any such extraordinary revelations from God. The way we now have to know the will of God concerning us in difficult cases, is to search and study the Scriptures, and where we find no particular rule to guide us in this, or that particular case, there we are to apply general rules."[16]

Fourth, God also tells us to use *conscience* to give direction when it is informed by Scripture and renewed by the Spirit. The apostle Paul stated, "And herein do I exercise myself, to have always a conscience void of offence toward God, and toward men" (Acts 24:16). Conscience is the knowledge of God's moral law written on the heart (Romans 2:14–15) and is therefore a reliable guide, but only if it agrees with Scripture.

When conscience speaks scripturally, it is of great value, for it condemns what is wrong and commends what is right in thoughts, words, and actions, thereby restraining much sin and promoting much good. Richard Sibbes said, "Conscience looks to God. It is placed as God's deputy and vice-regent in man."[7] Therefore, we should strive to keep a good conscience and to commit ourselves and our cause to God.

Finally, the Holy Spirit uses *the counsel of fellow believers* to direct His sheep in right paths. Whether from a classic book or from a treasured friend, good counsel proves for God's people that "a word fitly spoken is like apples of gold in pictures of silver" (Proverbs 25:11). A mature Christian whose mind is saturated with Scripture can often see a dilemma more objectively and offer a wise solution to our dilemma. Solomon commends such counsel many times in his Proverbs. He says, "Where no counsel is, the people fall: but in the multitude of counsellors there is safety" (Proverbs 11:14). Again, "The way of a fool is right in his own eyes: but he that hearkeneth unto counsel is wise" (Proverbs 12:15). Generally speaking, it is not wise to seek counsel from an unconverted friend in spiritual, moral, or ethical issues. Also, bear in mind that not every child of God is fit to dispense godly counsel. Discernment must be used in selecting whom to approach for advice, and all advice must be prayerfully laid beside Scripture.

These five means of discovering God's will afford great comfort to God's people. Yet, perplexing situations may still arise, for, as my father often told me, "believers often go to the grave with more questions than answers." In such times we must remember that we do not lead ourselves or choose our own paths; it is the Shepherd who leads us. We need not understand all things but only faithfully follow the direction of His staff.

The Staff of Uplifting

A shepherd's staff often has a crook, or hook, at the end. He uses the crook to extricate sheep from perilous situations such as a pit, ravine, ditch, or thicket of thorns. Kenneth Bailey explains, "When a lamb cannot scramble down a ledge or falls into a crevice or down a bank into a stream, the shepherd is able, with the crook in his staff, to catch the lamb by a leg or a shoulder and gently lift it back onto the path."[18]

Child of God, how has sin plummeted you into situations from which you could not extricate yourself? Can you number the miry depths into which you have sunk? Sins of omission and commission have plunged you into misery and trouble which daily threaten to overwhelm you.

Christ does not forget us at such times. Though we may seem to have forfeited all claims to His care, He is "a very present help in trouble" (Psalm 46:1). He does not deal with us after our sins or reward us according to our iniquities (Psalm 103:10). He does not burden us with the full penalty of our misdeeds. He comes after us in the wilderness, not resting until He has discovered the pit into which we have fallen. He then extricates us from the mire and lifts us tenderly out of our difficulties and iniquities by His Spirit. He brings us words of healing and hope from the Holy Scriptures. Then we learn by experience that the Bible was written "that we through patience and comfort of the Scriptures might have hope" (Romans 15:4).

If we are too weak to walk, He places us on His shoulders and brings us back to the fold, satisfied with no other recompense than that we are safe. As the prophet Ezekiel wrote, "For thus saith the LORD GOD; behold, I, even I, will both search my sheep, and seek them out. As a shepherd seeketh out his flock in the day that he is among his sheep that are scattered; so will I seek out my sheep, and will deliver them

out of all places where they have been scattered in the cloudy and
dark day" (Ezekiel 34:11-12). How patient Christ and His Spirit are in
preventing us from being overwhelmed by the sorrows that we have
brought upon ourselves!

Sometimes the mere touch of our Shepherd's staff is enough to
remind us of His loving presence with us. Keller writes,

> Sometimes I have been fascinated to see how a shepherd will
> actually hold his staff against the side of some sheep that is a
> special pet or favorite, simply so that they "are in touch." They will
> walk along this way almost as though it were "hand-in-hand." The
> sheep obviously enjoys this special attention from the shepherd
> and revels in the close, personal, intimate contact between them.
> To be treated in this way by the shepherd is to know comfort in a
> deep dimension. It is a delightful and moving picture.[19]

In the same way, Christ communicates with us by His Word and
Spirit, to say, "I am here. I am with you. I love you. Do not be afraid."
In those moments, Christ dwells in the heart by faith, and the believer
experiences the divine love that passes knowledge (Ephesians 3:16-19).
He hears the Spirit saying, "Fear thou not; for I am with thee: be not
dismayed; for I am thy God: I will strengthen thee; yea, I will help
thee; yea, I will uphold thee with the right hand of my righteousness"
(Isaiah 41:10). Then, the sheep of God can say with all their hearts,
"Yea, though I walk through the valley of the shadow of death, I will
fear no evil: for thou art with me; *thy rod and thy staff they comfort me.*"

Part 5

Psalm 23:5
"Thou preparest a table before me in the presence of mine enemies:
thou anointest my head with oil; my cup runneth over."

15

Divine Provision

Thou preparest a table before me in the presence of mine enemies.
—Psalm 23:5a

The Good Shepherd provides food for His people.[1] To *prepare a table* means to gather food, cook it, and serve it in a meal. Joseph, a type of Christ, hosted his famished brothers in Egypt and sent them back to Israel with an abundance of provisions (Genesis 42–45). The Lord was the Host of His redeemed people, Israel, in miraculously providing food and water in the wilderness, even though the unbelieving Israelites did not trust Him to "furnish a table in the wilderness" (Psalm 78:19).[2] When Elijah ran for his life from wicked Queen Jezebel, he awoke one day in total exhaustion to find that the Lord had sent an angel to serve him bread and water in the wilderness. That sustained him for forty days and forty nights (1 Kings 19:1–8). Perhaps David reflected on God's provision for His people in the wilderness of Sinai as he cared for his father's sheep in the wilderness of Judea. The

Great Shepherd provides His sheep with all they need for body and soul as they travel through a hostile world.

We must see this provision as primarily a spiritual feast. To prepare a table is the same language used when Wisdom in Proverbs 9 "furnishes" a table for her guests, and invites those who seek understanding to feast in her house (Proverbs 9:2). Christ is our Wisdom, and He lovingly prepares a table for His sheep even in the presence of their enemies. They learn to say with Job, "I have esteemed the words of his mouth more than my necessary food" (Job 23:12). Like Paul, they can say, "Blessed be the God and Father of our Lord Jesus Christ, who hath blessed us with all spiritual blessings in heavenly places in Christ" (Ephesians 1:3).

Just as the Shepherd leads His sheep in paths of righteousness, He reveals His glory as He extends spiritual hospitality to those who come to Him by faith. A Middle Eastern scholar who grew up in a family of shepherds wrote, "In the East, a man's fame is spread by means of his table and lavish hospitality rather than by his possessions. Strangers and neighbors alike discuss tables where they have been guests. Such tales spread from one town to another and are handed down from one generation to another."[3] God lavishly blesses His people "with all spiritual blessings in heavenly places in Christ ... to the praise of the glory of his grace" (Ephesians 1:6).

Christ's Labor to Prepare Abundant Provision for Us

Preparing nutritious and delicious food for one's family and guests is hard work. Being a good host requires careful planning, money, and effort. It is less satisfying if one's guests are not grateful. In spite of the foolishness of His own flock as well as the multitude of enemies surrounding them, the Lord provides for His flock. As the Good Shepherd, Jesus Christ finished His task of providing abundant spiritual provisions for His elect, though it cost Him the high price of His own blood.

"Good Shepherd, Thou preparest a table before me" reveals nothing less than God's amazing grace. Yet we also find such a table prepared in the gospel of Jesus Christ, in the covenant meal of the Lord's Supper, and in the eternal banquet of His glorious kingdom.

The preparations for this table were made before the world began (2 Timothy 1:9). Christ knew that He would find His sheep in the rough country of a sin-cursed earth, cut off from all supplies, lost and perishing. So in the counsel of peace, the Son covenanted with the Father to redeem the people whom the Father gave Him as the sheep of His pasture. The Holy Spirit calls Jesus "the Lamb slain from the foundation of the world" (Revelation 13:8) to testify of Christ's willingness from eternity to be bound with the cords of love to His own sheep and to be sacrificed for their sins.

As God gave manna to Israel to eat, the Father sent the Son to be the bread of life for His people, and the Son voluntarily came to do His Father's will (John 6:32–38). As the Lord opened springs of clean water for Israel to drink in the wilderness, Christ promised from eternity to open a wellspring of eternal life for sinners (Titus 1:2; John 4:14). He promised that Satan and all other enemies of Christ's sheep would never conquer them but would instead be crushed under Christ's feet (Genesis 3:15; Romans 16:20).

Because of Christ's preparations, His servants may eat, drink, and rejoice (Isaiah 65:13). Their enemies will look on in envy, but they cannot interrupt this holy feast. "No weapon that is formed against thee shall prosper; and every tongue that shall rise against thee in judgment thou shalt condemn. This is the heritage of the servants of the Lord, and their righteousness is of me, saith the LORD" (Isaiah 54:17).

Christ's labor to prepare abundant food for His sheep is an unfathomable mystery (Philippians 2:5–8). It involved His willingness to lay aside His eternal and divine glory, His position, and His prerogatives as the sinless Son of God. It meant humbling Himself, making Himself "of no reputation" to suffer privation, ridicule, false accusations, rumor, gossip, and false charges. People would brand Him as a glutton, drunkard, friend of sinners, and an imposter. But no amount of suffering, whether physical, mental, or spiritual, could stop Christ from preparing a table for us.

His coming to earth as Jesus of Nazareth was an act of utter self-sacrifice that culminated in His death on the cross of Calvary. He laid down His life for His sheep in utter selflessness. This was redeeming love. This was God fulfilling His eternal counsel. This was the satisfaction that God's justice demanded, according to the terrific summons of Zechariah 13:7, "Awake, O sword, against my Shepherd, and against the man that is my fellow, saith the LORD of hosts." This was God in Christ delivering men from their iniquities, their selfishness, and their self-destructive instincts as lost, helpless sheep.

Eternity will be spent probing the depths of this mystery, though God's sheep learn to ask even here on earth: "Good Shepherd, hast Thou gone through such unspeakable suffering to prepare a feast for me? Have my sins made salvation such a costly task for Thee? O God, who am I, that Thou dost think on me? How will I ever comprehend the eternal miracle that 'Thou preparest a table for me' at such cost and in the presence of my enemies?"

Christ's Labor to Bring Abundant Provision to Us

When David says, "Thou preparest a table *before* me," he implies that everything was prepared before his very eyes; all he must do now is enjoy the feast. The sheep do not have to find their way to this table, for the Shepherd who prepared their food brings it to them. As Paul argues in Romans 10, there is no need for us to ascend into heaven to bring Christ down or to descend into the deep to bring Christ up. In the gospel the salvation of God has come to us. The table has been prepared and the feast spread before us.

"Before me" implies that God brought this table to David, and David to this table. Apart from God's grace, we have no legs to run to Christ, no hands to reach for His food, no mouth to taste it, and no appetite to enjoy it. We need a Savior who not only prepares the gospel table of grace, but who also prepares us for His grace and feeds us with His grace, for without Him we can do nothing. Even as Christ offered Himself to sinners as "the bread of life," calling them to believe, He said, "No man can come to me, except the Father which hath sent me draw him" (John 6:35, 44). Isaac Watts expressed the depth of our need and the fullness of divine grace in this verse:

> While all our hearts and all our songs join to admire the feast,
> Each of us cry, with thankful tongues, "Lord, why was I a guest?
> Why was I made to hear thy voice, and enter while there's room,
> When thousands make a wretched choice, and rather
> starve than come?"
> 'Twas the same love that spread the feast that sweetly drew us in;
> Else we had still refused to taste, and perished in our sin. [4]

I need a Savior who will not forsake me after meriting salvation for me on Calvary, for I am still helpless without the Shepherd to apply salvation to me. I need grace to lift up my heart by faith to heaven where Christ Jesus is my Advocate at the right hand of the Father. Only then may I be nourished in my soul with Christ's crucified body and shed blood as the true meat and drink of eternal life. [5]

You might have a fairly substantial savings account at a local bank, but you cannot use it without proper authorization to withdraw from the account or write a check from it. Likewise, a homeless person may walk past wealthy banks, knowing there are millions of dollars in their vaults, but he is still hungry. So it is with the gospel. Merely knowing about the feast prepared by Christ will not help us if we have not been invited to the table.

The Lord prepares a feast prepared only for the spiritually impoverished whom He has chosen. Psalm 132 says, "For the LORD hath chosen Zion; he hath desired it for his habitation.... I will abundantly bless her provision: I will satisfy her poor with bread" (vv. 13, 15). To eat from His table, however, they must first recognize their spiritual poverty. Jesus Christ said, "Blessed are the poor in spirit: for theirs is the kingdom of heaven" (Matthew 5:3). Sadly, it is possible to be spiritually poor but still think you are rich and need nothing (Revelation 3:17).

By contrast, Zion's poor are spiritual beggars, dependents upon God's mercy. They have not merely learned to say the right words in confessing their sins. They have also laid all their sins before the Lord, pleading, "Enter not into judgment with thy servant: for in thy sight shall no man living be justified" (Psalm 143:2).

Awareness of sin in the mind and repentance from sin in the heart are miles apart in God's eyes. Asking for forgiveness can go far. Witness Saul's confession to David: "Thou art more righteous than I" (1 Samuel 24:17). Witness Judas Iscariot tossing thirty pieces of silver before the Sanhedrin, declaring, "I have sinned in that I have betrayed the innocent blood" (Matthew 27:4). But the feast of the gospel requires more than remorse and regret; it requires each person to turn away from sin to God, trusting Christ to save him from the penalty and power of sin. The heart must be cut free from all grounds of salvation except Jesus Christ. Such penitent, thirsting sinners are welcomed at Christ's feast, for salvation is by free grace alone. The invitation is simple and clear: "Ho, every one that thirsteth, come ye to the waters, and he that hath no money; come ye, buy, and eat; yea, come, buy wine and milk without money and without price" (Isaiah 55:1).

At His table the Lord Jesus Christ receives His guests with gracious love. He bestows every dish of this lavish feast with the generosity of a Prince. When He blesses, He makes the soul like that of Naphtali, "satisfied with favour, and full with the blessing of the LORD" (Deuteronomy 33:23), enabling His redeemed bride to say, "He brought me to the banqueting house, and his banner over me was love" (Song of Solomon 2:4).

The overflowing love of the Lord Jesus Christ draws His people to His table. His love teaches them that the abundance of divine provision is due to His divine person. He is the great I AM. Do they desire peace? "He is our peace." Do they need salvation? He declares, "I am your salvation." Do they long for comfort? He points them to Himself, saying, "I am your consolation; fear not." God makes Christ Jesus everything to believers: "wisdom, and righteousness, and sanctification, and redemption" (1 Corinthians 1:30).

Oh, how richly Jesus Christ provides for sin-sick souls! He is the salvation of God, the sum of all covenant blessings. In Him dwells all of God's fullness. He is the treasury of all-sufficient grace, and His sheep receive grace upon grace. Christ is everything that His people need for time and eternity.

In Christ, believers find a salvation that can never be aborted, a righteousness that can never be tarnished, a title that can never be clouded, a judgment that can never be repeated, and a justification that can never be annulled. They find a position that can never be invalidated, a seal that can never be violated, an inheritance that can never be revoked, a wealth that can never be depleted, and a peace that can never fade. In Christ, they find a love that can never fail, a grace that can never run out, a strength that can never be exhausted, a forgiveness that can never be rescinded, a comfort that can never be exhausted, an Intercessor who can never be disqualified, a Victor who can never be conquered, a hope that can never be disappointed, and a glory that can never be dimmed! Yes, Christ is all.

Through Christ we also have access to the Father (Ephesians 2:18), who gave His Son that whoever believes on Him will not perish but have everlasting life (John 3:16). From Christ flows the river of the water of life, which the Holy Spirit gives to the believer, in whom it springs up and will never dry up (John 4:14; 7:37–39).

To live by this Savior in the presence of enemies is rich, even if we are poor. To feed on this Christ is to be filled with all good things, even if we are hungry. To be satisfied with this divine food is to experience grace that will triumph over sin. Though we still live in the land of the curse and must walk through the valley of the shadow of death, we can still say with grateful hearts, "Thou preparest a table before me in the presence of mine enemies."

Christ's Labor to Lead Us in Victory over Our Enemies

As the Good Shepherd, Christ suffered and died on Calvary to provide abundant provisions for His flock. As the Great Shepherd, Christ now sits at the right hand of His Father to furnish a table for His sheep in the presence of their enemies. As the Chief Shepherd, Christ will soon return to earth in victory to gather all His sheep into heaven, far beyond the reach of their enemies. Truly, the Lord's sheep do not lack divine provision, now or in eternity.

Your enemies, true believer, will not gain the final victory over you, for you will be safely beyond their reach on the other side of the grave. You will be beyond the reach of Satan, who will no longer strike at your heels. You will be beyond the reach of this world that hates you and opposes you. You will be beyond the reach of your besetting sins, which will be cast off forever when you die.

While you are on this side of the grave waiting for your transition to glory, commit your enemies to Christ. Your King will handle them on your behalf far more effectively than you can imagine.

That was evident in the life of Martin Luther as he struggled to lead the Reformation. Meditating on this psalm, he wrote in 1536:

> In this way I also have been preserved by the grace of God the past eighteen years. I have let my enemies rage, threaten, slander, and damn me, take counsel against me without ceasing, invent many evil devices, and practice many a piece of knavery [deceptive plotting]. I have let them worry anxiously how they might kill

me and destroy my teaching, or rather God's. Moreover, I have been happy and of good cheer—at one time better than another—and have not worried greatly about their raving and raging, but have clung to the staff of comfort and found my way to the Lord's table. That is, I have committed my cares to the Lord God, into which He had led me absolutely without my will or counsel.[6]

In the midst of his trials, Luther found comfort in the victory of Christ. The Christian cannot boast in this victory as if it came from himself. After every statement of what we have done for the Lord, we must add, "yet not I, but the grace of God which was with me" (1 Corinthians 15:10). We should glorify God for everything that His grace accomplishes. Luther said,

> Until now I have not only held off all my enemies, but by the grace of God have also accomplished so much that, when I look behind me and consider how matters stand in the papacy, I really must be surprised that things have gone so far. I should never have dared to imagine that even one tenth of what is now evident would happen. He that has begun a good work will also bring it to completion (Philippians 1:6), even though nine more hells and worlds were gathered together in a heap.[7]

We must not be surprised if as followers of Christ we attract the hostile attention of Christ's enemies. Some of a Christian's most bitter enemies may be church members and leaders. Even as we feast in Christ's presence on God's grace, these enemies will surround us with hatred and lies, for they despise grace.[8] We see that in the life of Christ Himself. After Christ called Levi, saying, "Follow me," Levi prepared a great feast in his home for Jesus and Levi's fellow tax collectors. The scribes and Pharisees protested this fellowship with sinners, asking Christ, "Why do ye eat and drink with publicans and sinners?" Christ replied, "They that are whole need not a physician, but they that are sick. I came not to call the righteous, but sinners to repentance" (Luke 5:27-32). Meanwhile, the sinners in Levi's home could only listen to Jesus with wonder and joy, proclaiming, "Thou preparest a table before me in the presence of mine enemies."

Christ's dining with sinners provoked the Pharisees and scribes to attack Him another time, after which the Lord Jesus told the parable of the prodigal son. Rather than backing away from criticism, Christ made a feast the climax of the parable as the father celebrated the return of his lost son. This table was also prepared in the presence of an enemy, who was the prodigal's self-righteous older brother (Luke 15). The Pharisees did not miss the point, then or later when Jesus welcomed into His presence people such as the sinful woman of Capernaum and the chief tax collector Zacchaeus (Luke 7:36–50; 19:1–10). Repeatedly, when Christ ate with repentant sinners to welcome them into the kingdom, they could say, "Thou preparest a table before me," while referring to the judgmental Pharisees by adding, "in the presence of mine enemies."

Sinners are enemies not only of God's righteousness but also of God's grace. The kingdom of Satan resists both the law and the gospel. That should not surprise us, because if we are honest with ourselves, we too have been enemies of grace, and would have remained so had grace not given us new natures. We should not hate our enemies but love them, pray for them, and remember that they are the willing but enslaved victims of the spiritual forces of demonic evil.

Therefore, child of God, seek grace from the Lord as you face great enemies within and without. "Be strong in the Lord, and in the power of his might" (Ephesians 6:10). "Be strong in the grace that is in Christ Jesus" (2 Timothy 2:1). Strengthen yourself by remembering that your enemies will serve to your eternal advantage.

In this life, God uses your enemies to compel you to sit closer to Him, to feed at His table, and to gather with His people. The day will come when God will vindicate you in glory and cast your enemies into everlasting darkness where there shall be weeping and gnashing of teeth. While you wait, you may eat the hidden manna and drink from the secret spring, which bubbles up in the besieged city and enables you to defy the encircling forces of the enemy.

Joseph Hall (1574–1656) testified to the Christian's experience of conflict in this life:

> What shall I do, Lord? I strive and tug, what I may, with my natural corruptions; and with the spiritual wickednesses in high places (Ephesians 6:12), which set upon my soul; but sometimes I am foiled, and go halting [limping] out of the field. It is thy mercy that I live, being so fiercely assaulted by those principalities and powers. It were more than wonder that I should escape such hands without a wound. Even that holy servant of thine, who strove with thine angel for a blessing, went limping away, though he prevailed. What marvel is it that so weak a wretch as I, striving with many evil angels for the avoidance of a curse, come off with a maim or scar?[9]

Yet, in the midst of these struggles against sin and Satan, Hall could also testify of victory through his Savior, Jesus Christ:

> But, blessed be thy name, the wounds that I receive are not mortal; and when I fall, it is but to my knees: whence I rise with new courage and hopes of victory. Thou, who art the God of all power, and keepest the keys of hell and death, hast said, "Resist the devil, and he will flee from you." Lord, I do and will, by thy merciful aid, still and ever resist. Make thou my faith as steadfast as my will is resolute. Oh, still "teach thou my hands to war, and my fingers to fight" (Psalm 144:1). Arm thou my soul with strength; and at last, according to thy gracious promise, crown it with victory.[10]

Believer, are your enemies so afflicting you that you are driven to your knees in prayer? Haven't you also seen how those who are against you actually help you by making you more dependent on the Lord?

In eternity, you will partake of the King's high table, free of all enemies. You will no longer be an enemy to yourself, for all enemies and enmity will be kept out. Only friends and divine love will be let in. Oh, imagine what it will be like to be forever with your King, without hindrance, without obstacle, and without any enemy!

How wonderful it will be to see the Chief Shepherd sitting upon His throne and to set us at His right side as invited sheep rather than on His left as damned goats. Once you too were a goat, and your salvation seemed impossible. But with God, all things are possible. One day all of God's sheep will enter the gates of Paradise to feast with Abraham, Isaac, and Jacob at the table of the Lord.

You will then be more than an inhabitant of heaven, more than a sheep of God, and more than a child of heaven. Indeed, you will then be the bride of heaven described in John's vision in Revelation 19:6-9:

> And I heard as it were the voice of a great multitude, and as the voice of many waters, and as the voice of mighty thunderings, saying, Alleluia: for the Lord God omnipotent reigneth. Let us be glad and rejoice, and give honour to him: for the marriage of the Lamb is come, and his wife hath made herself ready. And to her was granted that she should be arrayed in fine linen, clean and white: for the fine linen is the righteousness of saints. And he saith unto me, Write, Blessed are they which are called unto the marriage supper of the Lamb.

Are you ready for that Day of Days? Will Christ's coming mean eternal victory for you or eternal defeat? Can you meet your Maker with what you have received from Him? For your own soul's sake, weigh your life in the balance of His Word. The angel of death can come for you at any moment. All men are appointed to die, and after death comes judgment (Hebrews 9:27).

"Surely I come quickly," Christ promised. Blessed is the Bride who can reply, "Even so, come, Lord Jesus. The grace of our Lord Jesus Christ be with you all. Amen" (Revelation 22:20-21).

16

Divine Anointing

Thou anointest my head with oil.

—Psalm 23:5b

We saw in the last chapter that the Shepherd prepares a feast for His people even in a hostile world. He also blesses them with divine anointing. Imagine a banquet where the host greets his guests warmly. Before the meal begins, the host provides water to wash the guest's feet, which is much appreciated after walking in sandals down hot and dusty roads. The host then takes a vial of oil and pours a little on the guest's head. The sweet, spicy oil refreshes the guest's dry skin and makes his face shine with happiness.

Anointing someone's head with oil seems strange to us today, but in Scripture it is rich with meaning. Oil is a sign of joy and satisfaction.[1] Pouring perfumed oil on the head expresses celebration and joy.[2] It was customary to honor a guest at a banquet by anointing his head with fragrant oil, a custom that continues in the Middle East today.[3] Thus, when David wrote, "Thou anointest my head with oil," he was saying that the Lord not only provided for his physical needs, but also blessed him with honor as a beloved guest.

Anointing is a symbol of our richest spiritual privileges in Jesus Christ. When God called men to serve His people, such as Aaron the priest, Moses as leader, the kings of Israel, and the prophet Elisha, these servants were prepared for their work by being anointed with oil.[4] The Hebrew word for "anointed one," whether a prophet, priest, or king, is *mashiach*, translated as "Messiah."[5] When translated into Greek, "anointed one" becomes *Christos* or "Christ," the title given to our Lord Jesus. He is the great Prophet, Priest, and King of His people.

The ceremonial anointing with oil was an outward sign of the gift of the Holy Spirit to bless, seal, and empower God's servants (1 Samuel 16:13; Isaiah 42:1). Anointing with oil was a sign of the greater anointing with the Holy Spirit. Jesus said of Himself: "The Spirit of the Lord is upon me, because he hath anointed me to preach the gospel to the poor" (Isaiah 61:1; Luke 4:18). Luke wrote, "God anointed Jesus of Nazareth with the Holy Ghost and with power: who went about doing good, and healing all that were oppressed of the devil; for God was with him" (Acts 10:38). Foreseeing Christ's work, the psalmist wrote, "God, thy God, hath anointed thee with the oil of gladness above thy fellows" (Psalm 45:7; Hebrews 1:9).

We need this Anointed One in all three of His offices. We can hardly call ourselves His sheep unless we feel our need for Him in all three roles. Francis Turretin (1623-1687) explained how Christ meets our every need:

- The threefold misery of man introduced by sin—ignorance, guilt, and the tyranny and bondage by sin—required this conjunction of a threefold office. Ignorance is healed by the prophetic; guilt by the priestly; the tyranny and corruption of sin by the kingly.

- Prophetic light scatters the darkness of error; the merit of the

Priest takes away guilt and procures reconciliation for us; the power of the King removes the bondage of sin and death.

- The Prophet shows God to us; the Priest leads us to God; and the King joins us together and glorifies us with God.

- The Prophet enlightens the mind by the Spirit of illumination; the Priest by the Spirit of consolation provides rest for the heart and conscience; the King by the Spirit of sanctification subdues rebellious affections.[6]

The Lord helps His sheep realize their need for the anointed Prophet, Priest, and King by His Word and Spirit. The Holy Spirit uncovers a sinner's unrighteousness and reveals Christ's righteousness. The Spirit convicts the sinner of his need for the anointed Priest to free him from sin and guilt through Christ's sacrifice, intercession, and blessing. And the Holy Spirit helps the sinner know how desperately he needs the anointed King to save him, heal him, and make him holy.

Thus the Holy Spirit makes believers partakers of Christ's anointing. Psalm 23 tells us that the Shepherd-King, Jesus Christ, delights to share His own anointing with His sheep for their great joy (Isaiah 61:1, 3). In union with Jesus Christ, every believer is anointed or baptized with the Holy Spirit (1 Corinthians 12:13; 2 Corinthians 1:21–22). The Spirit flows over Christ to His church (John 7:37–39), just as fragrant oil runs down from the head to the body (Psalm 133). As Calvin said, "He received the Holy Spirit in full perfection with all His graces, that He may lavish them upon us."[7] As a result, we share in the work of His offices, though Christ alone is the Mediator. For example, John wrote, "Ye have an unction [anointing] from the Holy One, and ye know all things .... But the anointing which ye have received of him abideth in you, and ye need not that any man teach you: but as the same anointing teacheth you of all things, and is truth, and is no lie, and even as it hath taught you, ye shall abide in him" (1 John 2:20, 27).

Psalm 23 is a song of spiritual experience. It is not just a declaration of truth, though this is also precious to the believer. It is truth made real to the soul through the exercise of faith. What does it mean to experience the anointing of our Shepherd-Host? What leads a believer to say with David, "Thou anointest my head with oil"?

Experiencing the Anointing of the Spirit of Christ

The Bible speaks of oil more than two hundred times. A special kind of oil, "an oil of holy ointment," was used to consecrate the tabernacle, the ark, the holy vessels, and the priests of the tabernacle including Aaron and his sons (Exodus 30:22–33). This oil could not be used for any other purpose. It was reserved for sacred use as a symbol of the Holy Spirit and His sanctifying power.

Without the Holy Spirit, God's children become restless, fretful, weak, dim-sighted, and sick. True believer, pause to admire the love, power, and grace of the divine Spirit. Is it not His hand that brings every blessing of salvation purchased by Jesus Christ? Do you not owe Him an incalculable debt of praise?

Consider only a few of His titles. He is "the holy Spirit of God"; therefore, together with the Father and the Son He is true and eternal God (Ephesians 4:30). He is also "the Spirit of Christ," for He is given by Christ and bears witness to Him (1 Peter 1:11). He is "the Spirit of life," for He gives physical life to all living things (Genesis 1:2; Psalm 104:30) and spiritual life to all who are in Christ Jesus (Romans 8:2). He is "the Spirit of truth," in opposition to everything that is false, and the teacher of all truth (John 14:17, 26). He is "the Spirit of grace and supplication," as the giver of the graces of true conversion, and the One who sustains us in our praying (Zechariah 12:10; Romans 8:26). He is "the Spirit of power," as opposed to all that is weak and insufficient, and is the enabler of every spiritual good (2 Timothy 1:7). And He is "the Spirit of holiness" who raised Christ from the dead and who raises us up to a new and godly life (Romans 1:4).

Child of God, the Holy Spirit is within you and for you, even when you cannot see Him. You are totally dependent upon God's Spirit, but you do not have the ability to anoint yourself anymore than a helpless sheep can. Moreover, you need the continuous anointing of God's gracious Spirit to counteract the recurring problems of sin and temptation. Are not the Holy Spirit's fresh applications your sure antidote against fresh transgressions? Yet, despite your fears, you will receive divine, continuous, and fresh anointing (Psalm 92:10), for the Holy Spirit lives within you. The apostle Paul asks, "What? Know ye not that your body is the temple of the Holy Ghost which is in you, which ye have of God, and ye are not your own?" (1 Corinthians 6:19). Why should there be famine in your soul when the Holy Spirit is in you?

The Spirit motivates His sheep to lay all of their needs at the shepherd's feet. The sinner groans, "Save me, or I perish. Take not Thy Holy Spirit away from me. Grant me the power, light, and guidance of Thy Spirit for Thy own Name's sake." Jesus Christ then sends His Spirit to anoint this soul with the oil of joy (Isaiah 61:3). The oil is delightful, for when God gives it to His child, his service to God becomes pleasant and Christ helps him bear his burdens. This oil lasts, too, for "the anointing which ye have received of him abideth in you, and ... ye shall abide in him" (1 John 2:27). Above all, this oil empowers, for it signifies freedom from bondage and fear and imparts strength for daily life and Christian service as well as for spiritual warfare against sin, self, Satan, and world. The oil of the Spirit sets all divine graces in motion, effectively producing power to endure, to pray, to serve, to worship, to live, to hear, and to engage in all that is required for true godliness.

Consider the power of God's anointing. By the Spirit, the prophets, priests, and kings of old served God and overcame their enemies. They were anointed to show that God Himself had appointed them to an office and would generously qualify that person for his work. Holy oil was poured upon a person in such great abundance that it ran down his beard and the skirts of his garments (Psalm 133:2). Without the authority and power of God's anointing, the offices of His servants would be impossible.

Those anointed ones in the Old Testament find their fulfillment in the anointing of the incarnate Son of God as Prophet, Priest, and King. In turn, His office-bearers and children are anointed as the fruit of Christ's work. Experiential union with Christ is a guarantee for God's people that they shall ever be anointed with fresh oil.

Though Christ's anointing was revealed in time at His miraculous conception (Luke 1:35), His baptism (Luke 3:22), and His ascension into glory (Psalm 45:7), He was never anointed literally with oil for an office, for this anointing took place from eternity. Old Testament anointing was only a shadow of Christ's eternal anointing; each found fulfillment in Him. However generously the Holy Spirit may have been given to other people, this gift was received in a limited measure. But Christ received the Spirit without measure (John 3:34), not from an earthly vial but from a heavenly fountain. The fullness of the Spirit came upon Him (John 1:33), and He declared, "The Spirit of the Lord God is upon me, because the Lord hath anointed me" (Isaiah 61:1).

Christ's anointing has two aspects: appointment and qualification. Christ's appointment took place in eternity when the Son of God was chosen by the Father to His threefold office. In turn, the Son agreed to represent the elect who were given to Him by the Father. His qualification, which respects His human nature only (for nothing can be added to the divine nature), took place in the fullness of time under the influence of God the Holy Spirit, as is evident from Luke 2:40, "And the child grew, and waxed strong in spirit, filled with wisdom; and the grace of God was upon Him."

Indeed, there never was a time when Jesus was not filled with the Holy Spirit. The Holy Spirit was with Christ the whole time of His earthly sojourn. The Spirit formed Christ's holy humanity as He "came upon" Mary and overshadowed her with "the power of the Highest"

(Luke 1:35). The Spirit came upon Christ at His baptism, "descending upon him like a dove" (Matthew 3:16; Mark 1:10). The Holy Spirit was an abiding presence in the Son of God (John 1:32–34). He filled Christ with power to overcome Satan's temptations, power to preach the gospel, and power to work miracles (Luke 4:1, 14, 18). The Spirit was the constant companion of the Servant of the Lord, for God had promised, "I will put my spirit upon him" (Isaiah 43:1; Matthew 12:18).

The sanctifying work of the Spirit is inseparable from the electing love of the Father and the atoning blood of Christ. Believers are "elect according to the foreknowledge of God the Father, through sanctification of the Spirit, unto obedience and sprinkling of the blood of Jesus Christ," says 1 Peter 1:2. Thus believers have a triple foundation. The Father reconciled them to Himself by free grace, the Son redeemed them by free grace, and the Spirit abides in them by free grace. This is a threefold cord that cannot be broken.

Some Christians fear that they lack the blessings of the anointed. Indeed, this is a gospel paradox. Christ is anointed Prophet to proclaim His wisdom to people who are empty of knowledge. Christ is anointed Priest to represent people who have given themselves over to sin, death, hell, and Satan. Christ is anointed King to protect a weak flock from all enemies. Christ cannot fail to anoint His people, for He has been anointed for them from eternity. Therefore, they may boast in Him, "Thou anointest my head with oil," exchanging "beauty for ashes, the oil of joy for mourning, and the garment of praise for the spirit of heaviness" (Isaiah 61:3).

Experiencing the Anointing of the Offices of Christ
Unfathomable though it may be, the anointed Christ graciously makes His people partakers of His anointing by means of His Spirit (1 John 2:27). Though there is only one Mediator between God and man (1 Timothy 2:5), believers share the privileges of Christ's anointed

offices. He is the Christ, and they are Christians. The Heidelberg Catechism says,

> *But why art thou called a Christian?*
>
> Because I am a member of Christ by faith, and thus am partaker of His anointing; that so I may confess His name [as a prophet], and present myself a living sacrifice of thankfulness to Him [as a priest]; and also that with a free and good conscience I may fight against sin and Satan in this life, and afterwards reign with Him eternally, over all creatures [as a king].[8]

Christ anoints His people and brings them into the marvelous light of His gospel, making them both beneficiaries and partakers of His work as Prophet, Priest, and King.

When the ointment of Christ's Spirit flows down upon His chosen ones, they become prophets who know and "confess His name" in personal, domestic, social, and ecclesiastical life. Despite persecution and trials, they sing like the imprisoned Paul and Silas, and exclaim, "I would not exchange my prison songs for the entire world, for Thou anointest my head with oil." They fulfill God's purpose when He says, "This people have I formed for myself: they shall shew forth my praise" (Isaiah 43:21). Christ says of them, "Whosoever therefore shall confess me before men, him will I confess also before my Father which is in heaven" (Matthew 10:32).

These prophets of Christ are often beset by fears that cause them to speak when they should be silent, and to be silent when they should speak—even to the point that they may deny the name of Jesus (Matthew 26:72). But they also know seasons of victorious grace when their talk and walk clearly declare that the name of Christ is greater and more worthy of praise than their own name. Then their confession shows they have been anointed from on high, and they discover that "the secret of the LORD is with them that fear him; and he will shew them his covenant" (Psalm 25:14).

The Redeemer who washes His flock in His priestly blood also anoints them to be priests by the renewing of the Holy Spirit. He gives them priestly grace to present themselves as "a living sacrifice of thankfulness to him," even "a living sacrifice, holy, acceptable unto God, which is your reasonable service" (Romans 12:1). They are not presented as sin offerings to make atonement for them (for Christ has accomplished divine reconciliation once and for all), but as sacrifices of humble gratitude. They desire to offer a triune God their broken hearts and contrite spirits through the sanctification of the Mediator's offering (Psalm 51:17). At the same time they cling to the skirts of His robes in hope of receiving more of His consecrated oil.

As priests, Christ's anointing transforms believers into warriors who wrestle in prayer for themselves, their families, the church, government, and even their enemies. God promised Abraham many years ago, "I will bless thee ... and thou shalt be a blessing" (Genesis 12:2). This promise is fulfilled in the priestly work of believers. Their High Priest, ordained "for ever after the order of Melchizedek" (Psalm 110:4), teaches them to sacrifice, pray, and bless as priests. He makes them a "holy priesthood, to offer up spiritual sacrifices, acceptable to God by Jesus Christ" (1 Peter 2:5). In Christ, they become both the priests who offer sacrifices of praise, and the sacrifices that are offered, reflecting Calvin's seal of a hand lifting up a heart, with the motto: "My heart I offer to thee, Lord, promptly and sincerely."[9]

Finally, Christ anoints His people to participate in His kingship. Christ makes believers partakers of His royal freedom ("a free and good conscience"), calls them into royal warfare ("I may fight against sin and Satan in this life"), and promises to share His royal reign with them ("and afterwards reign with Him eternally, over all creatures"). Partaking in Christ's anointing, they are and shall be to all eternity "more than conquerors through him" (Romans 8:37).

Highly blessed are those who bear fruit that springs forth from their anointing into Christ's threefold office! Highly blessed are they who, conscious of this divine anointing, are able to say, "Abba, Father" (Romans 8:15). They have great assurance, knowing with Paul that "He which stablisheth us with you in Christ, and hath anointed us, is God; who hath also sealed us, and given the earnest of the Spirit in our hearts" (2 Corinthians 1:21–22).

God's Spirit performs for the spiritual man what natural oil supplies for the natural man. As oil heals the bruised and wounded man (Isaiah 1:6; Luke 10:34), the Holy Spirit heals the wounded soul from backsliding, spiritual illness, and weakness. As oil was burned in the temple to provide light (Exodus 25:6), the Holy Spirit illuminates the understanding of His flock, enabling them to know and understand God's Word. As oil refreshes the face as a soothing lotion (Psalm 104:15), the Holy Spirit refreshes believers in the midst of warfare and trials. As oil was a sign of welcome to an invited guest (Luke 7:46), the Holy Spirit welcomes the child of God, inviting him to feast in God's house beneath His banner of eternal love. As physical oil makes a person beautiful and fragrant (Est. 2:12), the Holy Spirit beautifies God's people in the likeness of Christ and perfumes them with His fragrant righteousness. The Lord takes delight in His people when He sees them anointed with His spiritual graces, which are exemplified in the Bridegroom's "chief spices" (Song of Solomon 4:14). When sanctified by Jesus, they become more beautiful before God through the Spirit. By faith they can say with Paul, "We are unto God a sweet savour of Christ" (2 Corinthians 2:15).

In various ways, oil represents the offices, operations, gifts, and graces of the Holy Spirit as He works in His people. He is a precious Spirit. Love Him. Cherish His work. Cooperate with what He does in you by His Word. Also, seek more grace to live and walk worthy of Him who so greatly dignifies you (1 Thessalonians 2:12). "By patient continuance in well doing seek for glory and honour and immortality, eternal life" (Romans 2:7), for that is why you have been anointed.

Do you need to be anointed with the Spirit's oil? Have you experienced what God has promised to you in His Word? Ask yourself these questions:

- Have I been "sanctified by the Holy Ghost" (Romans 15:16)?
- Do I have "joy in the Holy Ghost" (Romans 14:17)?
- Am I "a temple of the Holy Ghost" (1 Corinthians 6:19)?
- Do I "keep by the Holy Ghost" the good things that God has entrusted to me (2 Timothy 1:14)?
- Do I "pray in the Holy Ghost" (Jude 20)?
- Can I live apart from the Holy Spirit, whose sacred influence is the power of salvation and all Christian living?

If the Holy Spirit is so essential for all Christians, how much more office-bearers in the church—ministers, elders, and deacons—need the anointing of Christ's Spirit! It is impossible to fulfill any office in the church apart from God's Spirit (Acts 6:3, 5; 2 Corinthians 3:5–6). Church officers, does this drive you to Christ, confessing, "Lord, I believe Thou hast appointed me to this office. Oh, anoint and qualify me with Thy Spirit. In myself, I do not know how to pray in private, much less in public. I do not know how to teach, direct, and exhort others. I do not know how to care for material possessions of the church, comfort the poor, evangelize the lost, or perform numerous other duties. Lord, intervene for me. Give me the measure of Thy Spirit that I need to perform duties for Thy honor and the good of Thy congregation."

It is a wonder that the Lord is pleased to use us. Our anointed Christ patiently bears with our limitations and infirmities and is always ready to give grace and wisdom to those who lack it.

The body of Christ must not be quick to criticize their God-given office-bearers, particularly not in the presence of their children. Yes, encourage, and if necessary correct your church officers in private, but do not rail on them or gossip about them. Bear in mind that they have not placed themselves in office but have been called to it and installed in it by God the Holy Spirit (Acts 13:2; 20:28). Respect them for the sake of their office, and pray for them for the sake of the church. Never look at office-bearers as the ideal representatives of Christ, for they are imperfect men; rather, consider Jesus Christ as the Chief Office-bearer to be the ideal of the living church.

Instead of criticizing your church's leaders, examine your own responsibilities in your family, at work, in the church, and for the nation. Fathers, are you prophetic teachers, priestly intercessors, and royal leaders in both precept and example within your own family? Can the world see that you are Spirit-anointed?

Do you feel the need for daily anointing to meet your daily responsibilities? Do you pray, "Lord, anoint my head, heart, and hands with Thy holy oil"? Whether you are an office-bearer or church member, parent or child, husband or wife, remember that we all need the Holy Spirit's anointing, which flows from Christ at the right hand of the Father. Open yourself to as much oil as you possibly can hold. Bring all your empty vessels to Him in your prayers, for He delights to fill the needy with good things (Luke 11:13). Know who you are, and what you are, by the grace of God:

> Thou, Lord, hast high exalted me with royal strength and dignity;
> With Thy anointing I am blest, Thy grace and favor on me rest;
> I thus exult o'er all my foes, o'er all that would my cause oppose.[10]

17

Divine Joy and Liberty

My cup runneth over.
—Psalm 23:5c

The Shepherd has spread a feast for His people. He offers them rich food even though they must eat in the presence of enemies who hate God, His righteousness, and His servants. He welcomes His people by anointing them as favored guests. David describes the abundance and joy of this divine feast by exclaiming, "My cup runneth over." The image is of a cup of wine kept so full by the liberal pouring of the host that it overflows. A guest need not fear that the wine for this joyous banquet will ever be depleted. He may eat and drink with total liberty.

The *cup* in Scripture—literally, a drinking bowl in David's time—often refers symbolically to one's lot in life, whether of suffering or of joy. The Lord gives to the wicked a cup full of fire, wrath, and desolation.[1] But He offers His people the cup of salvation and rejoicing.[2] Therefore, David speaks in Psalm 23 of the abundance of joy in God his Savior as a cup or drinking bowl to be sipped with confidence that God's love and grace will never fail.

Luther said, "David is thus speaking here of spiritual power, joy, and intoxication—the power of God (Romans 1:16); and a joy in the Holy Spirit, as St. Paul calls it (Romans 14:17); and a blessed intoxication, in which the people are filled not with wine, for that is debauchery, but with the Holy Spirit (Ephesians 5:18)."[3]

The Joy of Drinking from the Cup of Salvation

Drinking from the cup of salvation is a wonder for those who have tasted the acidic bitterness of their sins. We all seek happiness. In our search for happiness, we try to forget that our fall in Adam has plunged us into a state of condemnation and spiritual death. We have chosen bondage instead of liberty and sorrow instead of joy. We blindly refuse to believe that true happiness will never be found until Christ restores our relationship with the God who once walked with us in Paradise. When the Holy Spirit begins to work in the hearts of His own, He moves them to admit that God has righteously excluded mankind from perfect happiness due to sin. God could justly damn sinners and leave them in misery forever. But through His Spirit, He teaches sinners about their sin, the law, and the attributes of God. They realize that they can never find salvation in themselves but only in Jesus Christ. The same God of justice who shuts out sinners from Paradise also sent His Son to set them free. Drawn out of the burning desert to drink in Christ's oasis, they are astonished to taste the sweet and refreshing love of God. As faith revels in freedom, they can truly say, "My cup runneth over."

Freedom comes when God the Father takes away the cup of wrath and replaces it with the cup of salvation. Who can describe the stark contrast between justly deserved punishment and salvation by free grace? Expecting God's anger, the sinner meets God's love; deserving wrath, the sinner obtains mercy. Fearing the sentence of death, "Depart from me, ye cursed, into everlasting fire, prepared for the devil and his angels" (Matthew 25:41), the sinner hears the reassuring words, "This cup is the new testament in my blood, which is shed for you" (Luke 22:20). The believer then exclaims with David, "My cup runneth over."

God's overflowing cup of salvation results from the death of the Lord Jesus Christ. Christ graciously consented from all eternity to drink the cup of God's wrath. In this, Christ was the substitute for each son and daughter of Jehovah. Christ drank the cup of suffering for thirty-three years. He drank of the cup filled with the curse of the law merited by our sin. Our sins nailed His hands and feet to Golgotha's cross. He was given vinegar to drink before He fully emptied the cup of avenging, punishing wrath on our account. Christ did not leave any of this bitter wine for His children to drink, for as Romans 8:1 says: "There is therefore now no condemnation to them which are in Christ Jesus." Christ now places before us the cup of salvation, "the cup of blessing which we bless" as we celebrate Communion with Him (1 Corinthians 10:16).

Salvation fills the hearts of God's people with joy when they embrace this cup, remembering that Christ said, "This cup is the new testament in my blood: this do ye, as oft as ye drink it, in remembrance of me" (1 Corinthians 11:25). The cup and table of Psalm 23:5 are symbols that point to "the cup of the Lord" at "the Lord's table" to celebrate Christ's broken body and shed blood (1 Corinthians 10:21).[4] This new covenant cup overflows with reconciliation, salvation, grace, and glory now and forever. The benefits of the covenant of grace are summed up in the great covenant promise: "I will be their God, and they shall be my people" (Jeremiah 31:33). In that covenant, God in Christ becomes the property of sinners, and sinners become the property of God. This covenant also promises life for the dead, light for the blind, deliverance for captives, food for the hungry, water for the thirsty, riches for the poor, robes of righteousness for the naked, rest for the weary, relief for the oppressed, freedom for captives, strength for the weak, instruction for the ignorant, peace for the troubled, and consolation for the afflicted.

God's covenant promises stabilize a Christian by assuring him of happiness that he cannot find on his own. Anne Dutton (1692–1765), a Calvinist poet and prolific writer, wrote about her experience of conversion:

> As a newborn babe, I earnestly desired the sincere milk of the Word; and was often laid to the promise-breast. My dear Lord Jesus was very familiar to me then: and I could not bear to live without a sensible communion with him daily ….

> But alas, all this while, babe-like, I rather lived upon promises given in, than upon Christ in them. I knew not how to believe without sight. So long as God's love flowed into my soul, and my love flowed out to him again, under the attraction of his first love: just so long I could believe. But when the sweet sensation abated, my faith began to sink with it ….

> And while I went this way to work, I never attained settled assurance. No, the soul that enters into this rest, by faith, must have something more stable than fleeing frames [of mind] to lean on ….

> And as I was lamenting my case, that word was brought to my mind, "Rejoice in the Lord always: and again I say rejoice" (Philippians 4:4). But my heart straightway replied, "I have not enjoyed God tonight, and how can I rejoice?"… I was pointed hereto, as with a finger: "in the Lord," not in your frames. "In the Lord," not in what you enjoy from him, but in what you are in him ….

> And to this end, the Lord the Spirit went on to reveal Christ more and more to me, as the great foundation of my faith and joy. He showed me my everlasting standing in his person,

grace and righteousness: and gave me to see my security in his unchangeableness, under all the changes that passed over me .... Thus the Lord began to establish me, and to settle my faith upon its solid basis.[5]

When examining the foundation of their salvation, too many Christians ride the roller coaster of sensible experience that goes up and down, instead of building their joy on the Lord Himself. They must learn to rest in the promises of the covenant, for this is the essence of drinking the cup of salvation.

This covenant cup fills the conscience of sinners with peace and their souls with refreshment. Drinking from this cup confirms our faith in the atoning death of Christ and reminds us that all our sins are forgiven for His sake, and all our remaining infirmities are covered by His perfect righteousness. In communion with the Lord of life, believers are blessed with wisdom, knowledge, righteousness, truth, and obedience. They are also given direction, security, help, comfort, patience, courage, contentment, meekness, and heavenly-mindedness.

When David wrote, "my cup *runneth over*," he was describing the abundance of God's blessing.[6] The Hebrew word translated "runneth over" means to be saturated or thoroughly filled to or over the very brim (Isaiah 55:10; Jeremiah 31:14). In a hot, arid land, the Lord promised His people, "Thou shalt be like a watered garden, and like a spring of water, whose waters fail not" (Isaiah 58:11; cf. Jeremiah 31:12). The metaphor of an overflowing cup speaks of water in unending supply, producing satisfaction and joy: "They shall be abundantly satisfied with the fatness of thy house; and thou shalt make them drink of the river of thy pleasures. For with thee is the fountain of life" (Psalm 36:8-9a). The divine Host will see to it that His honored guests have more than enough to satisfy their thirsting souls.

Above all, this joyous provision for God's children is the Lord Himself. David wrote, "The LORD is the portion of my inheritance and of my cup" (Psalm 16:5). He is *El Shaddai*, God Almighty, all sufficient, alone sufficient, and always sufficient, and believers walk before His face (Genesis 17:1). The believer can then exclaim, "How can I sink? God is my helper! How can I be eternally lost? God is my guide and my salvation! How can I be miserable? God is my joy!"

Because Christ was forsaken by God for our sins (Matthew 27:46), God is our God forever in Christ. He gives Himself to us as an everlasting, unchanging portion. Faith can make this claim, "Assuredly all of God is mine—all His fullness, all His attributes, all His love, all of Himself, for He has said, 'I am your God.'" Thus faith drinks from the endless ocean of God's grace.

What cup can hold your God, believer? If your soul were enlarged and made as wide as heaven, you could not contain the infinite God. The Father has reserved for you an exalted Christ to be your portion eternally. But how will you ever drink in all of Him? Behold His matchless godhead, His perfect manhood, His power, wisdom, beauty, and grace! Examine His works, His sinless life, His death, His triumph over hell and the grave, and the splendors of His second coming! Only by a miracle of grace can this consuming Fire dwell in the bush and not consume it. We would die if God showed us too much of His love today. The glory that God has prepared for His own is too great for our bodies and souls to contain.

The Liberty and Enlargement Experienced with an Overflowing Cup

The overflowing cup of the Lord is given to His people with freedom to enjoy. They need not feel like guests at the table of a stingy man who resents every sip taken from his supplies (Proverbs 23:6–7). Rather, they are free to drink abundantly, knowing there is always more. They are children of God so they may taste whatever the Father provides as they sit at the table with their Elder Brother, Jesus Christ, and the Spirit, who urges, "Eat, O friends; drink, yea drink abundantly, O beloved"

(Song of Solomon 5:1). Their Host delights to give, and it glorifies Him that they eat so much and drink so deeply, entirely at His expense.

Drinking deeply of the cup frees the soul from fears of wrath, condemnation, alienation, bondage, and death and brings it into a conscious state of grace, justification, friendship, and life with God (Romans 8:1-3, 15). It is a foretaste of eternal glory, which Paul calls "the glorious liberty of the sons of God" (Romans 8:21).

This overflowing cup of salvation causes hearts to overflow as well. Souls that were once constricted by the narrowness of self-love now expand in grace. The Lord changes them from black holes that absorb whatever they can and yet are never filled into blazing suns that radiate light and warmth to all around them. Instead of deserts that dehydrate whoever travels through them, they become refreshing streams of living water. Their souls overflow with so much grace that they bear much fruit.

This enlarged soul also overflows with *gospel humility*. Never is a soul as humble as when it is filled with the goodness of God's salvation. Nothing but the love of the gospel can transform a hard heart into a tender heart of true humility. As Joseph Hart wrote,

Law and terrors do but harden,
All the while they work alone;
But a sense of blood-bought pardon
Soon dissolves a heart of stone.[7]

When the Spirit reveals the gospel to a soul, God's love shines within. The soul then receives freedom to look away from itself to Christ. With eyes of faith, the believer beholds Christ who was given for him so that His precious names, offices, states, natures, and benefits overflow within him as he confesses, "He is mine, and I am His." The redeemed sinner rejoices that he is reconciled to God and restored to His family.

Then, child of God, you will find in Christ a blessed counterpart to yourself, which will keep you humble. Vile, weak, and defenseless in yourself, you will receive from Him wisdom, strength, righteousness, fullness of supply, and almighty protection. Dissatisfied as you are in yourself, you will learn that your only cause for rejoicing is in Christ as *Jehovah Tsidkenu*, "the LORD our righteousness" (Jeremiah 23:6).

You will be filled with higher thoughts of His excellence and deeper thoughts of your own failure. The knowledge of Christ's unmerited love combined with His wondrous condescension and self-sacrifice will inspire you as you despise yourself for your sins. The more Christ increases, the more you will decrease. You will confess with the centurion, "Lord, I am not worthy that thou shouldest come under my roof" (Matthew 8:8). You may also say like Simon Peter, "Depart from me; for I am a sinful man, O Lord" (Luke 5:8). Yet Christ is willing to abide forever with us.

Soul enlargement also overflows with *gospel peace.* "Thou wilt keep him in perfect peace, whose mind is stayed on thee: because he trusteth in thee," says Isaiah 26:3. Though a Christian cannot lose peace with God because it is grounded in Christ (Romans 5:1), he can experience variations in that peace (Philippians 4:7; Colossians 3:15). Samuel Bolton said there are different aspects to our experience of divine peace, but all depend upon walking with the Lord. He wrote, "There is a peace which flows from the soul's communion and converse with God in duty. There is peace as well as sweetness in every part of holiness." He also said, "There is a peace which flows from the sense and knowledge of God's grace implanted in the soul. When a man is able to trace out the work of grace in his soul, there must needs be peace and comfort in it." The smallest portion of spiritual peace "is worth a world."[8]

True peace comes from Jesus Christ, who decrees peace and merits peace. He is the peacemaker and peacekeeper of His own. He persuades His chosen ones that no real peace may be found outside of Him. "For there is one God, and one Mediator between God and men, the man

Christ Jesus" (1 Timothy 2:5). When one exercises faith in the Prince of peace, the God of hope fills the heart "with all joy and peace" (Romans 15:13). Sometimes a believer's soul is like the Sea of Galilee troubled by tossing waves and blowing winds. But when Jesus speaks in the power of His precious blood, saying, "Peace, be still," calmness fills the soul.

When a believer experiences the enlargement of his soul with humility and hope, he also overflows with *gospel gratitude*. Salvation's overflowing cup causes the redeemed sinner to return all blessings to the Lord. He asks, "What shall I render unto the LORD for all his benefits toward me?" (Psalm 116:12). The sinner meditates on the vastness of divine grace and credits all its blessings to God, saying in thanks, "Bless the LORD, O my soul, and forget not all his benefits: who forgiveth all thine iniquities; who healeth all thy diseases; who redeemeth thy life from destruction; who crowneth thee with lovingkindness and tender mercies; who satisfieth thy mouth with good things; so that thy youth is renewed like the eagle's" (Psalm 103:2-5).

Christ's cup overflows, "for in him dwelleth all the fulness of the Godhead bodily, and ye are complete in him" (Colossians 2:9-10). The grace provided by your Savior is immeasurable. Seek therefore, to drink more freely from the Lord's overflowing cup until you may confess with David, "My cup runneth over."

The Overflow of the Cup of Salvation into Obedient Service

Spiritual satisfaction produces spiritual service. It prompts the believer to say, "O LORD, truly I am thy servant; I am thy servant, and the son of thine handmaid: thou hast loosed my bonds" (Psalm 116:12, 16). The overflowing cup prompts the believer to live for Christ in doing God's will. The humble Christian then gladly sings:

I am, O Lord, Thy servant, bound yet free,
Thy handmaid's son, whose shackles Thou has broken;

Redeemed by grace, I'll render as a token
Of gratitude my constant praise to Thee.[9]

Salvation's cup does not offer the freedom to sin. Rather, it yields the rich fruit of gospel obedience. Not out of legality, but out of gratitude, the soul returns to the law to embrace its principles as a guiding rule for life. Psalm 119:32 says, "I will run in the way of thy commandments, when thou shalt enlarge my heart." Thus Christian liberty avoids falling into the swamp of antinomianism on one side, as well as falling off the cliff of legalism on the other.

Motivation is everything in Christian service. The hypocrite is possessed by the spirit of legalism and self-righteousness. The child of God is possessed by the Spirit of grace and a heart of thanks. How can you tell the difference? Samuel Bolton (1606–1654) gives the following guidelines:

- The principle that moves one spirit to duty is slavish, the other childlike.

- The man who does these things as his delight, while the other does them as a burden.

- One man does his duty from the conviction of conscience [guilt], the other from the necessity of his nature [grace].

- One man looks for satisfaction in the performance of the duty, the other does it as a means of communion with God, seeing God, and enjoying God.

- One man performs duty to live by it …. But the believer performs duty to live by Christ alone.[10]

Is it evident that freedom from sin and redemption prompts you to obediently serve your God? Does this service flow from salvation's liberating cup? Is your life a testimony that Christ redeems His flock from slavery so they may serve the living God? Has He broken your bonds of subjection to other lords, so that you might serve Him whose yoke is easy and whose burden is light (Matthew 11:30)?

The child of God is obligated to serve God on the basis of His worthiness, goodness, authority, and commandments. However, the believer obeys not by knowledge of the law, but by union with Christ, in whom he is made a new creature with a new law written upon his heart. He is moved to obey God by the secret operations of God's irresistible Spirit. Therefore, Paul could write to the church in Philippi, "As ye have always obeyed ... work out your own salvation with fear and trembling. For it is God which worketh in you both to will and to do of his good pleasure" (Philippians 2:12–13). Have you experienced that?

If so, seek the grace to abide in it. As Peter says, live "as free, and not using your liberty for a cloak of maliciousness, but as the servants of God" (1 Peter 2:16). Your freedom has been dearly bought, mercifully revealed, freely bestowed, and fully conveyed to you by the Spirit of Christ. Honor the Spirit, therefore, by praying for grace to drink daily from Christ's overflowing cup.

Keep your cup close to the fountain of the Lord's ever-bubbling spring. Refuse to turn from living waters to broken cisterns of man's making. If you need to drink much of the Lord's cup then seek grace to meditate much on God as Father, Son, and Holy Spirit. John Stevenson, a gifted nineteenth-century preacher, wrote,

> Meditate on the perfect nature, and the glorious majesty, of thy Almighty Father, who filleth heaven and earth with his presence! His holiness underived, unsullied, and incorruptible. His wisdom unsearchable and omniscient. His power unlimited and irresistible. His truth unerring. His faithfulness unfailing. His justice impartial. His goodness universal. His long-suffering unwearied. His mercy everlasting. His love unequalled in its tenderness, and surpassing knowledge in its greatness .... Think

of him as thy Creator, thy Preserver, thy Benefactor, thy Friend, thy Father! ...

Meditate on God the Son condescending for thy salvation to become thy Brother—bone of thy bone, flesh of thy flesh—like unto thee in all things, sin only excepted .... Think of him as thy Prophet, teaching and enlightening thy soul—as thy Priest, atoning for thy sins, redeeming thy person, sympathizing with thy sorrows, and interceding for thy shortcomings—as thy King, reigning over thee in love, and invested with all power in heaven and on earth; as hereafter to appear upon his glorious throne, and reign in universal righteousness.

Meditate on God the Holy Ghost .... Is he not the Author of the new birth, the Giver of spiritual life, the Quickener of the dead, the Sustainer of the living, the Teacher of the ignorant, the Baptizer of the elect, and the Intercessor in the saints? Is he not called the Spirit of life and love, of truth and judgment, of prophecy and promise, of wisdom and revelation, of counsel and might, of faith and holiness, of grace and of supplications, of glory and of God?[11]

Surely, the triune God is great enough to fill the cup of our meditations for all eternity.

Furthermore, empty your soul of all that is outside of God and Christ. Especially strive to empty yourself of your old nature. If God were to shed His love upon many of us, we would not have room enough to receive it, for we are filled to the brim with ourselves. God's gifts must drive us to the Giver. Do not base your security on past experiences or present graces. Abide in Christ, for "as the branch cannot bear fruit of itself, except it abide in the vine; no more can ye," Christ taught, "except ye abide in me" (John 15:4).

Finally, to keep your cup overflowing, share with others what you have received. Though spiritual life cannot be given from one to another, God's child may direct the world to the Fountain of life. Though not a preacher, he may speak to family and friends of the fullness of the Most High that dwells in Christ. He may strive to comfort the suffering and lift up those that are bowed down. His prayer will be to share the cup of salvation with as many as he can so that this song will become theirs:

> May he who taught the morning stars to sing
> Aye keep my chalice cool, pure, and sweet,
> And grant me so with loving hand to bring
> Refreshment to His weary ones—to meet
> Their thirst with water from God's music-spring;
> And, bearing thus, to pour it at His feet.[12]

John Trapp (1601–1669) said, "Those that have this happiness must carry their cup upright and see that it overflow into their poor brethren's emptier vessels."[13] God pours his cup to overflowing for us so that we might pour out living water to others.

Part 6

Psalm 23:6
*"Surely goodness and mercy shall follow me all the days of my life:
and I will dwell in the house of the LORD for ever."*

18

God's Gracious Pursuit

Surely goodness and mercy shall follow me all the days of my life.
—Psalm 23:6a

Though only six verses long, Psalm 23 is a key that unlocks vast treasures of the Shepherd-Lord for His people. After promising that His sheep shall lack nothing, the psalm says the Shepherd lavishes the additional blessings of goodness and mercy upon His sheep.

David rejoices in the promise that the Shepherd-Lord will give His sheep divine rest and refreshment. The Lord provides restoration for the diseased, cast down, and wandering sheep. He uncovers their sin and gives them His divine righteousness in justification, sanctification, and preservation. He walks beside them through darkness and disease for their spiritual growth and encouragement. As they experience His companionship, they find great comfort, for He defends them fiercely and leads them tenderly.

David also rejoices that his Shepherd is a gracious Host. He prepares a rich banquet to feed His people, even though they must dine in the sight of their enemies. He welcomes them as honored guests at His table, anointing them with His Spirit. He allows them to drink from the cup of His salvation with joy and liberty.

In the sixth verse of the psalm, David says the Shepherd leads His sheep every step of the way until they are home. Then, as Host, He welcomes them into His home as members of His household forever. It is no accident that the special divine name, "the LORD," appears in the first and last verses of the psalm, for it reveals not just what the Shepherd does, but also who He is. As Christ Himself says, "I am Alpha and Omega, the beginning and the end" (Revelation 21:6).

Divine Grace Granting Certainty

As a sheep of the Lord's beloved flock, David confesses, "Surely goodness and mercy shall follow me all the days of my life." His way is sure, for the Good Shepherd leads His flock. His way is safe, for the Shepherd defends His sheep. His way is sweet, for the Shepherd feeds those in His care. His prospects are bright, for he has the Shepherd's promises.

Despite facing lions and bears as a young shepherd, years of persecution from Saul, and his tragic transgression with Bathsheba which tore his family and kingdom apart, David could look to the future with hope. His life was stained with sin and pierced with sorrows, but God's ways are soaked with grace. Therefore, David was sure that his Shepherd would save and keep him to the end.

David's words express confidence and certainty in the Lord. His faith conquered doubt as he fixed his eyes on the sovereign love and almighty power of God. After all he had received from the Lord, David felt that it would be presumptuous and vile to doubt the Lord's ability or willingness to supply all his needs to the end of his life.

In this, David does not lose sight of his own unworthiness. He does not boast in himself but in God's grace. He is persuaded that the Lord will bless him "for his name's sake"—*soli Deo gloria*. Because of the gracious nature of God's love, David's confidence is not in the integrity of his own heart but in the unchangeableness of his God. David does not say that he will never falter in faith or fail in obedience, but he is convinced that the loving-kindness of the Lord will never be removed from him.

His expectations do not refer to temporal happiness, earthly grandeur, or the glory of Israel's royal crown. They refer to spiritual happiness, eternal riches, and a heavenly kingdom. By grace, this was David's hope in life and death. That hope is evident in some of his last recorded words, "Although my house be not so with God; yet he hath made with me an everlasting covenant, ordered in all things, and sure: for this is all my salvation, and all my desire, although he make it [my house] not to grow" (2 Samuel 23:5). David could forgo temporal blessings but could not relax his grip on God's promises.

David trusted in a covenant-keeping God for spiritual and eternal blessings, and he was not disappointed. The Father's love and faithfulness, the Mediator's atoning blood and priestly intercession, and the Spirit's life and power were the foundation on which David grounded his *surely*. Indeed, God's covenant was more than his desire; it was also his experience. David had been personally led by the Redeemer to the streams of God's grace. He had drunk of the Father's reconciling love, the Son's atoning righteousness, and the Spirit's purifying power.

The security of all believers is grounded in the triune God. He has set His seal on Christ's promise, "And I give unto them eternal life; and they shall never perish, neither shall any man pluck them out of my hand. My Father, which gave them me, is greater than all; and no man is able to pluck them out of my Father's hand" (John 10:28–29). God is in His almighty power, steadfast love, abiding faithfulness, and infinite wisdom makes it impossible for one member of the redeemed flock to perish. Christ has committed Himself to save each person chosen and given to Him by the Father. The Spirit has sealed them to the day of redemption, even though they grieve Him at times (Ephesians 1:13–14; 4:30).

If the Good Shepherd failed to bring His children through all temptations and dangers to eternal glory, then He would lose more than His children. Charles Spurgeon told about a Scottish minister who was visiting an old saint. She was dying, but she declared her confidence that her Savior would never let her perish eternally. The minister asked, "Suppose He did not keep his promise and you got lost?"

She responded, "He would be a greater loser than I."

"Why?" asked the pastor.

She replied, "It is true that I would lose my soul, but God would lose His honor and His glory if this was not true."[1]

The glory of God's name is the foundation of an elect sinner's salvation, for upon this foundation rests His covenant and eternal love. As Scripture testifies: "For the LORD will not forsake his people for his great name's sake" (1 Samuel 12:22). And, "For thy name's sake, O LORD, pardon mine iniquity; for it is great" (Psalm 25:11).

How blessed is the assurance that God completes what He begins in saving the elect. He has pledged to fulfill exceeding great and precious promises for them. The united testimony of all His saints is that God never forsakes the work of His hands. If He was determined to set His love on us from eternity, He will not forget us in time.

We must not only believe the doctrine of the perseverance of the saints, but we must also love this doctrine. It reveals the dazzling beauty of Jesus Christ who "is able also to save them to the uttermost that come unto God by him, seeing he ever liveth to make intercession for them" (Hebrews 7:25). As surely as He died, Christ lives to intercede for His elect at God's right hand. Therefore nothing can defeat God's purpose to make them like Christ (Romans 8:29–34). Believers, our Shepherd in heaven knows how to plead for us better than weak Moses did for the Israelites, for His uplifted hands never grow weary (Exodus 17:8–13). His words are like music in our ears, "I have prayed for thee, that thy faith fail not" (Luke 22:32). Sheep of Christ's pasture, this is the secret of your preservation, perseverance, and victory over sin and death. In Christ, your weakness triumphs over Satan's strength. We will not only be conquerors, but *surely* "*more* than conquerors through him that loved us" (Romans 8:37).

Divine Grace Guarding with Goodness and Mercy

David also says, "Surely goodness and mercy shall follow me all the days of my life." It is as if he said, "Since my salvation is rooted in God's name and covenant, two heavenly escorts will follow me through life: His goodness and His mercy." God in His glorious attributes of goodness and mercy follows us, protecting us all the way home. Kenneth Bailey wrote of a shepherd's provision, "On the way home at the end of the day, the shepherd knows that there is the danger of a wolf or some other predator following the returning herd in hope that a young or injured sheep might lag behind and become easy prey." Therefore, the shepherd's assistant, or his dog, or the shepherd himself will follow in the rear.[2]

To properly understand the concepts of goodness and mercy, we must view them in three different aspects: (1) a pure, essential sense, as they are found in God, who is goodness and mercy; (2) a general, common sense, as God shows common goodness and mercy to all His creation, including man; and (3) a special, saving sense, in which God reveals His saving goodness and mercy to His elect flock.

First, God is *goodness* (Mark 10:18). To be good is to be kind or benevolent. As Psalm 145: 9 says, "The LORD is good to all: and his tender mercies are over all his works." His goodness is absolute. He is not good as compared to bad. He is essentially, infinitely, and purely good. He is completely and independently good. He does not need to increase his goodness or take it from anything outside of Himself. His goodness is self-sufficient. God is the total sum of all goodness. His love is the overflow of His goodness in giving to others. He delights in the goodness that He sees in His sheep which comes from Himself.

The Lord's goodness makes all His works and words good. Psalm 119:68 says, "Thou art good, and doest good; teach me thy statutes." Thomas Manton (1620–1677) wrote,

> He is ... originally good, *autagathos*, good of himself, which nothing else is; for all creatures are good only by participation and communication from God. He is essentially good; not only good, but goodness itself; the creature's good is a superadded quality, in God it is his essence. He is infinitely good; the creature's good is but a drop, but in God there is an infinite ocean or gathering together of goodness. He cannot be better, he is *summum bonum*— the chiefest good; other things are good in subordination to him, and according to that use and proportion they bear to him .... Beyond God there is nothing to be sought or aimed at; if we enjoy him we enjoy all good to make us completely happy. He is eternally and immutably good, for he cannot be less good than he is; as there can be no addition made to him, so no subtraction, or aught [anything] from him.[3]

God is also *merciful*. The Hebrew word for mercy is also translated "goodness" (Exodus 34:6) or "lovingkindness" (Psalm 17:7), which means loyal or faithful love. God's love is displayed throughout the universe and throughout history (Psalm 136). It refers particularly to God's love for those in covenant with Him. Ad Deuteronomy 7:9 says, "Know therefore that the LORD thy God, he is God, the faithful God, which keepeth covenant and mercy with them that love him and keep his commandments to a thousand generations."[4] His mercy is great (1 Kings 3:6), abundant (Psalm 86:5), and everlasting for His covenant people (Psalm 103:17). Goodness and mercy are inseparable (Psalm 136:1), but there is a difference. Generally speaking, goodness is for all the creatures of God's hand, regardless of their merit, while mercy is shown to those in need, who cannot help themselves, and who do not deserve it.

Thus, "mercy" in this text highlights God's kindness to those in need. Anyone who has gone to prison for his crimes and been released, or has had some life-threatening disease and been healed, or has faced a raging storm at sea and been saved, has experienced God's mercy (Psalm 107). Yet mercy is not merely a response from God but an attribute of His very nature. When John Duncan was told that a young man said there was no mercy in God from everlasting to everlasting, for there cannot be mercy without misery, his Hebrew professor replied, "God is unchangeable; mercy is an attribute of God. The man is confounding mercy with the exercise of mercy. There could not be the exercise of mercy till there was misery; but God was always a merciful God. You might as well say there could not be justice in God till there were creatures towards whom to exercise punitive justice."[5] Mercy is the essence of who God is.

Second, God reveals His *common goodness and mercy* to all His creatures, even the impenitent (Psalms 33:5; 136:25; 145:15–16). As Psalm 145:9 says, "The Lord is good to all: and His tender mercies are over all His works." This goodness and mercy, however, do not save a sinner from sin and misery. They will only add to a sinner's condemnation if the Lord does not pursue the sinner with saving goodness to change the soul into a vessel of mercy (Romans 9:23).

Third, there is God's *saving goodness and mercy*. That is what David had in mind when He says they will pursue him all his life until he enters the courts of the Lord in heaven. The psalmist speaks of these blessings as if they were two guardian angels commissioned to attend him on his lifelong journey. The name of one is Goodness; the other, Mercy. David could say, "In prosperity and adversity, health and sickness, life and death, black days and bright days, days of fasting and days of feasting, goodness and mercy shall follow me until my last breath."

Thomas Watson wrote that God's mercy displays His unique glory and beauty in the following ways:

- It is the great design of the Scripture to represent God as merciful. This is a loadstone [magnet] to draw sinners to him.

- Mercy is his darling attribute, which he most delights in (Micah 7:18).

- The bee most naturally gives honey, it stings only when it is provoked; so God does not punish till he can bear sin no longer.

- Mercy sweetens all God's other attributes.

- To have health is a mercy, but to have Christ and salvation is a greater mercy; it is like the diamond in the ring.[6]

It may seem too presumptuous for a Christian to claim that goodness and mercy will always follow him. You might ask, "How can I say that when I feel hounded and pursued by affliction, sin, persecution, disease, trouble, or death?"

God's idea of goodness is vastly different from ours. We think of goodness as the fulfillment of our earthly desires, but we really do not know what is good for us. God's idea of goodness embraces all that glorifies Him in the salvation of His elect. His promise "that all things work together for good to them that love God, to them who are the called according to his purpose," is qualified by His definition of goodness: "For whom he did foreknow, he also did predestinate to be conformed to the image of his Son, that he might be the firstborn among many brethren" (Romans 8:28–29). To make us like His Son, God must often enrich us by impoverishing us and exalt us by humbling us. William Cowper captured this paradox when he wrote,

God moves in a mysterious way,
His wonders to perform.

He plants his footsteps in the sea
And rides upon the storm.

Deep in unfathomable mines
Of never-failing skill
He treasures up his bright designs
And works his sovereign will.[7]

Though God's goodness is often wrapped in mystery, the believer can confess that he is rich in the blessings of grace. The meeting of the estranged brothers Esau and Jacob illustrates this point (Genesis 33). Esau had prospered in accumulating earthly possessions during the years of separation from his brother. That induced him to respond to Jacob's generous gifts with the confession, "I have enough, my brother; keep that thou hast unto thyself" (Genesis 33:9). What Esau didn't know, however, was that Jacob had also prospered, which caused Jacob to respond, "Take, I pray thee, my blessing that is brought to thee; because God hath dealt graciously with me, and because I have enough" (Genesis 33:11).

Though Esau and Jacob both said they had enough, their confessions were dramatically different. Esau attributed his success to himself, "*I* have enough." Jacob attributed success to the Lord. He said he had prospered "because God hath dealt graciously with me." Therefore, it is not surprising that the Holy Spirit uses two distinct words in the Hebrew language which are here translated "enough." Esau's "enough" signifies plenty, abundance, and sufficiency, while Jacob's "enough" literally means "everything."

Thus Esau could say, "Jacob, behold all my possessions and my great abundance. I have plenty. I have all I will ever need in this temporal life." But Jacob could say, "Esau, I have everything, for I have the wealth of a triune God at my disposal. I have God's goodness and mercy; I have God Himself. I have everything I need for soul and body, for time and eternity."

By claiming goodness and mercy, Jacob included himself in the rich confession of Paul to the Corinthians: "For all things are yours; whether Paul, or Apollos, or Cephas, or the world, or life, or death, or things present, or things to come; all are yours; and ye are Christ's; and Christ is God's" (1 Corinthians 3:21–23).

Do you have Esau's "enough" or Jacob's "everything?" Can you claim the blessing of the psalmist, "Happy is he that hath the God of Jacob for his help, whose hope is in the LORD his God" (Psalm 146:5)? To possess the goodness and mercy of God is to have everything even if we own nothing. To live without God is to have nothing even if we own everything. With God we are rich, though poor; without God we are poor, though rich.

Divine Grace Pursuing God's People

"Surely goodness and mercy shall follow me all the days of my life," David says. Literally, the Hebrew word for "follow" means to hunt, pursue, or chase. In other words, "Goodness and mercy will refuse to leave me alone; they will accompany me, follow behind me, surround me, guard me, and protect me. They will be my lifelong escorts."

David is blessed by the full spectrum of God's grace. As a believer he profoundly benefits from special or saving grace, both in this life and for the life to come. Ultimately, he does not focus on God's goodness that is common to all but on the saving mercies of God that are promised only to the sheep of God (Isaiah 55:3).

Because of these saving mercies, believers can also rejoice that God's lovingkindness will pursue them to the end of their earthly pilgrimage. Fear and unbelief will not destroy that assurance. The true sheep of God may say of God's pursuing grace:

> Still with unhurrying chase,
> And unperturbed pace,

Deliberate speed, majestic instancy,
Surely, goodness and mercy shall follow me.[8]

Goodness and mercy followed David in confronting the giant
Goliath, the persecution of Saul, the mocking of Michal, the betrayal
of Ahithophel, the cursing of Shimei, the rebellion of Absalom, and
the machinations of Adonijah. Through all these trials, God refused
to let David utterly fall. In the same way, God's goodness and mercy
will pursue every sheep of the Lord, preserving them in a state of grace
so they never fall away. They will never lose the seed of regeneration
or the jewels of faith, hope, and love.

Just as sovereign love led Christ to pay the ransom for our sin, so
the sovereign power of Christ keeps His flock from destruction. As
our Savior, He is "able to keep you from falling, and to present you
faultless before the presence of his glory with exceeding joy" (Jude 24).
While the Lord has given us a new nature, we do not have the power in
ourselves to persevere. That is granted to us by the indwelling presence
and power of the Spirit of Christ. The branch cannot live severed from
the vine, nor can a limb survive apart from the body. Likewise, true
believers are preserved only in Christ.

Believer, don't you owe all thanks to God for this grace? Wasn't
it grace that first taught you that you were without God, Christ, or
hope in the world? Wasn't it grace that stopped you from drinking in
iniquity as an ox drinks in water? Wasn't it grace that revealed Jesus
Christ to your hell-bound soul, as the sweet Savior? Wasn't it grace
that would not let you rest until you had experienced that "Christ is
mine, and I am His"? Isn't it grace that still moves you to beg for more
access to the throne of God, for more strength to fight the daily battles
of faith, and for increasing knowledge of God's goodness and mercy?

Do not think that God has ceased pursuing you because you are
now His. He will not rest until He has all your heart, your soul, your
mind, and your strength. His goodness and mercy will pursue you

in all your backsliding, coldness in prayer, and neglect of the means of grace dispensed in the church. His voice will speak to you through every Bible reading, every sermon, and every good word of counsel (or rebuke) from a friend. His hands will reach out to you in every mercy, every blessing, and every sin-chastening trial. His heart will continue to pursue you until you enter into His glory and see His face.

What should amaze us is that God pursues us in *grace*. The word *follow* in Psalm 23:6 commonly means to pursue in order to attack, persecute, and destroy. We might expect such punishment if we discovered that God was pursuing us. We might think He has come to hunt us down as criminals, for we have broken His laws. But no, the Lord seeks us not to punish us as we deserve but to show us "the exceeding riches of his grace in his kindness toward us through Christ Jesus" (Ephesians 2:7). He pursues us in gracious love.

If you have received grace from God, then mercy and goodness will surely follow you until your dying breath. You have been brought into a state of grace, and grace will pursue you wherever you go. Grace will make you reign with Jesus Christ. Blessed by His goodness and kept by His mercy, you may sing:

> Lord, though I walk 'mid troubles sore,
> Thou wilt restore my faltering spirit;
> Though angry foes my soul alarm,
> Thy mighty arm will save and cheer it.
> Yea, Thou wilt finish perfectly
> What Thou for me hast undertaken;
> May not Thy works, in mercy wrought
> E'er come to naught or be forsaken.[9]

You may also say with Philip Doddridge:

> Grace first contriv'd a way
> To save rebellious man,

And all the steps that grace display;
Which drew the wondrous plan.

Grace taught my wandering feet
To tread the heavenly road,
And new supplies each hour I meet,
While pressing on to God.

Grace all the work shall crown,
Through everlasting days;
It lays in heaven the topmost stone,
And well deserves the praise.

19

At Home with the Shepherd

And I will dwell in the house of the LORD for ever.
—Psalm 23:6b

Though believers experience the presence of their Shepherd throughout this life, they know they are not yet home. They are pilgrims traveling through a strange land, and their hearts long for a heavenly country, where their heavenly Shepherd dwells. While they live by God's promises and experience His grace in this life, they live by faith, not by sight, and hope for what they have not yet received. They identify with Abraham and the other patriarchs, of whom is said, "These all died in faith, not having received the promises, but having seen them afar off, and were persuaded of them, and embraced them, and confessed that they were strangers and pilgrims on the earth" (Hebrews 11:13). Like Christian in John Bunyan's *Pilgrim's Progress*, they are still traveling the narrow road to the Celestial City.

David concludes his magnificent psalm with his eyes on the future: "And I will dwell in the house of the LORD for ever." This moving conclusion portrays the return of the flock to the safety and pleasures of the fold in their true home. In the imagery of the Host and His guests, these too-good-to-be-true words speak of being welcomed and received into the family home. "The house of the LORD" is a biblical expression intimating the place where God dwells with His people, whether in the tabernacle, the temple, the church, or ultimately in heaven.[1]

In the house of the Lord the godly yearn to live in God's presence and see His glory. David says in Psalm 27:4, "One thing have I desired of the LORD, that will I seek after; that I may dwell in the house of the LORD all the days of my life, to behold the beauty of the LORD, and to enquire in his temple." Christ tapped into this hope of believers when He said, "In my Father's house are many mansions: if it were not so, I would have told you. I go to prepare a place for you. And if I go and prepare a place for you, I will come again, and receive you unto myself; that where I am, there ye may be also" (John 14:2–3). This hope will be fulfilled when Christ's petition is granted, "Father, I will that they also, whom thou hast given me, be with me where I am; that they may behold my glory" (John 17:24a).

Hoping to Dwell in the House of the Lord

David loved the house of the Lord on earth. In David's early days the tabernacle was at Nob (1 Samuel 21:1), while the ark was at Kirjath-jearim (1 Samuel 7:1–2; 1 Chronicles 13:5–6). Since the royal palace of Saul at Gibeah was within a few hours' journey of both places, David could frequently attend the holy services of the tabernacle at Nob more than when he was living in his father's house at Bethlehem.

David was never disappointed by going to God's house. He knew that the cloud of God's presence covered the tabernacle, and that the brightness of His glory shone within the sanctuary. He went with the multitude "to the house of God, with voice of joy and praise, with a multitude that kept holyday" (Psalm 42:4). He had seen God's power and glory in the sanctuary (Psalm 63:2), and confessed, "LORD, I have loved the habitation of thy house, and the place where thine honour dwelleth" (Psalm 26:8). From personal experience, he knew that God's dealings with His people were closely connected with "the house of the Lord"; therefore, David desired to dwell there forever.

The revelation of the glory of God and communion with God moved David to vow that he would never depart from the house of God. Every aspect of worship in the tabernacle represented the Messiah to come. When David saw a lamb slain for a burnt offering, he thought of the coming Messiah who would be led "as a lamb to the slaughter" (Isaiah 53:7). In bloody sacrifices, David saw the necessity of Christ to offer up His blood once and for all for sinners (Psalm 40:6-8). He saw that without the shedding of blood there could be no remission of sin, no approach to God, and no communion with Him (Psalm 51:6). In the many priestly cleansings, David saw the necessity of the Messiah to be both Justifier and Sanctifier of His people in order to forgive and cleanse His people (Psalm 51:2). In the smoke that rose to the heavens he saw the necessity of Christ as Advocate (Psalm 141:2). In the golden candlestick he saw the Messiah as the true Light, so that Jehovah's face could shine upon him with grace and mercy (Psalm 36:9). The table of shewbread pointed David to the coming Savior as the Bread of Life (Psalm 78:23-25). All the furniture of the tabernacle and the tabernacle itself directed David to Christ as his justification, sanctification, light, nourishment, intercession, and salvation (Psalm 36:8).

David loved God's house because he found Christ in it. And in finding Christ, he found communion with God (Psalm 63:2). In finding communion with God, he found the glory of God. No wonder God's house was his joy and delight! He longed to search after Christ in all the types, shadows, and ceremonies of the tabernacle. The more he saw of Christ, the more he found comfort in sorrow, deliverance from doubt, victory over unbelief, solutions to problems, answers to prayers, strength in weakness, and above all, forgiveness of sins and peace with God. Oh, how unforgettable were his experiences of "times of refreshing ... from the presence of the Lord" (Acts 3:19)! What access to God David enjoyed in this tabernacle! He could draw near to his Father like a child, confessing his sins in assurance of forgiveness (Psalm 32:5). In difficulties, David found guidance in God's unerring wisdom at the house of the Lord; in danger, he found sure refuge in God's almighty presence and power; in darkness and death, he learned to rest on the truth and faithfulness of his God, who promised never to leave nor forsake him. So David declared, "As for me, I will come into thy house in the multitude of the mercy: and in thy fear will I worship toward thy holy temple" (Psalm 5:7).

This same God still makes His house beautiful for His people today. From the newest believer to the most advanced in grace, all God's people are welcomed to the house and ordinances of God and can say, "How amiable [lovely] are thy tabernacles, O Lord of hosts" (Psalm 84:1). It is good for God's people to be in the house of the Lord to glorify God and meet with Christ in His sanctuary, for God's house is the gate of heaven (Genesis 28:17). To find Christ in sermons, in sacraments, in singing, and in prayers of supplication makes God's house delightful and precious. Believers may sit down under the shadow of the Almighty and experience that His fruit is sweet to their taste (Song of Solomon 2:3–4).

When worshiping God, His children desire to linger in His house, yet they must inevitably go back to a world of trials, temptations, opposition, and affliction. With David, they long for a better country than this earth has to offer.

The house of the Lord on earth was not the ultimate object of David's praise when he exclaimed, "I will dwell in the house of the Lord for ever!" He looked beyond this present world, to a "house not made with hands, eternal in the heavens" (2 Corinthians 5:1). With Abraham before him, David "looked for a city which hath foundations, whose builder and maker is God" (Hebrews 11:10).

When the true believer bids farewell to the house of God below, he finds another home above. The departed saint reaches the summit of Mount Zion and enters the city of the living God, the heavenly Jerusalem (Hebrews 12:22–24). He joins the innumerable company of angels and saints, whose names are written in heaven. He appears in peace and reconciliation before God, the Judge of all, and forms an everlasting fellowship with the spirits of the just made perfect. He comes to Jesus "the mediator of the new covenant, and to the blood of sprinkling, that speaketh better things than that of Abel" (Hebrews 12:24).

Oh, how blessed is a believer's translation from the church on earth to the church in heaven! Goodness and mercy have followed him throughout life, and now goodness and mercy surround him on every side. Who shall describe the unspeakable joy of his soul as he enters into glory? How satisfied he will be with all he sees and hears! With grateful adoration he will worship his faithful God who has fulfilled all His promises and surpassed even the believer's highest expectations. Who can conceive of the joy and gratitude with which he will join in the song of his redeemed brethren: "Unto him that loved us, and washed us from our sins in his own blood, and hath made us kings and priests unto God and his Father; to him be glory and dominion for ever and ever. Amen" (Revelation 1:5–6)!

The soul in heaven dwells in a perfected state. It can do no wrong, see no iniquity, hear no evil, and receive no spiritual harm. The Redeemer, now seen in His glorified human form, fills the believer's thoughts, is the theme of the soul's conversations, and is the object of the soul's adoration. The soul burns within itself while Christ reveals what He has suffered and the glory that is now His. It experiences inexpressible delight in Christ's presence and praises Him in high, holy, and celestial strains.

How imperfect are our highest conceptions of the beauty, blessedness, holiness, and glory of God's eternal house. To know it as it is, we must be caught up, as Paul was, into the "third heaven," but even then its realities cannot be described in earthly language (2 Corinthians 12:2, 4). As great as is the happiness and glory that the departed saint enjoys in his purely spiritual condition, there is more to come. His mortal body will be raised out of the dust and no longer be natural and corruptible, but be transformed into a Spirit-dominated and immortal body, made fit for heaven (1 Corinthians 15:44). Gathered from the dust of the grave by the hand of the Creator, it will become a pure and crystal vessel prepared to receive the believer's glorified soul. Joy will abound in the house of the Lord on resurrection morning, when the souls of the saints are joined with their resurrected, glorified bodies. They will be delivered from the bondage of corruption and be introduced into the glorious liberty of the children of God (Romans 8:21). "So shall we ever be with the Lord" (1 Thessalonians 4:17).

When the Great Shepherd appears in the heavens, there will be joy unequalled in heaven and earth. The "times of the restitution of all things" will gladden all the holy angels and every redeemed human being (Acts 3:21). The trumpet will sound to proclaim that "the year of my redeemed has come" (Isaiah 63:4). Universal liberty will be granted to all God's elect. The bond slaves of corruption will finally be emancipated. The prison house of the grave will be thrown open, and its bodies resurrected. There will be a continuous season of spiritual peace, harmony, joy, brotherhood, happiness, and prosperity. All the saints will be arrayed in white and shining garments; as victors, they will wave palm branches and wear crowns of life and righteousness received from the hand of Christ.

The dead in Christ will rise first, and the saints who are still alive will be changed into the likeness of their Lord. Then in one blessed company they will all be caught up in the air to meet their glorious Redeemer (1 Thessalonians 4:13-18). He has already changed their vile bodies into the likeness of His glorious body—incorruptible, powerful, spiritual, and heavenly (Philippians 3:21; 1 Corinthians 15:42-44,

49). So in soul and body the redeemed saints will now be the perfect possession of their Lord. Their names will be confessed before the angels of God (Luke 12:8), and they will possess their everlasting inheritance. They will forever dwell in the house of the Lord and surround the throne of the Lamb!

The pilgrims will rest in their true home (Hebrews 11:13). As good and faithful servants, they have completed their work, which the Lord declares to be well done. They are then invited to enter into their Master's joy (Matthew 25:21). The runners of the race have finished their course and have won the prize of their high calling (Philippians 3:14; 2 Timothy 4:7). The soldiers of Christ have fought the good fight of faith, secured victory by grace, and received the crown of righteousness (2 Timothy 4:7–8).

The little flock of sheep need not fear anymore, for they see that their Father's good pleasure was to give them the kingdom (Luke 12:32). They were poor but now find treasure in heaven, inheritance in light, fullness of joy, and an eternal weight of glory (Psalm 16:11; Matthew 6:20; 2 Corinthians 4:17). All doubts of their acceptance are gone. Faith has given way to sight; hope has given way to fruition. They see that the One who went before them has indeed prepared a place for them (John 14:2). They are safe within their fold. They are welcomed at the table that their gracious Host has prepared for them. They behold the King in His beauty (Isaiah 33:17) and live in the enjoyment of His love. The reigning Lamb leads them to fountains of living water and wipes away all their tears (Revelation 7:17). The Lord God Almighty is their unfading portion, their ever-open temple, their everlasting light, and their eternal glory (Revelation 21: 22–23).

They dwell in the house of the Lord and are forever blessed because they are surrounded by the Triune God.

Preparing to Dwell in the House of the Lord

Will you be among those who dwell in the house of the Lord forever? I hope that after reading this book, you understand that only those who have the Lord as their Shepherd in this life will dwell in His house in the life to come. We have no right to hope that Christ will bring us into His Father's house unless we are following Him today.

Perhaps you really don't care. You may find it interesting to read about people's beliefs, and even find Psalm 23 to be a beautiful poem, but you do not see any need to follow Christ and to submit your whole life to His Word. If Christ is not your Shepherd and Lord, then someone or something else will be. It might be drugs. A note found with the body of a young drug addict who committed suicide said this:

> King Drugs are my shepherd, I shall always want.
> They make me to lie down in the gutters.
> They lead me beside the troubled waters.
> They destroy my soul.
> They lead me in the paths of wickedness for the effort's sake.
> Yea, I shall walk through the valley of poverty and will fear all evil
> For you, Drugs, are with me.
> Your needle and capsule try to comfort me.
> You strip the table of groceries in the presence of my family.
> You rob my head of reason. My cup of sorrow runs over.
> Surely drug addiction shall stalk me all the days of my life
> And I will dwell in the house of the damned forever. [2]

Substitute your own idols in the place of King Drugs, and you will see the end result of your addiction. The world, sin, and Satan, which you serve, demand much from you, and their wages bring death. You will bring destruction upon yourself if you continue on this hell-bent course.

Jesus Christ is the Good Shepherd. To be His sheep, you must recognize the sinfulness of your heart and your actions, repent by turning from sin to God, and rely upon Christ to save you by the power of His death and resurrection. This kind of conversion results in a changed life. As the sheep of Christ follow Him, they are characterized more and more by:

- desire for Him
- delight in Him
- admiration for Him
- confidence that He does no wrong
- trust in Him
- humility before Him
- tender reverence in His presence
- following Him in childlike obedience
- biblical like-mindedness with Him
- knowing everlasting love from Him

Are you a sheep of Christ? If not, cry out to Him to save you. Ask the Lord to show you yourself and to show you Christ. Seek the graces of genuine repentance and faith in Christ alone for salvation. Go to a church that preaches the Word of God to the glory of Christ. Read your Bible every day, and do not give up until the Lord Jesus rescues you.

If you are one of Christ's sheep, your Shepherd is leading you on a pathway to the Father's house, where you will dwell with Him forever. Let me therefore conclude this book with some counsel for you on the way to the Celestial City.

Cultivate Holy Desires for Heaven

Seek grace to maintain a true, biblical balance between godly contentment with your present home in this world, and godly longing for the mansion that is being prepared for you. Like the apostle Paul, learn to "groan, earnestly desiring" your eternal home in heaven, while you "walk by faith, not by sight" in this world (2 Corinthians 5:2, 7).

Learn to be content with what you are given, remembering that Christ has said, "In the world ye shall have tribulation: but be of good cheer; I have overcome the world" (John 16:33). Do not envy wicked people who prosper (Psalm 73:3). You have a better inheritance, better company, and a better future than they do. Keep your eyes on the Shepherd, and trust in Him to supply all you need.

Let holiness keep you poor in spirit and dependent upon God's generosity. Remember that Christ alone is your righteousness before God. Persevere in faith and obedience, and your eyes will see salvation in Christ. Whatever may be the judgment of your own ignorance and of the world's malice, the Good Shepherd is leading you the right way. You will confess this with amazement and praise when He brings you into the heavenly city to dwell forever with Him.

He who has cared for you from eternity will never leave you nor forsake you, even if you have much to complain about and say, like Jacob: "Few and evil have the days of my life been" (Genesis 47:9). You have a good portion in this life, though your means may be scanty, your body weak and sickly, your children disobedient, and your crosses heavy. Psalm 37:16 says, "A little that a righteous man hath is better than the riches of many wicked." Furthermore, you will one day have a mansion in heaven, which Christ Jesus has prepared for you. In this place you will enjoy fellowship with your Master, away from all corrupt self, all bitter sin, and all the vanity of this world. Go then, in God's strength, and boast of His righteousness (Psalm 71:16). Make this your triumph song: "I will dwell in the house of the Lord for ever!"

Seek grace to be less at home in this world, and to long for the world to come. In that eternal dwelling, you will find your forgiving Father; your Elder Brother, Jesus; and your Sealer, Guide, and Comforter, the

Holy Spirit! Long for your heavenly dwelling, for there God is honored as holy, His eternal law of love is obeyed, and His will is celebrated. Long for your eternal dwelling, for it is full of love and holiness. Long for your eternal dwelling, for it is your abiding rest. There will be no more pain, trouble, and weariness in heaven. There will be no more sin, Satan, or sorrow. Peace will reign forever. Long for your heavenly dwelling, for there you will be perfect in soul and body. You will regain the lost likeness of your Creator. It is the glorious home of your glorious Lord, and you will dwell with Him forever.

Meditate on Heaven's Glorious Activities
Seek grace to meditate much on what you will be doing within the walls of the heavenly Jerusalem. Meditate on heaven's holy *worship*, the great and continuous activity of the redeemed (Revelation 19:1-8). Worship your King with holy reverence this side of the grave to prepare for worship on the other side. Consider how much of this worship will take the form of holy music. The Book of Revelation contains more songs than any other book in the Bible, save the Psalms. Seek grace to learn more experiential gospel notes in this life so you may sing them more fully in the life to come.

Meditate on heaven's holy *service*, knowing that as the servants of God and of the Lamb, you will work for Him in eternal happiness (Revelation 22:3). Consider how the work of serving Christ secures the rewards of His grace, and that one of those rewards will be increasingly more opportunities to serve Him when He returns (Matthew 24:45-46; 25:14, 19, 21, 23). Though we know little of this work, there will be many activities in heaven that will supersede the work we do for Christ in this earth. But heavenly service will not burden us with exhaustion, weariness, or failure. Seek grace to be your Master's willing servant in this life, if you desire to be his eternal servant.

Meditate on heaven's holy *authority*, too, knowing that you will reign with Christ over the earth (Revelation 1:6; 5:10; 22:5). As the

Heidelberg Catechism says, be faithful now to "confess His name" as a prophet, to present yourself daily "a living sacrifice" to Him as a priest, and to "fight against sin and Satan in this life" as a king, so that you may "afterwards reign with Him eternally, over all creatures."[3]

Meditate on heaven's holy *fellowship*. You cannot have too much communion with God in this life in preparation for the unspeakably rich communion with Him that will be your portion in the life to come. Consider also the great friendships we will enjoy with other believers in heaven. Richard Whately (1787–1863) said, "The extension and perfection of friendship will constitute a great part of the future happiness of the blessed." He explained, "The highest enjoyment doubtless to the blessed, will be the personal knowledge of their great and beloved Master; yet I cannot but think that some part of their happiness will consist in an intimate knowledge of the greatest of his followers also."[4]

Philip Melanchthon (1497–1560) said much the same in his memorial address on Luther:

> We remember the great delight with which he recounted the course, the counsels, the perils, and escapes of the Prophets, and the learning with which he discoursed on all the ages of the Church, thereby showing that he was inflamed by no ordinary passion for these wonderful men. Now he embraces them and rejoices to hear them speak and to speak to them in turn. Now they hail him gladly as a companion, and thank God with him for having gathered and preserved the Church.[5]

In heaven, Luther and Calvin have been reunited. No discord will mar heaven's angelic music. All who sing to the Lamb are one in mind and spirit.

Meditate too on heaven's *education*. Be assured that heaven will also require us to develop and grow. As fallen creatures, we cannot fully comprehend the riches of God's greatness and goodness; therefore, we need to continually learn more about Him. God seats us with Christ in the heavenly places for this purpose: "That in the ages to come he might shew the exceeding riches of his grace in his kindness toward us through Christ Jesus" (Ephesians 2:7). The higher God's heavenly pilgrim ascends, the greater will be the scope of his joy. He will be astonished by new views of God, new revelations of His purposes, and new draughts from the fountain of living water. Heaven will be a school where classes are never dismissed. We will sit as eternal students at Christ's feet to learn of Him ever more deeply, richly, and fully.

Meditate also on heaven's holy *joy and peace* in seeing, knowing, and loving God, for there you will enjoy Him forever! Your eternal mansion will not be rented from a landlord but will be a mansion given to you by your heavenly Father through His Son. Then we shall know the full meaning of Zephaniah 3:17, "The LORD thy God in the midst of thee is mighty; he will save, he will rejoice over thee with joy; he will rest in his love, he will joy over thee with singing."

In heaven, God's glory in Christ will be our light, our water, our food, and our life. Not only will we dwell in His glory, but His glory will dwell in us. John Howe (1630–1705) wrote,

> This communicated glory fills up the whole soul, causes all clouds and darkness to vanish, leaves no place for any thing that is vile or inglorious; it is pure glory, free from mixture of anything that is alien to it. And it is itself full. The soul is replenished, not with airy, evanid [faint, vanishing] shadows; but with substantial, solid glory, a massive, weighty glory (2 Corinthians 4:17).[6]

All our desires will be fulfilled by God in Christ (Matthew 5:6). Paul's prayer will find its grand fulfillment in every believer: "to know the love of Christ, which passeth knowledge, that ye might be filled with all the fulness of God" (Ephesians 3:19).

The wedding day of Christ's bride will be celebrated. The eternal Sabbath of the church will begin. Jesus will enfold His people in His glory. They will never wander from Him or be separated from Him again but will gaze upon their Shepherd-Lord and unceasingly praise Him. With their Beloved they will bask in His love and feast on the eternal smile of His approval–forever!

Meditate on heaven, and say in your soul, "The LORD is my shepherd; I shall not want .... And I will dwell in the house of the LORD for ever."

Also, turn Psalm 23 into a prayer: "Jehovah-Shepherd, be Thou my Shepherd. Suffer me never to want. Make me to lie down in patches of grass completely satiated. Lead me beside restful waters. Refreshen my soul. Even in dry inhospitable desert terrain, covered with numerous circling and confusing paths, lead me rightly for Thy Name's sake. And when I walk through ravines with shadows of death, let me fear no evil. Abide with me. Let Thy rod and Thy staff comfort me. Prepare a banquet before me in the presence of mine enemies. Anoint my head with oil; and make my drinking bowl overflow its brim. Let Thy goodness and mercy pursue me all the days of my life, so that I may dwell in the house of the Lord forever!"[7] Amen.

Notes

Introduction

1. C. H. Spurgeon, *The Treasury of David* (London: Marshall Brothers, 1881), 1:353.

2. F. B. Meyer, *The Shepherd Psalm* (Chicago: Moody Press, 1976), 11–12.

Chapter 1

1. John Calvin, *Commentary on the Book of Psalms*, trans. James Anderson (repr., Grand Rapid: Baker, 2003), 1:391.

2. Abraham Hellenbroek, *A Specimen of Divine Truths*, trans. Joel R. Beeke (Grand Rapids: Reformation Heritage Books, n.d.), 36.

3. William Huntington, "God the Guardian of the Poor and the Bank of Faith," in *The Works of the Reverend William Huntington* (London: for E. Huntington, by T. Bensley, 1811), 3:108.

4. See the Dutch Reformed "Form for the Administration of the Lord's Supper," in *Doctrinal Standards, Liturgy, and Church Order*, ed. Joel R. Beeke (Grand Rapids: Reformation Heritage Books, 2003), 137.

5. *The Psalter with Doctrinal Standards, Liturgy, Church Order, and Added Chorale Section* (1965; repr., Grand Rapids: Eerdmans, 2003), no. 255, stanzas 1, 3 [Psalm 95].

6. J. R. MacDuff, *The Shepherd and His Flock* (London: James Nisbet, 1876), 228.

7. Heidelberg Catechism, Q. 1, in *The Reformation Heritage KJV Study Bible* (Grand Rapids: Reformation Heritage Books, 2014), 1988.

8. Hellenbroek, *A Specimen of Divine Truths*, 36.

Chapter 2

1. Heidelberg Catechism, Q. 127, in *The Reformation Heritage KJV Study Bible*, 2005-6.

2. Ralph Erskine, "True Lovers of God Highly Privileged," in *The Sermons and Other Practical Works of the Reverend and Learned Ralph Erskine* (London: R. Baynes, 1821), 9:97.

3. *Letters of Samuel Rutherford*, ed. Andrew A. Bonar (1891; repr., Edinburgh: Banner of Truth, 2006), 422.

4. Westminster Shorter Catechism, Q. 1, in *The Reformation Heritage KJV Study Bible*, 2053.

5. Heidelberg Catechism, Q. 89-90, in *The Reformation Heritage KJV Study Bible*, 2000.

6. Rutherford, *Letters*, 347.

7. *Psalter*, no. 422, stanza 6 [Psalm 89].

8. Heidelberg Catechism, Q. 1, in *The Reformation Heritage KJV Study Bible*, 1988.

9. Heidelberg Catechism, Q. 114, in *Reformation Heritage KJV Study Bible*, 2003.

10. Stephen Charnock, "The Subjects of the Lord's Supper," in *The Works of Stephen Charnock* (1865; repr., Edinburgh: Banner of Truth, 1985), 4:451.

Chapter 3

1. Martin Luther, "Psalm 23," trans. W. M. Miller, in *Luther's Works*, ed. Jaroslav Pelikan (St. Louis: Concordia, 1955), 12:158-59.

2. Heidelberg Catechism, Q. 125, in *The Reformation Heritage KJV Study Bible*, 2005.

3. *Matthew Henry's Commentary* (Peabody, Mass.: Hendrickson, 2003), 2:579 [2 Kings 7:1].

4. Charles C. Colton, *Lacon: Or, Many Things in a Few Words* (New York: S. Marks, 1824), 1:105.

5. *The Psalter*, no. 222, stanzas 1, 5, 9 [Psalm 81].

6. Thomas Watson, *The Lord's Prayer* (Edinburgh: Banner of Truth, 1965), 14.

7. Wilhelmus à Brakel, *The Christian's Reasonable Service*, ed. Joel R. Beeke, trans. Bartel Elshout (Grand Rapids: Reformation Heritage Books, 1995), 4:173.

8. Watson, *The Lord's Prayer*, 14.

9. Heidelberg Catechism, Q. 47, in *The Reformation Heritage KJV Study Bible*, 1994.

10. John Flavel, *The Fountain of Life*, in *The Works of John Flavel* (1820; repr., Edinburgh: Banner of Truth, 1968), 1:415.

11. Watson, *The Lord's Prayer*, 14.

12. Ralph Erskine, "True Lovers of God Highly Privileged," in *Select Sermons of Ralph Erskine* (London: Houlston and Wright, 1863), 1:238.

13. William Bridge, *Sermons on Faith*, in *The Works of the Rev. William Bridge* (London: Thomas Tegg, 1845), 2:372.

14. John Trapp, *A Commentary on the Old and New Testaments*, ed. Hugh Martin (London: Richard D. Dickinson, 1867), 1:92.

Chapter 4

1. John Bunyan, *The Pilgrim's Progress*, in *The Works of John Bunyan*, ed. George Offor (1854; repr., Edinburgh: Banner of Truth, 1991), 3:96–97.

2. Thomas Shepard, *The Sincere Convert*, in *The Works of Thomas Shepard* (Boston: Doctrinal Tract and Book Society, 1853), 1:65.

3. Shepard, *The Sincere Convert*, in *Works*, 1:107.

4. Genesis 1:1; 1 Timothy 1:15; Matthew 11:26.

5. *The Works of Thomas Goodwin* (Grand Rapids: Reformation Heritage Books, 2006), 4:418–19.

6. Samuel Rutherford, *The Covenant of Life Opened* (Edinburgh: A. Anderson, 1655), 304.

7. David Dickson, *The Summe of Saving Knowledge* (Edinburgh: George Swintoun and Thomas Brown, 1671), 17; cf. Joohyun Kim, "The Holy Spirit in David Dickson's Doctrine of the *Pactum Salutis*," *Puritan Reformed Journal* 7, no. 2 (July 2015): 112–26.

8. See John 17:1, 6, 12.

9. See Romans 11:36; Revelation 4:11.

10. *The Confessions of Aurelius Augustine*, trans. J. G. Pilkington (Edinburgh: T & T Clark, 1886), 26–27 [2.2].

11. *The Psalter*, no. 31 [Psalm 17].

Chapter 5

1. Kenneth E. Bailey, *The Good Shepherd: A Thousand-Year Journey from Psalm 23 to the New Testament* (Downers Grove: IVP Academic, 2014), 40.

2. Augustine, *Confessions*, 1.1, in *A Select Library of the Nicene and Post-Nicene Fathers of the Christian Church*, ed. Philip Schaff (Buffalo: The Christian Literature Co., 1886), 1:45.

3. Bailey, *The Good Shepherd*, 39–40.

4. Phillip Keller, *A Shepherd Looks at Psalm 23* (Grand Rapids: Zondervan, 1970), 36.

5. Keller, *A Shepherd Looks at Psalm 23*, 36.

6. Keller, *A Shepherd Looks at Psalm 23*, 39.

7. Keller, *A Shepherd Looks at Psalm 23*, 40, 42.

8. Keller, *A Shepherd Looks at Psalm 23*, 43.

9. Keller, *A Shepherd Looks at Psalm 23*, 116.

10. Keller, *A Shepherd Looks at Psalm 23*, 46.

11. Bailey, *The Good Shepherd*, 41.

12. *The Psalter*, no. 368 [Psalm 132].

13. George Swinnock, *The Christian Man's Calling*, in *The Works of George Swinnock* (1868; repr., Edinburgh: Banner of Truth, 1992), 1:202.

14. Luther, "Psalm 23," in *Luther's Works*, 12:161.

15. *The Psalter*, no. 381 [Psalm 138].

16. Cf. Westminster Confession, 11.4 and 18.2–4.

17. The saying is attributed to Martin Luther.

18. Augustine, *On Christian Doctrine*, trans. J. F. Shaw, 1.5, in *The Works of Aurelius Augustine*, ed. Marcus Dods (Edinburgh: T & T Clark, 1892), 9:10.

19. Richard Sibbes, *A Description of Christ*, in *The Works of Richard Sibbes* (1862–1864; repr., Edinburgh: Banner of Truth, 1973), 1:17.

Chapter 6

1. Phillip Keller, *A Shepherd Looks at Psalm 23* (Grand Rapids: Zondervan, 1970), 56–57.

2. Keller, *A Shepherd Looks at Psalm 23*, 52.

3. Keller, *A Shepherd Looks at Psalm 23*, 55.

4. Shepard, *The Parable of the Ten Virgins Unfolded*, in *Works*, 2:281.

5. *The Psalter*, no. 55 [Psalm 23].

6. Robert Murray M'Cheyne, *A Basket of Fragments* (1848; repr., Inverness, Scotland: Christian Focus Publications, 1975), 30.

Chapter 7

1. Heidelberg Catechism, Q. 12, in *The Reformation Heritage KJV Study Bible*, 1989.

2. See Keller, *A Shepherd Looks at Psalm 23*, 60-61.

3. George Swinnock, *The Gods Die Like Men; Or, Magistrates Are Mortal*, in *The Works of George Swinnock* (1868; repr., Edinburgh: Banner of Truth 1992), 4:129.

4. Keller, *A Shepherd Looks at Psalm 23*, 62-63.

5. "Form for the Administration of Baptism," in *Doctrinal Standards, Liturgy, and Church Order*, ed. Joel R. Beeke (Grand Rapids: Reformation Heritage Books, 2003), 126.

6. William Jenkyn, *An Exposition upon the Epistle of Jude*, ed. James Sherman (Edinburgh: James Nichol, 1865), 162.

7. Excerpts of Jeremy Taylor, "A Prayer Against Pride," *The Golden Grove, Or A Manual of Daily Prayers*, in *The Whole Works of the Right Reverend Jeremy Taylor*, ed. Charles P. Eden (London: Longman, et al., 1865), 7:640-41.

8. See Keller, *A Shepherd Looks at Psalm 23*, 68.

Chapter 8

1. For more on backsliding and its solution, see Joel R. Beeke, *Getting Back into the Race: The Cure for Backsliding* (Adelphi, Md.: Cruciform Press, 2011).

2. Kenneth E. Bailey, *The Good Shepherd: A Thousand Year Journey from Psalm 23 to the New Testament* (Downers Grove, Ill.: IVP Academic, 2014), 44-45.

3. The Heidelberg Catechism, Q. 126, in *The Reformation Heritage KJV Study Bible*, 2005.

4. Westminster Shorter Catechism, Q. 98, in *The Reformation Heritage KJV Study Bible*, 2061.

5. Thomas Watson, *The Doctrine of Repentance*, Puritan Paperbacks (Edinburgh: Banner of Truth, 1987), 18.

6. Watson, *The Doctrine of Repentance*, 19.

7. Heidelberg Catechism, Q. 89, in *The Reformation Heritage KJV Study Bible*, 2000.

8. Watson, *The Doctrine of Repentance*, 45.

Chapter 9

1. See Thomas Boston, *Human Nature in Its Fourfold State* (Edinburgh: Banner of Truth, 1964).

2. Augustus Toplady, "Rock of Ages," stanza 2.

3. John Bunyan, *Grace Abounding to the Chief of Sinners*, in *The Works of John Bunyan*, ed. George Offor, 3 vols. (1854; repr., Edinburgh: Banner of Truth, 1991), 1:35–36.

4. Psalter 83, stanza 1.

5. Toplady, "Rock of Ages," stanzas 1, 3.

6. John Kent, "Who but the soul that's led to know," in William Gadsby, *A Selection of Hymns for Public Worship* (London: J. Gadsby, 1854), no. 113.

7. Heidelberg Catechism, LD 23, Q. 59, in *The Reformation Heritage KJV Study Bible*, 1995.

Chapter 10

1. Halvor Ronning, on a tour of Israel with the author on May 21, 2015.

2. Keller, *A Shepherd Looks at Psalm 23*, 70.

3. Keller, *A Shepherd Looks at Psalm 23*, 71–74.

4. Westminster Shorter Catechism, Q. 35, in *The Reformation Heritage KJV Study Bible*, 2056.

5. Heidelberg Catechism, Q. 89–90, in *The Reformation Heritage KJV Study Bible*, 2000.

6. John Owen, *Pneumatologia, Or, a Discourse Concerning the Holy Spirit*, in *The Works of John Owen* (1850–1853; repr., Edinburgh: Banner of Truth, 1965), 3:574–75.

7. William Gurnall, *The Christian in Complete Armour*, two vols. in one (1864; repr., Edinburgh: Banner of Truth, 1964), 1:16.

8. Gurnall, *The Christian in Complete Armour*, 1:516.

9. Canons of Dort, 3rd/4th Head, Art. 12, in *The Reformation Heritage KJV Study Bible*, 2017.

10. Thomas Shepard, *Meditations and Spiritual Experiences*, in *The Works of Thomas Shepard* (Boston: Doctrinal Tract and Book Society, 1853), 3:431.

11. Shepard, *Meditations and Spiritual Experiences*, in *Works*, 3:439.

12. Alexander Whyte, *Thomas Shepard: Pilgrim Father and Founder of Harvard* (1909; repr., Grand Rapids: Reformation Heritage Books, 2007), 144.

13. Gurnall, *The Christian in Complete Armour*, 1:417–18.

14. For more detailed instructions about pursuing holiness through divine sanctification, see Joel R. Beeke, *Holiness: God's Call to Sanctification* (Edinburgh: Banner of Truth, 1994).

15. Jonathan Edwards, "Concerning the End for which God Created the World," in *The Works of Jonathan Edwards, Volume 8, Ethical Writings*, ed. Paul Ramsey (New Haven: Yale University Press, 1989), 523–24.

16. Thomas Shepard, *The Parable of the Ten Virgins*, in *Works*, 2:81.

17. John Newton, *Cardiphonia*, in *The Works of the Rev. John Newton*, 6 vols. (London: Hamilton, Adams, and Co., 1824), 2:81.

Chapter 11

1. Bailey, *The Good Shepherd*, 41.

2. Keller, *A Shepherd Looks at Psalm 23*, 83.

3. M. P. Krikorian, cited by Bailey, *The Good Shepherd*, 47.

4. John Preston, "The Doctrine of Self-deniall," in *Fovre Godly and Learned Treatises*, 3rd ed. (London: by T. C. for Michael Sparke, 1633), 225.

5. Richard Sibbes, *The Church's Visitation*, in *The Works of Richard Sibbes* (1862–1864; repr., Edinburgh: Banner of Truth, 1973), 1:378.

6. *The Psalter*, no. 427 [Psalm 118].

7. M. P. Krikorian, cited by Bailey, *The Good Shepherd*, 47.

8. *Diaries and Letters of Philip Henry*, ed. Matthew Henry Lee (London: Kegan Paul, Trench and Co., 1882), 62

9. Jonathan Edwards, "Resolutions," no. 56, in *The Works of Jonathan Edwards, Volume 16, Letters and Personal Writings*, ed. George S. Claghorn (New Haven: Yale University Press, 1998), 757.

10. John Owen, *Of the Mortification of Sin in Believers*, in *The Works of John Owen* (1850–1853; repr., Edinburgh: Banner of Truth, 1967), 6:20.

11. Central Intelligence Agency, *The World Factbook*, https://www.cia.gov/library/publications/the-world-factbook/geos/xx.html (accessed Mar. 13, 2015).

12. George Swinnock, *The Fading of the Flesh*, in *Works*, 3:425.

13. *Memoirs of Thomas Halyburton*, ed. Joel R. Beeke (Grand Rapids: Reformation Heritage Books, 1996), 226, 265–66, 293.

14. James Hervey, "Subject of Conversation with Some Young Christians," in John Brown, *Memoirs of the Life and Character of the Late Rev. James Hervey*, 3rd ed. (London: Ogle, Duncan, and Co., 1822), 513–14.

15. Hervey, "Subject of Conversation with Some Young Christians," in Brown, *Memoirs*, 514.

Chapter 12

1. Martin Luther, "Psalm 23," in *Luther's Works*, 12:168.

2. John Flavel, *A Practical Treatise of Fear*, in *The Works of John Flavel* (1820; Edinburgh: Banner of Truth, 1968), 3:252.

3. Ebenezer Erskine, "Courageous Faith," in *The Whole Works of the Rev. Ebenezer Erskine* (London: William Baynes and Son, 1826), 1:670.

4. Heidelberg Catechism, Q. 47, in *The Reformation Heritage KJV Study Bible*, 1994.

5. *The Psalter*, no. 20 [Psalm 11].

6. Flavel, *The Method of Grace*, in Works, 2:118.

7. Thomas Watson, *A Body of Divinity* (Edinburgh: Banner of Truth, 1965), 216.

8. *Fides Christum mihi donat, charitas ex fide me proximo.* Cited in Thomas Adam, *Private Thoughts on Religion* (Poughkeepsie: Rudd and Stockholm, 1814), 188.

9. Watson, *A Body of Divinity*, 219.

10. Watson, *A Body of Divinity*, 219.

Chapter 13

1. Richard Marius, *Martin Luther: The Christian between God and Death* (Cambridge, Mass.: Belknap Press, 1999), 289.

2. Shorter Catechism, Q. 21, in *The Reformation Heritage KJV Study Bible*, 2054.

3. Canons of Dort, Fifth Head, Art. 8, in *The Reformation Heritage KJV Study Bible*, 2021.

4. *The Psalter*, 362, stanza 3 (Psalm 130).

Chapter 14

1. Peter Craigie, *Psalms 1–50*, Word Biblical Commentary 19, 2nd ed. (Nashville: Thomas Nelson, 2004), 207; Keller, *A Shepherd Looks at Psalm 23*, 93.

2. Bailey, *The Good Shepherd*, 50, 52.

3. John Goldingay, *Psalms, Volume 1: Psalms 1–41*, Baker Commentary on the Old Testament: Wisdom and Psalms, ed. Tremper Longman III (Grand Rapids: Baker Academic, 2006), 351.

4. Bailey, *The Good Shepherd*, 52.

5. M. P. Krikorian, cited in Bailey, *The Good Shepherd*, 50.

6. Keller, *A Shepherd Looks at Psalm 23*, 98.

7. Bailey, *The Good Shepherd*, 51.

8. Keller, *A Shepherd Looks at Psalm 23*, 96.

9. Leslie C. Allen, *Ezekiel 20–48*, Word Biblical Commentary 29 (Nashville: Thomas Nelson, 1990), 14.

10. Ralph H. Alexander, "Ezekiel," in *The Expositor's Bible Commentary, Revised Edition*, ed. Tremper Longman III and David E. Garland (Grand Rapids: Zondervan, 2010), 7:752.

11. Heidelberg Catechism, Q. 1, in *The Reformation Heritage KJV Study Bible*, 1988.

12. Keller, *A Shepherd Looks at Psalm 23*, 99.

13. "Form for the Administration of Baptism," in *The Psalter*, 126.

14. Thomas Watson, *The Christian Soldier: Or, Heaven Taken by Storm* (New York: Robert Moore, 1816), 27.

15. Ezekiel Hopkins, *An Exposition upon the Commandments*, in *The Works of Ezekiel Hopkins*, ed. Charles W. Quick (Philadelphia: The Protestant Episcopal Book Society, 1867), 1:237.

16. John Flavel, *Divine Conduct: Or, the Mystery of Providence*, in *The Works of John Flavel* (1820; repr., Edinburgh: Banner of Truth, 1968), 4:468.

17. Richard Sibbes, *A Commentary upon the First Chapter of the Second Epistle of Paul to the Corinthians*, in *The Works of Richard Sibbes* (1862-1864; repr., Edinburgh: Banner of Truth, 1981), 3:209 [2 Cor. 1:12].

18. Bailey, *The Good Shepherd*, 52.

19. Keller, *A Shepherd Looks at Psalm 23*, 101.

Chapter 15

1. "The image shifts to a gracious host (though the message remains the same as the shepherd)." *The Reformation Heritage KJV Study Bible*, 780 [Psalm 23:5].

2. Craigie, *Psalms 1–50, Second Edition*, 207.

3. George M. Lamsa, quoted in Bailey, *The Good Shepherd*, 54.

4. Isaac Watts, "How Sweet and Awful Is the Place," in *Trinity Hymnal—Baptist Edition* (Suwanee, Ga.: Great Commission Publications, 1995), no. 271.

5. Cf. "Form for the Administration of the Lord's Supper," *The Psalter*, 139.

6. Luther, "Psalm 23," in *Luther's Works*, 12:175.

7. Luther, "Psalm 23," in *Luther's Works*, 12:175.

8. Regarding the link between Psalm 23:5 and the offense that Christ's eating with sinners gave to the Pharisees, I am indebted to Bailey, *The Good Shepherd*, 57–58.

9. Joseph Hall, *The Breathings of the Devout Soul*, sec. 22, in *The Works of Joseph Hall* (Oxford: D. A. Talboys, 1837), 8:219–20.

10. Hall, *The Breathings of the Devout Soul*, sec. 22, in *Works*, 8:220.

Chapter 16

1. Psalms 36:8; 63:5, 11–12; Isaiah 55:2; Jeremiah 31:14. The particular Hebrew word used here can be translated "fatness."

2. Deuteronomy 28:40; 2 Sam. 14:2; Psalm 104:15; Amos 6:6; Matt. 6:17.

3. Luke 7:46; see Bailey, *The Good Shepherd*, 58.

4. Exodus 29:7; Leviticus 8:12; Judges 9:8; 1 Samuel 9:16; 10:1; 1 Kings 19:16.

5. Leviticus 4:3; Psalms 18:50; 105:15; etc.

6. Francis Turretin, *Institutes of Elenctic Theology*, ed. James T. Dennison, Jr., trans. George Musgrave Giger (Phillipsburg, N.J.: P & R Publishing, 1994), 2:393

[14.5.8]. I have divided Turretin's paragraph into bullet points for the ease of the modern reader.

7. John Calvin, "Calvin's Catechism (1545)," Q. 41, in *Reformed Confessions of the Sixteenth and Seventeenth Centuries in English Translation, Volume 1, 1525–1552,* ed. James T. Dennison, Jr. (Grand Rapids: Reformation Heritage Books, 2008), 474.

8. Heidelberg Catechism, Q. 32, in *The Reformation Heritage KJV Study Bible,* 1992.

9. See Barbara Carvill, "The Calvin Seal," *Calvin College,* http://www.calvin.edu/about/history/calvin-seal.html (accessed Mar. 24, 2015).

10. *The Psalter,* no. 250, stanza 4 (Psalm 92).

Chapter 17

1. Psalms 11:6; 75:8; Isaiah 51:17, 22; Jeremiah 25:15; Ezekiel 32:31–33.

2. Psalms 16:5; 116:13. Christ used this symbolism in the same way when He instituted the Lord's Supper.

3. Luther, "Psalm 23," in *Luther's Works,* 12:176.

4. Bailey, *The Good Shepherd,* 59.

5. Anne Dutton, *A Brief Account of the Gracious Dealings of God with a Poor, Sinful, Unworthy Creature,* in *Select Spiritual Writings of Anne Dutton: Eighteenth-Century, British-Baptist, Woman Theologian, Volume 3, Autobiography,* ed. JoAnn Ford Watson (Macon, Ga.: Mercer University Press, 2006), 25–28.

6. The same Hebrew word appears in Psalm 66:12, where it is translated "wealth" (KJV) or "abundance" (ESV).

7. Joseph Hart, "Nothing but Thy Blood, O Jesus," http://www.hymnary.org/text/nothing_but_thy_blood_o_jesus (accessed March 25, 2015).

8. Samuel Bolton, *The True Bounds of Christian Freedom,* Puritan Paperbacks (Edinburgh: Banner of Truth, 1964), 156–57.

9. *The Psalter,* no. 426, stanza 9 (Psalm 116).

10. Bolton, *The True Bounds of Christian Freedom*, 140–42.

11. John Stevenson, *The Lord Our Shepherd: An Exposition of the Twenty-Third Psalm* (New York: Robert Carter, 1845), 189–90.

12. Frances Havergal, "The Song Chalice." http://cavaliersonly.com/poetry_by_christian_poets_of_the_past/frances_havergal_-_page_3, accessed July 25, 2015.

13. John Trapp, *A Commentary on the Old and New Testaments*, ed. W. Webster (London: Richard D. Dickinson, 1868), 2:484 [Psalm 23:5].

Chapter 18

1. C. H. Spurgeon, "Entangled in the Land," sermon 2,188, in *The Metropolitan Tabernacle Pulpit* (London: Banner of Truth, 1970), 37:83.

2. Bailey, *The Good Shepherd*, 60.

3. Thomas Manton, "Several Sermons upon the CXIX Psalm," in *The Complete Works of Thomas Manton* (London: James Nisbet and Co., 1872), 7:236.

4. See also Deuteronomy 7:12; 1 Kings 8:23; Nehemiah 1:5; 9:32; Psalms 89:28; 106:45; Isaiah 54:10; 55:3; Daniel 9:4.

5. David Brown, *Life of the Late John Duncan*, 2nd ed. (Edinburgh: Edmonston and Douglas, 1872), 422.

6. Thomas Watson, *A Body of Divinity* (Edinburgh: Banner of Truth, 1965), 93–94.

7. William Cowper, "God Moves in a Mysterious Way," http://www.hymnary.org/text/god_moves_in_a_mysterious_way (accessed March 26, 2015).

8. The first three lines are from Francis Thompson, "The Hound of Heaven," *The Oxford Book of English Mystical Verse* (1917), http://www.bartleby.com/236/239.html (accessed March 27, 2015). In the context of the original poem, the lines speak of God's relentless and loving pursuit of a man who flees God and unsuccessfully seeks satisfaction in nature. However, the same God who pursues the unconverted unto repentance, continues to pursue the believer.

9. *The Psalter*, no. 429, stanza 4 (Psalm 138).

Chapter 19

1. Among the almost three hundred texts using the expression "house of the Lord" or "house of God," see Genesis 28:17; Exodus 23:19; 2 Chronicles 3:1; Psalms 42:4; 122:1; Micah 4:1; 1 Timothy 3:15; Hebrews 10:21; 1 Peter 4:17.

2. Adapted from "The Psalm of the Addict," http://www.bartleby.com/73/852.html (accessed March 27, 2015). The original read, "King Heroin."

3. Heidelberg Catechism, Q. 32, in *The Reformation Heritage KJV Study Bible*, 1992.

4. Richard Whately, *A View of the Scripture Revelations Concerning a Future State* (Philadelphia: Lindsay and Blakiston, 1855), 214–15.

5. Philip Melanchthon, *Funeral Oration over Luther*, appendix in James W. Richard, *Philip Melanchthon: The Protestant Preceptor of Germany, 1497-1560* (London: G. P. Putnam's Sons, 1898), 390.

6. John Howe, *The Blessedness of the Righteous*, in *The Works of the Rev. John Howe, M.A., As Published During His Life* (London: William Tegg and Co., 1848), 2:78.

7. I am indebted to Dr. Halvor Ronning for several ideas in this paraphrasing of Psalm 23 into a prayer according to the shepherding conditions in Israel.